How Should We Live?

How Should We Live?

A PRACTICAL APPROACH TO EVERYDAY MORALITY

John Kekes

The University of Chicago Press
Chicago and London

The University of Chicago Press, Chicago 60637
The University of Chicago Press, Ltd., London
© 2014 by The University of Chicago
All rights reserved. No part of this book may be used or reproduced in any
manner whatsoever without written permission, except in the case of brief
quotations in critical articles and reviews. For more information, contact
the University of Chicago Press, 1427 E. 60th St., Chicago, IL 60637.
Published 2014
Paperback edition 2019
Printed in the United States of America

28 27 26 25 24 23 22 21 20 19   1 2 3 4 5

ISBN-13: 978-0-226-15565-4 (cloth)
ISBN-13: 978-0-226-63907-9 (paper)
ISBN-13: 978-0-226-15579-1 (e-book)
DOI: https://doi.org/10.7208/chicago/9780226155791.001.0001

Library of Congress Cataloging-in-Publication Data

Kekes, John, author.
    How should we live? : a practical approach to everyday morality /
John Kekes.
        pages   cm
    Includes bibliographical references and index.
    ISBN 978-0-226-15565-4 (cloth : alk. paper)
    ISBN 978-0-226-15579-1 (e-book)
    1. Ethics. 2. Conduct of life. I. Title.
    BJ1012.K4234 2014
    170 — dc23

                                              2014007329

For JYK

Contents

Acknowledgments

The views I defend in this book have been formed partly in response to the works of those with whom I disagree. I acknowledge with gratitude that I have learned a great deal from them. I hope they will not think that I have misunderstood their theories and ideals.

I am indebted to three readers engaged by the University of Chicago Press for their sympathetic reports and exceptionally helpful suggestions for revision. I have followed most of their recommendations, and the resulting work is the better for it.

The readers were the excellent selections of my editor, Elizabeth Branch Dyson. I thank her for that and for her friendly, perceptive, and conscientious help in making the original submission into a book.

A slightly different version of chapter 2 was published in *Philosophy* 86 (2011): 333–51. I am grateful for permission to publish this article as a chapter.

I dedicate this book to my wife with love and gratitude for making it possible and for much else.

1   Introduction

Such is the disorder and confusion of human affairs, that no perfect
or regular distribution of happiness and misery is ever, in this life, to be
expected. Not only the goods of fortune, and the endowments of the body
(both of which are important), not only these advantages, I say, are un-
equally divided between the virtuous and the vicious, but even the mind
itself partakes, in some degree, of this disorder, and the most worthy
character, by the very constitution of the passions, enjoys not the highest
felicity. . . . In a word, human life is more governed by fortune than
by reason . . . and is more influenced by particular humours, than
by general principles.

DAVID HUME, "The Sceptic"[1]

The Problem and the Project

This book is about two ways of trying answer the question of how we
should live. One relies on ideal theories, the other on a practical approach. I defend the view that we should turn away from ideal theories
and turn toward a practical approach. Ideal theorists have for many
millennia sought an overriding ideal whose acceptance is required by
reason, an ideal that guides how everyone, always, everywhere should
live. I do not think such an ideal has been or can be found. The ideals
that guide how we should live are many. They vary with the possibilities and limits that exist at different times, in different contexts, and for
different persons. Reason does exclude some ideals, but it allows that in

civilized circumstances many reasonable ideals remain, none is over-riding, and there is a variety of reasonable ways of living.

In giving reasons against ideal theories and for a practical approach, I begin with real lives. Real lives are lives as they are, not as they should be. Ideal theories are about how lives should be, not as they are. One main reason why real lives are not as they should be is that conflicts stand in their way. Ideal theories are intended to resolve these conflicts and transform lives as they are to come closer to how they should be.

Chapters 2 through 10 each begin with a story about the conflicts of a real person living a real and ordinary life. The stories are drawn from life and are meant to be true to it. I have changed some of the facts to avoid identifying the person, but the changes do not affect the types of conflicts that are faced, given irrelevant differences, not only by the person in the story but also by countless others, including perhaps even readers of this book.

These conflicts are not dramatic choices between life and death or good and evil. Nor are they about the morality of torturing terrorists in dire emergencies, or about killing if it saves lives, or about making choices behind the veil of ignorance. They do not concern the social problems we currently face about abortion, euthanasia, capital punishment, pornography, the legalization of drugs, and the sexual abuse of children. The conflicts are within ourselves between our various responsibilities; ways of using our limited time, energy, and money; balancing long- and short-term satisfactions; controlling our temper; doing too much or not enough; dealing with people we dislike; and so on. They stand in the way of living as we should. We all have to cope with them, but how we do that is vulnerable to the same kind of conflicts as the ones with which we have to cope.

Ideal theorists propose an ideal that should guide us in resolving our conflicts and transforming our lives from what they are to what they should be. They suppose that the ideal they favor is overriding because living according to it is more important than any other ideal that might conflict with it. In each chapter I consider an ideal proposed by an influential contemporary ideal theorist as the key to resolving our conflicts, including those of the person in the story, and motivating us to live as we should. The ideals are absolutist morality, individual autonomy, reflective self-evaluation, unconditional love, strong evaluation, narrative unity, inescapable reflection, and necessary truthfulness. They are defended, in the order of discussion, by Thomas Nagel,

Christine Korsgaard, Harry Frankfurt (in two chapters), Charles Taylor, Alasdair MacIntyre, Donald Davidson, and Bernard Williams (also in two chapters).

There is, of course, a large body of interpretive and evaluative work on the details of each of these ideals. My concern, however, is not with such details, but with the most basic assumption on which each of the ideals rests. The assumption is that reason requires that we should live by recognizing the overriding importance of a particular ideal. I think this assumption is mistaken, and I intend to show that reason allows us to live according to a wide variety of ideals, none of which is always overriding.

I will be critical of each of the theories I discuss, but I acknowledge that I have learned much from them. I have arrived at the practical approach I defend by asking why I cannot accept any of these theories. I have concluded that none of them would enable the person in the story, or us as we face very similar conflicts, to resolve the conflicts and transform our lives from what they are to what they should be.

I emphasize now, and will do so again, that I recognize that all the ideals I will discuss are important; we cannot live a civilized life without them. I am not opposed to the ideals, but to ideal theories that inflate the importance of a fine ideal beyond reasonable limits and claim that it should always override any consideration that conflicts with it. My doubts about ideal theories are strengthened by their history. Not one of the many proposed ideal theories has been accepted by all, or most, or even the majority of those who think about such matters. The reason for these disagreements is not the shortage of proposed ideals, nor that their critics have failed to understand them. The reason is that no ideal theory can possibly succeed. They are meant to be universal guides of all lives in all contexts. But our characters, experiences, preferences, and conflicts vary and change, as do our conditions and contexts. No theory about how all lives should be lived could possibly be a guide to individually variable lives. The history of ideal theories, therefore, is the history of very intelligent people banging their very learned heads against a very solid wall.

The critical aim of the book is to show that currently available ideal theories cannot deliver what their defenders promise. Its constructive aim is to answer the obvious question that if ideal theories cannot succeed in doing what they are meant to do, then how can we deal with the conflicts that stand in the way of transforming our life to approximate more closely how it should be? The answer is that we should follow the practical approach. It is an approach, not a theory, because it is impossible to have the sort of theory that would be a reasonable guide to how we should live, given the enormous variety of characters, conditions, contexts, and conflicts with which we must cope. Each chapter, except the introductory and the concluding ones, is both critical and constructive. In the earlier chapters the emphasis is on criticism, rather than constructive claims. In later chapters the emphasis gradually shifts toward constructive claims.

Conflicts

One type of conflict that stands between our lives as they are and how they should be is caused by our incompatible beliefs, emotions, and desires that guide how we should live. Strong emotions make us reluctant to act on reasonable beliefs. Love and hate, confidence and fear, pride and shame, loyalty and self-interest often drive us in opposite directions. We pursue what we want and ignore the cautious warnings of what we know or feel would be prudent. The strength of our conflicting beliefs, emotions, and desires keeps changing depending on their objects, ambient influences, old and new experiences, and our shifting moods and competing interpretations. The importance we attribute to work, leisure, health, money, food, sex, politics, religion, and death varies, often daily, depending on which of our conflicting beliefs, emotions, and desires have the temporary upper hand. We are often assailed by regret, remorse, guilt, and shame for what reason has led us to do or fail to do. These and other bad feelings about ourselves undermine the confidence we need to have in order to guide our future.

We want to avoid such conflicts and form stable, coherent, and realistic attitudes, but the conflicts affect also our efforts to form such attitudes. Nevertheless, we have to cope with our conflicts in much of what we do. For this, however, we must pay the price of going against some of our beliefs, emotions, or desires. We are naturally reluctant to do that, so we dither in irresolution or deceive ourselves by denigrating what we would like but cannot have.

Another type of conflict we routinely have to face is between the various aesthetic, economic, legal, medical, moral, personal, political, prudential, religious, scientific, and other ideals we hold. Our evaluations of what is good or bad and better or worse are guided by these ideals. But they routinely motivate us to act in conflicting ways. Honoring one often excludes the possibility of honoring another. When we encounter such conflicts, we have to make a choice, and whatever we choose inevitably involves going against one of the ideals to which we are committed and which we now must violate. Since how we want to live is guided by these conflicting ideals, choosing between them forces us to act contrary to how we want to live.

A third type of conflict arises from our dissatisfactions with ourselves. We may think we are too fearful, lazy, accommodating, resentful, undisciplined, hasty, or overconfident, and realize that our faults prevent us from living as we want. We often know why we have failed and what we should have done not to fail. This gives us an ideal of what our better future self would be if it were free of the faults that handicap us now. The present faulty self, however, is the only one we have. Whatever we do must be done by it. Its faults will affect what we do, and that will stand in the way of changing our unsatisfactory present self into a future self we think would be better. The present self is how we are, the future self is how we think we should be, and they often pull us in incompatible directions. This conflict affects all of us who are in some way dissatisfied with ourselves. And few of us are without such dissatisfactions.

A consequence of these familiar conflicts among our attitudes, ideals, and present and future self is that we often do not know how to act. Yet we must cope with the conflicts, act in one way or another, or die from inanition. But whatever we do, we have to act contrary to part of what we are. Disorder and confusion are natural and understandable consequences of such conflicts. And when we do act because we are forced to do something, the conflicts are only temporarily resolved. Our attitudes, commitments, and faulty present and desired future self remain as conflicting as they were before. Their conflicts are likely to persist and stand in the way of transforming our life from what it is to what we think it should be, and thus make us dissatisfied with how we live. This is one reason why Hume's skeptic is right: "the mind partakes" in the disorder and confusion of human affairs.

Real Lives

There are formidable obstacles to facing these conflicts and their implications for our life. We need to be honest, calm, relaxed, and a little
thoughtful, have at least a modest historical perspective, and neither
ignore nor deny the conflicts that stand in the way of living as we think
we should. It is hard to accept that the causes of many of our serious
dissatisfactions with how we live are conflicts within us and that they
are likely to persist and make us uncertain about how to make our life
better. A much easier way is to look elsewhere, ignore the unpleasant
facts, collude in their sentimental falsification, nurture false hopes, and
console ourselves with wishful thinking rather than face the possibility
that we are the causes of many of our dissatisfactions.

We can readily accept that others confuse comforting wishes with
distressing reality, allow fears to overwhelm their judgment, make
themselves busy with unnecessary activities rather than acknowledge
unpleasant facts, invent excuses for not doing what they do not want
to do, misdescribe their motives, pretend that their vices are virtues,
simulate feelings they should but do not have, worship false gods, passionately support unworthy causes, value what is shoddy, and deny their
faults. It is more difficult, however, to face the fact that some of these
falsifying stratagems may well be also our own. For facing them requires us to acknowledge that if some of our dissatisfactions are caused
by conflicts within us, then our efforts to cope with them may also be
beset by the sorts of conflicts with which we are trying to cope. As Lucy
said: "The trouble with you, Charlie Brown, is that you are you."

Our conflicts do not make it impossible to live as we want, only very
difficult: many of us try, but few succeed. One main reason for our frequent failures is that the conflicts are between parts of our nature, of
our self, character, temperament, lasting dispositions, aversions, preferences, and habits. Our nature is complex, has depths of which we may
not be aware. The conflicts, however, are close to its surface. They are
familiar, obvious, and we routinely encounter them in ourselves and
others. But the hard fact is that our efforts to cope with them are also
vulnerable to the same kind of conflicts. This is one main reason why
life is difficult and our dissatisfactions are many. Conflicts cast doubt
on the widely held assumption that if we do not fall afoul of external
contingencies beyond our control and follow reasonable ideals of how
we should live, then nothing will stop us from living according to them.

The assumption is false. Even if contingencies from outside ourselves do not assail us and we are committed to reasonable ideals of how we should live, conflicts inside ourselves often prevent us from living according to them.

We should certainly try to live as reasonably as we can, but conflicts may nevertheless stand in our way. I say *may*, not *will*. It is possible to live reasonably, but it takes fortunate circumstances and considerable lifelong efforts. These conditions are rarely met, and their coincidence is even rarer. If in doubt, ask yourself: how many people do you know, yourself included, who try to live according to reasonable ideals, do not falsify the facts, and are free of conflicts that jeopardize their—our— efforts? How many of us could truly say, or could have it said of us, that we live as we want and actually like our life enough not to want it to be different in various ways?

In asking these questions, I am not supposing that the key to living as we want is to live successfully according to reasonable ideals. There are other ways of living reasonably and succeeding at it. But even if we do not deliberately or otherwise aim to live according to reasonable ideals, most of us know without much soul-searching what would make our life better. And when we know it, we rely on some perhaps undeveloped, or inarticulate, or weakly held ideals in the background. Knowing that, however, is not enough. We also have to live according to them, and that remains difficult, partly because the internal conflicts that stand in the way are part of our nature and may prevent us from living in the way other parts of our nature motivate us to try to do. The mind partakes in causing the resulting disorders and confusions, and that is another reason why Hume's skeptic is right.

Concentrating on these conflicts is not an amateur venture into scientific psychology but an attempt to understand the significance of facts that have been long familiar to reflective observers of the ways in which we jeopardize our own efforts. Many facts are prior to scientific attempts to explain their causes. We can watch a falling star, get into debt, or resent an authority without theorizing about astronomy, Keynesian economics, or psychoanalysis. We can reason in ignorance of the rules of logic, expect objects to fall without knowledge of gravity, and note the resemblance between children and their parents even if we have never heard of genetics. Likewise, the conflicts in our nature and the resulting problems have been familiar a hundred, three hundred, a thousand, and two thousand years ago. Psychologists may try to explain their causes, and I applaud their efforts, but my concern is not with their causes, whether evolutionary, cultural, psychoanalytic, or neurological, but with the conflicts themselves, with the problems they present to how we want to live, and with what we can and cannot do about them.

These conflicts are not momentary lapses, to which we are all occasionally prone. Nor do they afflict only a few of us. They are part of human nature. No one is quite free of them. Self-control may enable us to cope with them, as some may learn to control their reactions to pain and fear, but we must all learn to live, as well as we can, with the conflicts, pains, and fears we encounter in ourselves. The question is how we might learn that.

Ideal theorists have had much to say on this subject, but I do not think they have come to terms with the seriousness and implications of these internal conflicts. Ideal theories have a very long history of trying to do that, although they have not been so named until recently. I am not sure who first used the label, but it is certainly used in 1971 by Rawls in A Theory of Justice. I turn now to some of the best known ideal theories that have been proposed in the past.

Ideal Theories

Plato's Socrates says that the unexamined life is not worth living. He suggests thereby that more examination may make life more worth living.[2] Whether this is true surely depends on what the examination reveals. We may find that we are stupid, craven, weak, ignorant, unjust, cruel, and so forth. We may be assailed by guilt, shame, or self-loathing. And the results of the examination may embitter us, make us misanthropic, and sap our very will to carry on. Is it plausible to suppose that Pascal, Rousseau, Schopenhauer, Kierkegaard, Nietzsche, Flaubert, and Proust were made more satisfied with their lives by their extensive self-examination than they would have been if they had let sleeping dogs lie?

Aristotle seems to think that we are distinguished from animals by our capacity for rationality.[3] I put this tentatively because all commentators I know of agree that the relevant passages are obscure. It is certainly true that we tend to give reasons for whatever we happen to believe, feel, or want, but the reasons are often very bad. Self-deception, wishful thinking, prejudice, superstition, and dogmatism are well-known problems that stand in the way of rationality, and none of them seems to handicap animals. We could just as well be distinguished from animals by our capacity for irrationality. Why, then, focus on what we would be like if the familiar problems did not handicap us, rather than on what we, handicapped by them, really are?

Kant says that only the good will is unconditionally good; the categorical imperative commands us to be motivated by it; and following its command is a requirement of reason.[4] Yet we are often motivated by ill will, act contrary to the categorical imperative, and even when we do what Kant says reason requires of us, we often cause great harm to others and ourselves, which, according to Kant, should not deter us from doing our duty. Why labor to construct this elephantine architectonic system about what we ought to do and pay very little attention to the conflicts that prevent us from doing what reason and morality supposedly require us to do?

Mill writes of "the social feelings of mankind; the desire to be in unity with our fellow creatures, which is already a powerful principle in human nature, and happily one of those which tend to become stronger, even without express inculcation, from the influences of advancing civilization."[5] And his most recent acolyte, Steven Pinker, claims in an eight-hundred-page book laden with misleading statistics that violence has declined because proportionally fewer people are killed in wars.[6] Oddly, he does not bother to notice that there are other measures of violence than counting corpses on battlefields. No one can reasonably suppose that there has been a decline, during the past hundred years, of concentration camps; terrorism; religious, ethnic, and tribal massacres; organized crime; and deaths caused by preventable poverty, famine, and epidemics.

Consider what more realistic writers say of the real world. "The hundred years after 1900 were without question the bloodiest in modern history, far more violent in relative as well as absolute terms than any previous era." "By any measure, the Second World War was the greatest man-made catastrophe of all time."[7] Estimates of the total number of people killed in various forms of organized violence during the past one hundred years or so range between 167 million and 188 million.[8] And "archeological, anthropological, as well as all surviving documentary evidence indicates that war, armed conflict between organized political groups, has been the universal norm in human history."[9] For more of the same, see note 10.[10] But these and a multitude of similar awful facts do not dampen the Whiggish sentimentalism Mill and his followers share.

Of course it is good to do as the ideal theorists say we should. We should examine how we live, be rational, act out of good will, and cultivate our social feelings. As our past and present show, however, their admonishments have had no discernible effect on our inhumanity to one another and have left unaltered the persistent pattern of irrationality, immorality, and imprudence that runs through the history of all times, nations, and civilizations. Our conflicts stand between what these ideal theorists tell us our lives should be and what they really are. Yet the oddest assortment of distinguished past and present ideal theorists assure us, contrary to facts they cannot fail to know, that human beings are basically rational and good.[11]

If we are as ideal theorists suppose, then they need to explain why the awful facts of the past and the present are not contrary to their comforting view of humanity. Their explanations must sooner or later acknowledge that there are conflicts that prevent us from living in ways that allow our supposed basic rationality and goodness to shine through. But if these conflicts are acknowledged, then the futility of the repeated admonishments by ideal theorists to examine our life, be more rational, act more out of good will, and nurture our social feeling will also have to be acknowledged. The conflicts will stand in the way of heeding their admonishments.

The contemporary efforts to construct ever more complex ideal theories can connect with our lives only if they recognize the seriousness of our conflicts and propose reasonable ways of resolving them. I do not think the theories of Plato, Aristotle, Kant, Mill, and their followers have done that. Their theories fit some of the facts and ignore or attempt to explain away contrary facts. They advocate a supposedly overriding ideal that they claim reason requires us to live by, but if the conflicts that are part of our nature stand in our way, then their theories are merely elaborate blueprints for castles built on air. They earnestly solemnize the sentimental ditty Bing Crosby memorably crooned:

Accentuate the positive
Eliminate the negative
Latch on to the affirmative
Don't mess with Mister In-Between.

The Argument

I argue critically throughout the book that we should turn away from ideal theories because they misrepresent reality and that makes them dangerous illusions. They are illusions because reason does not require us to accept any ideal as an overriding guide of how we should live. They are dangerous because they stand in the way of facing and coping with the conflicts that are part of our nature and stand in the way of our efforts to live according to our commitments to a variety of ideals. I also argue constructively that we should turn toward the practical approach as a reasonable alternative to ideal theories. It is an approach that takes different forms in different contexts, not a theory. It does not lend itself to a simple statement. What it is and what forms it takes will emerge from understanding how the real people in the stories I tell in each chapter cope with their conflicts.

By way of an initial indication of what to expect, I mention without supporting reasons that the practical approach is not theoretical; it is particular, not general; concrete, not abstract; context-dependent, not universal; accepts that we can only cope with our conflicts, but not resolve them once and for all. It is committed to a variety of often conflicting ideals according to which reason allows but does not require us to live. It is an attempt to work out a reasonable pluralistic alternative to absolutist ideal theories and various forms of relativism.

I do not think it can be reasonably denied that conflicts are part of our nature. But it will be denied that they are permanent parts. I cannot prove the contrary. What I can and will do instead is show that the reasons that have been given for denying that conflicts are permanent parts of our nature are unconvincing. It is, of course, possible that there may be other and better reasons than those that have been given. I can say only that I do not know of any. As things now stand, it seems to me that the best we can do will not eliminate, but sometimes allow us to cope with, them.

I realize that by expressing doubts about widely accepted ideal theories, I am opposing a prevailing consensus. I do not do this lightly or willingly. It seems to me, however, that the practical approach to how we should live and cope with our conflicts is better than nurturing dangerous illusions about it. By stressing that conflicts are parts of our nature, I do not mean that we are at their mercy. There is much that we can and should do to cope with them and make our lives better. It is a mistake to suppose, however, that if we do what we can, we will eliminate these conflicts. We cannot reasonably expect that the exceptionally fortunate physical, psychological, social, political, and moral conditions required for coping successfully with our conflicts will regularly coincide. They may on rare occasions coincide, but it is an illusion to expect that if we are reasonable and try hard enough, we can make them coincide. Of course we should do what we can, or our lives will be even worse.

If the world were made for us, or we for the world, then the disorder and confusion of our affairs would not be formidable problems. As things are, however, "there is no pre-established harmony between the furtherance of truth and the well-being of mankind."[12] Facing the truth is generally better than being deceived by untruth, but it is yet another illusion to suppose that facing the truth about how our lives really are would allow us to transform them into what they should be. Or so I will argue.

The title of each chapter, except the first and the last, is the ideal I consider in that chapter. The epigraph that follows each title is intended to indicate in a few unargued, succinct, but I hope perspicuous sentences a serious problem for the ideal theory I consider in the chapter. Readers who cannot restrain their curiosity should feel free to read the epigraphs one after another. Following each epigraph is a story I tell about a real life and its conflicts. Then comes my account of an ideal theory prescribing how reason requires us to live so as to resolve the conflicts described in the story. In roughly the second half of each chapter, I give reasons why the ideal theory cannot deliver what its defenders promise and how the practical approach enables us to do better.

2 Absolutist Morality

There exists a great chasm between those, on one side, who relate everything to a single central vision, one system less or more coherent and
articulate, in terms of which they understand, think and feel—a single,
universal, organising principle in terms of which alone all that they are
and say has significance—and, on the other side, those who pursue
many ends, often unrelated.

ISAIAH BERLIN, "The Hedgehog and the Fox"[1]

Ideal theorists and defenders of a practical approach are on opposite
sides of the great chasm Berlin writes about in "The Hedgehog and
the Fox." According to ideal theorists, reason requires making a commitment to an ideal that is always overriding. I deny it; I think reason
allows living with commitments to a variety of ideals, none of which is
overriding. Ideal theorists and defenders of a practical approach agree
that we all have various commitments to aesthetic, moral, personal, political, religious, or scientific ideals, among others, and that we should
live according to them. They also agree that our commitments often
conflict, that the conflicts stand in the way of living as we think we
should, and that we need a reasonable way of coping with the conflicts.
They disagree, however, whether coping with them requires commitment to an overriding ideal or whether it can be done reasonably case
by case. This chapter is about the ideal theory according to which the
overriding ideal should be morality. I call this view of morality absolutist. There are, of course, nonabsolutist views of morality, and what I say

in criticism of absolutist morality does not apply to them. Here are two classic statements of the absolutist view.

According to Kant, "there is a practical law, which commands absolutely of itself and without incentives, and that the observance of this law is duty. . . . For, duty is to be practical unconditional necessity of action and it must therefore hold for all rational beings . . . and *only because of this* be also a law of the will of every rational being."[2] He writes in a subsequent work that, given this practical unconditional necessity of action, there can be no conflicting duties. "A *conflict of duties* . . . would be a relation between them in which one of them would cancel the other (wholly or in part).—But since duty and obligation are concepts that express the objective practical *necessity* of certain actions and two rules opposed to each other cannot be necessary at the same time, it is a duty to act in accordance with one rule[;] to act in accordance with the opposite rule is not a duty but even contrary to duty; so a *collision of duties* and obligations is inconceivable."[3]

John Stuart Mill writes that "justice is a name for certain classes of moral rules, which concern the essentials of human well-being more nearly, and are therefore of more absolute obligation, than any other rules for the guidance of life." He adds: "This is the highest standard of social and distributive justice; towards which all institutions, and the efforts of all virtuous citizens should be made in the utmost possible degree to converge." And he concludes that "justice is a name for certain moral requirements, which, regarded collectively, stand higher in the scale of social utility, and are therefore of more paramount obligation, than any others."[4]

There are also numerous contemporary defenders of morality as an overriding ideal.[5] A full list of them would be very long, especially if it included the plethora of articles. I hope it will suffice to say that in both past and present thinking, absolutist morality has been and continues to be widely favored as an overriding ideal that should guide how we live.

Absolutist moralists (from now on called simply moralists) think that conflicts about how we should live should be resolved by evaluating our conflicting commitments from the moral point of view. Moral commitments may conflict with nonmoral commitments, but reason requires that such conflicts should be resolved in favor of the moral ones. According to moralists, commitment to morality as the overriding ideal is required by reason, and it is unreasonable not to make such a commitment. Defenders of a practical approach agree that moral commitments are important, but they do not think reason requires that they should always be overriding. They may be overriding in some cases but not in others.

In this chapter I discuss and give reasons against Thomas Nagel's ideal theory of absolutist morality as an overriding ideal. I think Nagel and other ideal theorists are mistaken in their search for an overriding ideal and that the practical approach is right in regarding that search as misguided. But the view I defend in this chapter is the much more modest one that reason allows both moralism and a practical approach but does not require either. The dispute, then, is about the reasons for and against commitment to morality as an ideal that should be followed by everyone, always, and in all contexts. If moralists are right, conflicts among our various commitments need not be permanent parts of life, because we can and should resolve them by appealing to morality. If the practical approach is right, conflicts are unavoidable consequences of having commitments to a variety of ideals but to no overriding ideal. I begin with a story about someone who is committed to morality as an overriding ideal.

The School Teacher

The School Teacher is approaching forty, divorced, teaches history in high school, and has two teenage children who live with her. Her dominant attitude to life is moral. She values truth, justice, honesty, courage, and integrity above all else, and she does her best to live and act accordingly. She has not always been like that. She grew out of adolescence as confused, morally uncertain, fearful, and self-indulgent as most of us. But she became committed to morality and makes constant efforts to live and act so as to approximate more closely her moral ideal. This is not easy for her. She has to control her unruly beliefs, emotions, and desires that prompt her to act contrary to her moral commitments. Gradually, however, she has reached a stage in her life when she often, although not invariably, succeeds.

The School Teacher is not a fanatic. She cares about beauty, security, sex, comfort, and having a historical perspective. She has preferences about style, diet, housing, exercise, friends, and leisure. She wants to be a good mother, teacher, colleague, neighbor, and friend. She is active in local politics and has decided views about politics in general. But her commitment to morality is overriding. If her moral and nonmoral commitments conflict, as they do from time to time, she opts for the moral ones. She thinks and feels that her commitment to morality should override any of her nonmoral commitments when they conflict.

Do not think, as Susan Wolf says in a much-quoted article about moral saints, that the School Teacher would have to be a "very, very nice" do-gooder relentlessly bent on the moral improvement of the human condition. "The worry is," according to Wolf, that such a person would "have to be dull-witted or humorless or bland." "The ideal of a life of moral sainthood disturbs not simply because it is an ideal of a life in which morality unduly dominates," but because "it seems to require either the lack or the denial of the existence of an identifiable personal self."[6] The School Teacher is not a moral saint, but she tries hard to live and act according to her moral commitments, even when, and especially when, nonmoral commitments, whose force she recognizes, motivate her to act contrary to her moral commitments.

Her commitment to morality, however, exacts a heavy cost. She is becoming more and more friendless. People rightly sense that she judges them, weighs the moral acceptability of how they live and what choices they make. Even when she keeps mum about the minor moral failings she observers in others, they, being sensitive to criticism, suspect, usually correctly, that they are being adversely judged. The School Teacher knows, feels keenly, and minds the resulting cooling of her relationships. As her friends, lovers, colleagues, neighbors, and acquaintances get to know her better, they come to resent and fear her constant moral scrutiny of how they live and act. She knows this and forces herself to watch what she says and hide the disapproval she feels—justifiably, she is convinced. She finds that people are far more self-indulgent than they ought to be. And her commitment to morality does not allow her to ignore the more serious transgressions she observes. She knows in her heart that most people are at least as wanting from the moral point of view as she herself is. She has a dim view of humanity in general and of herself in particular, and she thinks it is the right view.

Her husband left because he could no longer stand her predictable responses that led her to cast an unblinking moral eye on whatever they discussed. Her preoccupation with morality fatigued and irritated him, and he did not want to take it any more. Her children are dependent on her for love and support, but what they often get are moral instructions of what they and their friends should or should not have done. They are impatient and when they complain to their father, whom they often see, he understands what bothers them. Her fellow teachers are exasperated by her scruples and the implied criticism of themselves. Her students' parents think she is too demanding. And her political allies tell her that political effectiveness demands the compromises her commitment to morality does not allow her to make or accept.

She knows that morality requires her to judge people and actions, without fear and favor, to be impartial, to make no exceptions, and to condemn the lies, broken promises, dishonesty, and injustice of whoever is guilty of them. But she knows also that it is not in her to condemn a charming liar as much as a boorish one, or to despise the expediency of a political ally as much as that of political opponent, and she feels ashamed at her inconsistency. Still, she judges her lovers, children, colleagues, and friends, and they sense this and feel betrayed by her. They expect her to be warm, loyal, understanding, and indulgent toward them, but she does not pretend to feel warm toward wrongdoers. She tells herself that her primary loyalty should be to morality and that she should be as unindulgent toward others as she is toward herself. The fact is that she does not much like anyone, including herself and her intimates. They realize this and sooner or later, in one way or another, make it known to her.

The School Teacher is intelligent and perceptive, and she knows all this. Not surprisingly, she has become dissatisfied with herself. She knows she should be more loving and easygoing and less judgmental, but she cannot reconcile that with her commitment to morality as an overriding ideal. Honesty does not permit her to ignore what she regards as serious transgressions, to be half-hearted in discharging her responsibilities. She feels guilty and ashamed about her own moral failures, and she is having second thoughts about the overriding moral ideal to which she has been trying to live up. She feels keenly the conflicts between her commitment to morality and her need for self-esteem and warm personal relationships. She finds it increasingly hard to bear the burden of her overriding moral commitment. Her resolve is weakening about continuing to live according to it. Yet she is convinced that her commitment is right and that compromising it would be shameful, and untrue to herself. What should she do?

Absolutist Morality

In several influential works Thomas Nagel has discussed the conflicts between moral and nonmoral commitments. "It is clear," writes Nagel, "that in most people, the coexistence of the personal standpoint with the values deriving from the initial judgment of the impersonal standpoint produces a division of the self." The personal standpoint is extremely important to a person, but from the impersonal standpoint, "*everyone's* life matters as much as his does, and his matters no more than anyone else's. These two attitudes are not easy to combine."[7]

The School Teacher's predicament is that she finds the two standpoints conflicting and does not know how to combine them, how to resolve their conflicts. Nagel, however, knows. He writes in *The View from Nowhere* that although "doing the right thing is part of living well it is not the whole of it, nor even the dominant part: because the impersonal standpoint that acknowledges the claims of morality is only one aspect of a normal individual among others"; nevertheless, "there are times when doing the right thing may cost more in terms of other aspects of the good life than it contributes to the good life in its own right" (197). Nagel thinks that when this happens, as it is and has been happening to the School Teacher and happens to us again and again, reason requires that we should resolve the conflict in favor of morality. "The correct morality will always have a preponderance of reasons on its side, even though it needn't coincide with the good life" (199). Put plainly, Nagel's view is that reason requires us to live and act morally, even if it makes our lives worse.

Why does reason require this? Because "impersonal moralities with universal pretensions . . . derive their content from a view of one's own actions *sub specie aeternitatis*." "A universal standpoint that does not distinguish between oneself and anyone else reveals general principles of conduct that apply to oneself because they apply to everyone. There is a natural tendency to identify this higher standpoint with the true self, weighed down perhaps by individualistic baggage. There is a further tendency to accord absolute priority in the governance of life to its judgments" (199). The School Teacher, of course, is not a philosopher and is not concerned with articulating what Nagel says is a requirement of reason, but she senses it. She thinks and feels that her moral self is her true higher self and that she should follow its promptings when they conflict with her personal commitments, regardless of the cost of doing so. Nagel would say that the School Teacher is right to think and feel this way. "Insofar as reasons are universal, the repeated applications of impersonal standards seems to yield the most integrated set of requirements that can be hoped for, taking into account reasons derived from all perspectives" (204).

This is a clear and forthright statement of a view shared by many contemporary ideal theorists, who, although they differ in their interpretations of the contents of universal reasons, impersonal standards, and the unified view that emerges from them, agree with the basic assumption that reason requires viewing "one's own actions *sub specie aeternitatis.*" Why should we accept this assumption? Why should we think that the School Teacher is right to accept it? Consider three reasons against accepting it.

One of them, amazingly enough, is Nagel's. He gives it close to the end of the same work from which I have been citing passages (*The View from Nowhere*). "The basic moral insight that objectively no one matters more than anyone else, and that this acknowledgment should be of fundamental importance to each of us even though the objective standpoint is not our only standpoint, creates a conflict in the self too powerful to admit an easy resolution. I doubt that an appealing reconciliation of morality, rationality, and the good life can be achieved within the boundaries of ethical theory" (205). In short, Nagel admits that he can give no reason for the assumption on which his view rests. The admission is a testimony to Nagel's honesty, but it leads one to ask what is the point of filling many pages with the futile search for the reason Nagel knows is needed but cannot find. I do not think the failure to find it is Nagel's fault. I think there is no such reason to be found. Conflicts are permanent features of our lives.

Another reason for rejecting the assumption is Montaigne's: "What is the use of these lofty points of philosophy on which no human can settle, and these rules that exceed our use and strength? I often see people propose to us patterns of life which neither the proposer nor his hearers have any hope of following, or, what is more, any desire to follow." The School Teacher, Montaigne would say, committed herself to an ideal to which it is psychologically impossible for human beings to live up. The conflicts that now beset her are caused by facts of life that she can no longer ignore. She, and we, must live in the world and respond to it as we find it. Innocence and purity are impossible dreams. "The virtue assigned to the affairs of the world is a virtue with many bends, angles, and elbows, so as to join and adapt itself to human weakness; mixed and artificial, not straight, clean, constant, or purely innocent." "He who walks in the crowd must step aside, keep his elbows in, step back or advance, even leave the straight way, according to what he encounters." "Whoever escapes with clean breeches from handling the affairs of the world, escapes by a miracle."[8]

Finally, I come to the reason Bernard Williams gives for rejecting the view that reason requires us to make a commitment to morality as an overriding ideal: "There can come a point at which it is quite unreasonable for a man to give up, in the name of the impartial good ordering of the world of moral agents, something which is a condition of his having any interest in being around in that world at all."[9] The personal necessarily precedes and is a condition of the impersonal. For even if we come to evaluate from an impersonal moral point of view the personal beliefs, emotions, and desires with which we come to maturity, we, the persons that we are, must want to live and act according to the impersonal point of view, and wanting that must come from the beliefs, emotions, and wants of the persons that we are, since it cannot come from anywhere else. If, impossible as it is, we became impersonal, there would be no person left to be impersonal.

These reasons against the assumption—for which Nagel admits to be unable to find reasons—are not the end of the matter. In *The Last Word* he makes a further attempt to provide the needed reasons. The reason Nagel is seeking is "something each individual can find within himself, but at the same time it has universal authority." "Whoever appeals to reason purports to discover a source of authority within himself that is not merely personal, or societal, but universal" (3). Of course we often discover within ourselves what is personal or societal, but the attempt "to identify what is subjective and particular, or relative and communal, in one's outlook leads inevitably to the objective and universal. That is so whether the object of our scrutiny is ethics, or science, or even logic" (16). "There are some types of thought that we cannot avoid simply *having*—that it is strictly impossible to consider merely from the outside." This is "true of practical reasoning, including moral reasoning" (20). "One cannot just *exit* from the domain of moral reflection: It is simply there. All one can do is to proceed with it in the light of whatever new historical or psychological evidence may be offered" (21).

According to Nagel, we cannot avoid moral commitments, and reason requires us to regard them as overriding. "Moral considerations occupy a position in the system of human thought that makes it illegitimate to subordinate them completely to anything else." Of course, "particular moral claims are constantly being discredited for all kinds of reasons, but moral considerations per se keep arising again to challenge in their own rights any blanket attempt to displace, defuse, or subjectivize them" (105). He thinks that moral commitments can be challenged only on moral grounds and that whether the challenge is reasonable depends on moral reasons. "Challenges to the objectivity of science can be met only by further scientific reasoning, challenges to the objectivity of history by history, and so forth" (21). Challenges to "our arithmetical or moral convictions . . . may lead us to reexamine them," but we "cannot simply leave those domains behind" (21).

It seems to me that Nagel offers dogmatic pronouncements in place of reasons. Consider how arbitrary and unreasonable it would be to claim that challenges to the objectivity of religion can be met only by further religious reasoning, or that challenges to the objectivity of mysticism, magic, or telepathy can only be met by further mystical, magical, telepathic reasoning. Consider the countless examples in which serious thinkers have challenged and rejected the objectivity of morality and its status as an overriding ideal on the grounds that it is the disguised expression of self-interest, ideology, religious belief, or the superego, rather than a requirement of reason. Can the challenges of the ancient sophists and skeptics, of Machiavelli, Hobbes, Marx, Nietzsche, Weber, and of the long tradition of thoughtful cultural relativists be dismissed as Nagel does, by saying that morality is a domain of thought "that it is strictly impossible to consider merely from the outside" (20)? Examples abound in which thinkers have again and again done what Nagel says is impossible to do. All these thinkers may be mistaken, but that would need to be shown, not simply asserted.

Nagel supposes that challenges to moral reasoning are demands for additional moral reasons. But serious challenges to morality consist in demanding reasons for all moral reasoning. That challenge cannot possibly be met by offering further moral reasons, as Nagel claims, but only by giving reasons why it is reasonable to reason morally, rather than to follow, for instance, prudential, ideological, religious, historical, or psychoanalytic reasons. Perhaps these nonmoral modes of reasoning are all illegitimate and their challenges to moral reasoning can be met. But whether or not that is so, their challenges cannot be met by giving moral reasons. The name for doing what Nagel insists on is begging the question. And the fallacy does not stop being one if the question begged is as basic as the one to which Nagel gives a dogmatic answer.

Suppose, however, that I am wrong and Nagel is right: "There are some types of thought that we cannot avoid simply *having*—that it is strictly impossible to consider merely from the outside" (20). Let us suppose further that morality is one of these types of thought. Why should we think that "moral considerations occupy a position in the system of human thought that makes it illegitimate to subordinate them completely to anything else" (105)? Why is it illegitimate to subordinate moral considerations to nonmoral ones? Who could reasonably suppose that since battery is morally wrong, one should not resort to it if there is no other way to prevent a teenager from spray painting his initials on Leonardo's *Last Supper*. Or that since stealing is morally wrong, one should not steal the folio of a hitherto unknown play of Shakespeare from a man who is about to use it as kindling. In general, it is unreasonable to suppose that moral considerations should always override conflicting nonmoral ones.

Nagel might say that what should be overriding are not particular moral commitments, like the ones just mentioned, but the most basic commitment to morality as overriding art, politics, history, religion, science, prudence, and so forth. Why should morality override them? Why should it be a requirement of reason to override our sanity, or protecting the life of our beloved, or the survival of great works of art, or of our cultural tradition, if it conflicts with a basic commitment to morality? I think that Frankfurt is right to say in response to views like Nagel's:

> The basic concern of morality is with how we conduct ourselves in our relations with other people. Now why should *that* be, always and in all circumstances, the most important thing in our lives? No doubt it is important; but as far as I am aware, there is no convincing argument that it must override everything else. Even if we were entirely clear what the moral law commands, it would remain an open question how important it is for us to obey those commands. We would still have to decide how much to care about morality. Morality cannot satisfy us about that.[10]

How could it be reasonable to claim that reason requires the School Teacher to resolve her conflicts in favor of continuing to regard her commitment to morality as overriding and thereby alienate herself from her life, cause serious damage to her self-respect, and do without the warm human relationships for which she yearns? The alternative is not to repudiate morality altogether, but to regard it as only one of her most important commitments. Morality may require her and us to be true to our commitments, but it does not require us to alienate others from ourselves. And if I am wrong, Nagel is right, and morality does require that of us, then that would be a good reason to say that morality should be revised so as to dispense with a requirement that is contrary to how it is reasonable to live.

Commitments

The conflicts of the School Teacher and the doubts about Nagel's defense of moralism make it natural to ask: Why do ideal theorists think that a commitment to morality as an overriding ideal should override any other commitment to any other ideal that may conflict with it? Ideal theorists need to answer this question, which arises not just about morality but also about religion, politics, economics, science, or any other ideal that is supposed to be an overriding guide of how we should live. It is not hard to understand that an ideal of how we should live is reinforced by knowing that other people share it. But why do ideal theorists insist that reason requires everyone to share it? And regardless of whether the ideal is shared by others, why should it be one that must always, in all contexts, be overriding? Why could an ideal not be a general guide that allows for circumstances in which it might be reasonably overridden by some other ideal? Why should it be a requirement of reason that a commitment we have made should always override whatever other commitments of ours might conflict with it? Why could not a commitment to morality allow that if a less important moral requirement conflicts with an important political requirement, then the moral requirement may be temporarily suspended, as is often done in familiar conflicts in which politicians must lie or break a promise in order to protect the interests of those whom they represent? Why must commitments be always overriding, rather than normally or generally overriding, thus allowing for exceptions in some cases? What reasons might lead us to make a commitment to an ideal and insist that it should always be overriding?

A superficial answer is that we might make such a commitment because we have been brought up by our parents or teachers to make it. Or we come to make it in later life because we are influenced by a charismatic teacher or by some life-changing experience, such as grief, gross injustice, or the collapse of our whole way of life. But this response is unconvincing because many of us reject our upbringing, resist charisma, find other ways of coming to terms with wrenching experiences, or may live on stoically in misery, or not at all. Why do many of us willingly make and continue to be guided by a commitment to an overriding ideal, while many others do not? A better answer is that such a commitment enables us to resolve our conflicts, whereas having a variety of commitments to a variety of ideals would lead to conflicts, rather than to resolving them. And our overriding commitment is likely to be reinforced by others who have made the same commitment. The usual sources of an overriding commitment, therefore, are both psychological and social, and they reciprocally strengthen one another.

Perhaps this is the right answer to the question of why we come to make a commitment to an overriding ideal and try to live according to it. But this combined psychological and social explanation of how we arrive at such a commitment does not come even close to a justification of it. The overriding commitments of fanatics, dogmatists, and ideologues who are ruled by some prejudice, passion, dread, or indoctrination are mistaken and often have disastrous consequences for themselves and others. Might it not be that an overriding commitment to morality is also mistaken? After all, many reigns of terror were motivated by just such moral commitments. Doubts about whether our commitment to morality should be overriding are legitimate, and they cannot be dismissed, as Nagel does, by the insouciant claim that "one cannot just *exit* from the domain of moral reflection: It is simply there" (*The Last Word*, 21). If questioning the legitimacy of overriding commitment to morality is to exit from morality, then one can certainly do so. I am doing it right now, and of course many others have done it. And such questioning need not be arbitrary: there may be reasons for it.

One reason is that not just moralists but all ideal theorists face a dilemma they can neither avoid nor satisfactorily resolve. In the same sense in which Nagel says that morality is simply there, economics, medicine, politics, and science are also simply there. Moralists insist that to each one of these areas of life that are simply there, morality may set reasonable limits. This is true, even if we may argue about what limits are reasonable. But it is also true that there are reasonable limits to morality set by economics, medicine, politics, and science. Morality must take into account the facts of life, and the facts limit what can be a reasonable view of morality. In that case, however, morality cannot be overriding, since it can be overridden by economic, medical, political, scientific, or other considerations. It is therefore not an adequate reason for regarding morality as overriding that it is simply there. There are other important areas of life that are simply there. They often conflict, and it is not required, but contrary to reason, to arbitrarily declare, as Nagel and other ideal theorists do, that such conflicts must always be resolved in favor of the ideal theory they happen to favor. Since ideal theorists claim that conflicts between ideal theories should always be resolved in favor of a particular ideal theory, they need to provide some reason for their claim. The dilemma they face is this: if, on the one hand, they provide the required reason in support of their claim that their ideal theory is overriding, then they cannot derive that reason from their ideal theory, since that would beg the question at issue; if, on the other hand, they cannot provide the required reason, then their claim that their ideal theory is overriding is arbitrary. Since there are undeniable conflicts between ideal theories, the claim that a particular ideal theory is always overriding is either question-begging or arbitrary.

Another reason for questioning moralism is that the commitment to morality as an overriding ideal may be mistaken. Such a commitment is an attitude to life that involves beliefs, emotions, and desires. Some such beliefs are about how our lives do and should proceed; the favorable or unfavorable circumstances that form the context in which we live; and the various other commitments we have made to family, work, or a cherished cause. And the beliefs are also about the particular responsibilities that follow from our various commitments. These beliefs may be true, false, or a mixture of both, depending on what the relevant facts are. But whether the beliefs are true, false, or mixed depends also on the relative importance we attribute to the relevant facts, such as to our success or failure in living according our beliefs, or to the relative importance we assign to family, work, money, politics, or religion.

Our beliefs about the facts and their relative importance may be false, or more or less false, for many reasons, but some among them are self-deception, fear, hope, stupidity, laziness, and other psychological obstacles that prevent us from forming an accurate view of the relevant facts. These obstacles range from reasonable defenses against the awfulness of our circumstances, through nonculpable weaknesses and shortcomings, to culpable vices. Generally speaking, however, it is very much in our interest that our attitude to life should be formed of true beliefs, because our success in living according to our commitment to the ideal we aim at depends on it. Part of the School Teacher's dissatisfaction with her life was caused by her conflicts, which, in turn, led to her correct judgment that she was failing to live as closely as she felt she ought to have to the commitment she had made to her overriding moral ideal.

Emotions are another component of the attitude we have to our life. It is natural to feel optimistic or pessimistic, hopeful or fearful, pleased or apprehensive, proud or ashamed, enthusiastic or demoralized, and so forth, about our life. Such emotions are natural in the sense that having them is readily understandable and it is their absence that requires explanation. If we have no such emotions, then something has gone very wrong in our life. Extreme hardship, constant struggle against grave threats, serious traumas, mental illness, or recurrent humiliation may make our life hard to endure. It is understandable why, if we are afflicted by such misfortunes, we would direct our emotions outward, toward the causes of our hardships, and respond to them by anger, fear, resentment, and the like, instead of directing them inward and allowing ourselves to add the burden of terrible feelings to the misfortune we are enduring. But in the normal course of events, in civilized circumstances, without very bad luck, it is normal for us to have emotions about how our life is going, regardless of whether or how much we are satisfied or dissatisfied with it.

Having emotions about our life, however, is one thing; whether they are reasonable is quite another. They may be unreasonable if they are directed toward the wrong object or, if directed toward the right object, they are disproportionally strong or weak. Our emotions about our success or failure in living as we want are unreasonable if they do not respond to the facts but to what we hope or fear the facts will turn out to be, or if we optimistically overreact with joy when all goes momentarily well, or pessimistically despair when we suffer insignificant setbacks. But emotions may also be reasonable when they are realistic responses to the facts that bear on whether we live as we want and when our responses are neither too strong nor too weak. Adapting Aristotle's requirement, we may say that emotions are reasonable when they respond to the right object, to the right extent, at the right time, with the right aim, and in the right way.[11]

Some moralists, especially Kantians, are skeptical about relying on our emotions, because they think that emotions are involuntary and we cannot control them. But this skepticism is unwarranted. Although we cannot control emotions directly, we can control them indirectly. There may be little we can do about having or not having particular emotions, but there is much that we can do to strengthen reasonable emotions and weaken unreasonable ones. The possibility of correcting them depends on our collateral beliefs. Reasonable emotions toward our life involve beliefs we take to be true: that we are loved, that our cause is doomed, that a goal is within our reach, that our friend is true, and so on. Any of these beliefs may turn out to be false. The realization that the beliefs we took to be true are in fact false will affect the emotions that are reactions to the belief about whose truth we have changed our mind. Our joy at being loved or shame at failure will not survive for long if we discover that the love was simulated or what appeared to be a failure was in fact a success. The emotion may linger then, like an aftertaste or the memory of a bad dream, but it is likely to weaken and gradually dissipate.

The indirect control we can exert over our emotions by relying on our beliefs is not one-directional, running only from beliefs to emotions, but reciprocal. Emotions may also exert reasonable indirect control over our beliefs about how we should live. This is not because it might be reasonable to allow emotions to influence our beliefs about what the facts are. It is always unreasonable to believe or disbelieve something only because we hope or fear that the belief is true or false. But it is not unreasonable to correct our beliefs about how we should live by taking into account our strong emotions about it. It may be reasonable to correct our beliefs about what justice requires by compassion for the wrongdoer, or to revise our beliefs about how we should live if we find living that way dispiritingly boring.

This is just the sort of experience that led to the School Teacher's conflicts. She found that her commitment to morality as an overriding ideal made her ashamed at what she took to be her failures, undermined her self-respect, and made impossible the warm relationships she yearned for. These understandable emotions caused her to question the beliefs that led her to live with bad feelings about herself and her life. She found that her emotions conflicted with her beliefs about how she should live. The point is not that reason requires that either her emotions or her beliefs should override the other, but that reason

27

allows that neither should be overriding and thus exclude the possibility of correction by the other. Life would have gone better for her if she had maintained her commitment to morality without insisting that it should be overriding.

No ideal theory could answer the question of what is the right mixture of reasonable beliefs and reasonable emotions. The right mixture depends on our character, our circumstances, and the particular beliefs and emotions in question. It is unreasonable to expect that an ideal theory could determine once and for all, universally for everyone, in all circumstances, what the right mixture of individual beliefs and emotions is. This does not mean, of course, that reason allows us to regard any mixture as right if we happen to think so. What we think about it may also be reasonable, unreasonable, or mixed. The point I have been stressing is that it does not make what we think unreasonable that it is context-dependent, does not hold for everyone, and does not fit into an ideal theory, regardless of what the ideal theory is.

The second reason, then, for doubting ideal theories is that they require us to make a commitment to an overriding ideal, but such commitments, as all others, may rest on unreasonable beliefs and emotions. Before it can be reasonable to regard a commitment as overriding, reason requires making as sure as we can that it is reliable. But whether it is reliable depends on the facts, and so the reliability of a commitment to an overriding ideal also depends on the facts. If our beliefs, emotions, overriding commitment, and ideal theory are mistaken about the facts, then we have reason to doubt them even though they are simply there. Since morality itself, not just particular moral requirements, also depends on the facts, it may be corrected, revised, or possibly even abandoned if the facts are not as moralists suppose. And since economics, medicine, politics, and science are better guides to the facts that it is their expertise to describe and explain than morality is, morality may be reasonably overridden by them if the facts warrant it. I conclude that ideal theorists are mistaken in claiming that morality or any other ideal theory is always overriding. This, of course, does not mean that morality or some other ideal theory may not be overriding in some contexts.

Overriding Commitments?

Aristotle says that "we must enjoin every one that has the power to live according to his own choice to set up for himself some object of the good life to aim at (whether honour or reputation or wealth or culture), with reference to which he will then do all his acts, since not to have one's life organized in view of some end is a mark of much folly. Then above all we must first define to ourselves without hurry or carelessness . . . what are the indispensable conditions of its attainment."[12] A life with an overriding commitment would be organized the way Aristotle enjoins. One requirement, among others, of an overriding commitment is to enable us to resolve conflicts between our beliefs, emotions, and desires that guide how we should live. According to ideal theorists, if we had only nonoverriding commitments, we could not resolve these conflicts, especially since both our commitments and our ideals may also conflict. This is why reason requires making a commitment to an overriding ideal and imposing coherence on our beliefs, emotions, and desires. Without it, we would be left with conflicts about how we should live.

We may not have a coherent guide to how we should live even if our beliefs, emotions, and desires are consistent. Consistent ones would not conflict, but they may nevertheless lead to disjointed actions. Consistent beliefs, emotions, and desires are compatible with a compartmentalized life that has separate and only marginally overlapping dimensions. Our beliefs might be preoccupied with work, our emotions might center on love, and our desires may lead us to pursue a variety of ideals. Such beliefs, emotions, and desires are consistent but not coherent. Coherence requires that there be a large area in which our beliefs, emotions, and desires overlap and are directed toward the same object. If we add that the object on which the beliefs, emotions, and desires center is the way in which we live, or, as Aristotle says, "some object of the good life to aim at," then we can see why a coherent life would be good to have. And we can see also why, according to this Aristotelian ideal, a life with conflicts would be bad to have.

The ideal is, then, to make our life better by making it more coherent. The way to do that, according to ideal theorists, is to make a commitment to an overriding ideal that would enable us to impose coherence on our beliefs, emotions, and desires about how we should live. What the School Teacher should do about her life, according to this ideal, is not to give up her commitment to an overriding moral ideal, but to make her beliefs, emotions, and desires more coherent. If she manages that, hard as it may be, she would have a good reason to live according to her overriding commitment. And, if she learns to impose coherence on her incoherent beliefs, emotions, and desires, she will have no reason against it. This is a widely held ideal, but there is nevertheless a strong reason against it.

The reason is that the achievement of the ideal is very unlikely, although not impossible. It is unlikely because it depends on having a character of great simplicity and single-mindedness, such as saints, monsters, and childlike innocents may possess, and also on having exceptionally fortunate circumstances in which the contingencies of life are mostly favorable. The coincidence of such character and circumstances is for the vast majority of us extremely unlikely. To base the ideal of how we should live on such a coincidence is patently unrealistic and a virtual guarantee of failure. Neither the School Teacher nor we can eliminate conflicts from our life. In order to understand why this is so, I continue the discussion of commitments.

Most of our commitments are not overriding: we normally follow their guidance, but they may conflict, acting on them may be too risky or costly, or we may have more urgent and pressing concerns, and then we prudently lay them momentarily aside. Such commitments may be, for instance, to a political cause, physical exercise, or saving for retirement. But if we find that the cause is hijacked by a corrupt politician, if there is a time-consuming emergency at work that leaves us no free time, or if our aged parents are in dire financial need, then we suspend our commitment, not because we abandon it, but because a more important commitment temporarily overrides it. We may also have an overriding commitment. It may be to a beloved person, creative life, religious faith, political ideology, or self-interest, or it may be to happiness, power, salvation, glory, duty, justice, the common good, and so on.

One reason for not making an overriding commitment is the realization of how damaging its violation would be. We do not want to find ourselves in one of those life-shattering situations in which we more or less inadvertently violate it. Thoughtlessness or self-deception may prevent us from recognizing the significance of what we are doing. Fear, self-indulgence, confusion, or weakness may make us unable to resist bribery, blackmail, threats, or flattery. We may find ourselves in some terrible situation, familiar from history and literature, that is not of our making and in which no acceptable alternative is open to us. Whatever the cause, the effect on us of violating an overriding commitment would be shattering. We would then not know how we could live with ourselves, as Oedipus, Othello, Macbeth, and other tragic figures could not, because we would have violated the overriding commitment that we were convinced we ought to have honored above all else. We would realize that we had been tried and found wanting, not by others, but by ourselves. An abyss would open up at the center of our being and we would face disintegration, madness, self-loathing. We would not know how to go on because the evaluative basis of our life would have been shattered. We may not be able to articulate these deterrents to forming an overriding commitment, but we may sense them, know that we are weak and fallible, not made for heroism, and conclude that we are unprepared to become a tragic figure.

This may give us reasons to make no overriding commitment and to regard nothing as always more important than something else. We may think that any commitment may be reasonably overridden under certain conditions and see no reason why we should burden ourselves with an uncompromising stand. Who knows what calamities we may have to face in the future and what emergencies or crises may arise. If we do not take anything deadly seriously, we are less open to the sort of lasting injury that may befall those who have an overriding commitment and are forced to choose between heroism and self-loathing. We should cultivate suppleness and the ability to withstand the inevitable buffeting we will suffer in life's treacherous waters. So goes one line of thought that is prudent rather than heroic.

Of course, there is also another line of thought. Commitment to an overriding ideal gives us a clear sense of identity, of what we are about, of what we most deeply care about. It provides a basis on which the evaluative dimension of our life can rest, the standard by which we can evaluate what is more and what is less important. Honoring it is the source of our self-respect. It defines our limits, what we must or cannot do, what we regard as possible or unthinkable. We appeal to it to resolve conflicts among our various other commitments. It makes our beliefs, emotions, and desires coherent.

If we have an overriding commitment, we see that violating it would leave us without a reasonable way of coping with conflicts, without a clear sense of what does and does not matter in the long run, for our life overall. We would be left at the mercy of external influences, bend as the wind blows, and lack a coherent sense of how we should live, face difficult situations, and resolve conflicts between our various emotions, contrary beliefs, and incompatible desires. If we have no overriding commitment, we may be safer than otherwise, but at the core of our being there will be no there there (as Gertrude Stein said in a rather different context). We may live more prudently, but we will have no clear sense of what we live for.

I have endeavored to show that there are reasons for living both with and without an overriding commitment. Ideal theorists find the first set of reasons more persuasive, I the second set. But there is yet another difference between them. Ideal theorists think that reason requires us to make an overriding commitment, whereas, according to a practical approach, reason allows us to live both with an overriding commitment and without it. I think this second difference counts in favor of a practical approach and against ideal theories.

A Dilemma

Ideal theories and a practical approach are two lines of thought that lead to familiar, easily recognizable, ideal types. They rarely occur in a pure form. When most of us face a difficult decision—say, about divorce, taking a serious risk, or whether to remain loyal to a cherished but corrupted cause—we wish we had an overriding commitment that would dictate what we should do. But when we actually face the dire consequences that may follow from honoring an overriding commitment we have made to living in a way that has gone wrong or threatens to do so, then we wish that our commitment were more flexible. We know that having an overriding commitment has costs and benefits, but we know also that living without one does too. In the lives of those who have not clearly opted for one or the other way—that is, in most lives—conflicts will remain permanent features.

These conflicts will not be only between particular commitments, but also between the two general attitudes. Ideal theorists defending an overriding commitment to some ideal are right in this: if we had made an overriding commitment, we would have a way of resolving conflicts in particular contexts. But they are wrong to suppose that this would free us from conflicts. For the conflict between ideal theories and a practical approach, between the two attitudes to life, would remain and make us hesitate to choose one of these general attitudes. An overriding commitment would give us a clear and firm sense of ourselves, and most of us want that. But having only flexible commitments would give us greater freedom and more possibilities in coping with the problems of life we inevitably encounter, and most us want that also. Our dilemma is to find some way of coping with the conflict between these two attitudes. If we opt one way, we lose something very important that we value. If we opt the other way, we lose something we value no less. The result is that facing the dilemma will make us ambivalent. But not facing it, which is what most of us do, will not make us less ambivalent about how we should live. It will make us continually veer between dissatisfaction with our life and indecision about how to cope with our conflicts.

Suppose we face the dilemma and say to ourselves that resolving it one way or another is preferable to living with conflicts. It is understandable to want this, but it will not overcome our dissatisfaction with whichever lemma we opt for. Opting for an ideal theory will enable us to resolve the conflicts we face. But the conflicts are between beliefs we hold, emotions we feel, and desires on which we want to act. To opt for one of the conflicting beliefs, emotions, or desires is to opt against the others. The unavoidable consequence will be that we have to go against something we believe, or suppress an emotion we feel, or act contrary to a desire we have. Having decided that a belief, emotion, or desire is more important and should override conflicting beliefs, emotions, or desires will resolve the conflict, but it will not make the overridden beliefs, emotions, or desires disappear. They will remain, and will remain frustrated. They will be persistent reminders that we have denied part of what we genuinely believe, feel, or want. We will still veer between dissatisfaction with the life in which we have been untrue to what we believe, feel, or want and indecision about how to cope with our conflicts.

Why, then, should we not opt against following an ideal theory? Why not say that we should cope with conflicts between our beliefs, emotions, and desires by balancing them as well as we can. We can be committed to them, but if they conflict, then the belief, emotion, or desire we have more reason to prefer in a particular context should prevail over the one we have less reason to prefer then and there. We would not have to be untrue to what we have overridden, but merely subordinate it temporarily to a belief, emotion, or desire for which we have better reasons. This is in fact the strategy most of us, consciously or otherwise, try to follow.

It is, however, an easier strategy to describe than actually to follow. For it leaves open a question that inevitably arises and that following the strategy requires answering: how can we tell that we indeed have better reasons to act on a particular belief, emotion, or desire than on one that conflicts with it? The conflict that the strategy was meant to enable us to cope with will not have disappeared; it will only have shifted. Our problem is no longer which of our conflicting beliefs, emotions, or desires should be overriding, but which of our conflicting reasons for our conflicting beliefs, emotions, or desires should be overriding. Of course, we may be able to find reasons for resolving that conflict as well. But there is no reason to suppose that those reasons will be less conflicting than the preceding ones. We derive our reasons from our beliefs, emotions, and desires. If they conflict, as they will, then the reasons we derive from them will also conflict. I do not see, therefore, how opting for an ideal theory would be an improvement over opting for a practical approach, or vice versa.

The human condition is that we have to live in the world, if we live at all. We have some latitude in deciding how we should respond to the problems we encounter. We decide on the basis of our beliefs, emotions, and desires, especially those that are informed by the ideals that guide how we should live. The ideals are various; the beliefs, emotions, and desires are many; they conflict and make us ambivalent about how we should live. We must cope with these conflicts, or we die. The problem is that we have no guidance beyond the conflicting beliefs, emotions, and desires about how we should cope. Our dilemma is whether we should face it by relying on an ideal theory or by adopting a practical approach to how we should live. Relying on either has advantages and disadvantages, and estimating their relative importance in forever-shifting circumstances is what makes the dilemma at once unavoidable and necessary to face again and again. According to a practical approach, reason allows but does not require either. But ideal theorists think that reason always requires everyone always to rely on an ideal theory. I have been arguing in this chapter that if the ideal theory is absolutist morality, then ideal theorists of this kind are mistaken.

3　Individual Autonomy

We are subject to infirmities, miseries, interrupted, tossed and
tumbled up and down . . . uncertain [and] brittle, and so is all we
trust unto. And he that knows not this, and is not armed to endure,
is not fit to live in this world.

ROBERT BURTON, *The Anatomy of Melancholy*[1]

The ideal of individual autonomy is at the core of many contemporary
ideal theories. The ideal is that we should be free to choose between
alternative ways of living on the basis of having understood and evaluated the alternatives. Autonomy includes free choice, but goes beyond
it because it requires that the free choice be based on understanding
and the favorable evaluation of the alternative chosen. It is implicit in
the ideal that we can resolve our conflicts by becoming more autonomous. I argue in this chapter that autonomy as an overriding ideal is
seriously flawed and does not help us to resolve our conflicts.

There are numerous ideal theorists who defend autonomy as an overriding ideal, but I will concentrate on Christine M. Korsgaard's theory
in *Self-Constitution*.[2] It is perhaps the best known and most discussed of
the available ideal theories of autonomy. As before, I begin with a story
about the conflicts in the real life of a real person.

The Lawyer

The Lawyer is in his mid-forties and has a law practice in a small town. He took the practice over from his father, who is now retired. The Lawyer is secure and comfortable, has a good family life, and occupies a respected place in his community. But he sees the future ahead of him and finds it uninspiring. His family life is affectionate but not passionate. The humdrum cases he competently handles no longer challenge or engage him. He is largely going through the motions, finding diminishing satisfactions in his life. He asks himself whether this is all he can expect until he, like his father, retires and plays golf with similarly dispirited partners. He is dissatisfied with both his professional life and the political conditions of his society.

He has always had an interest in politics and was quite active in it during his college days. Indeed, there was a time when he was undecided between pursuing a career in law or in politics. He picked law largely because his father expected it of him and because he wanted for himself the comfort, security, respect, and status his father obviously enjoyed. He also saw the risks and compromises involved in a political career. He opted for law and got the satisfactions of the conventional life he wanted. But now he finds that these satisfactions are meager. In this unquiet state, he thinks back to his choice of career, and although he does not quite regret the choice he made, he is questioning it. He asks himself whether he should not enter politics now and give up his law practice. He has not changed his political views, he thinks his country needs people like him and views like his, and that there are good reasons for exchanging his insufficiently satisfying professional life for active engagement in politics.

He is nothing if not reasonable, however, and after careful reflection he also sees that there are good reasons for continuing his law practice. He believes that the continued well-being of his family rests on his income and that his wife and children count on the affection he genuinely feels for them and shows day in and day out by the attention he pays to them. He also feels loyalty to the many clients who, throughout the years, have entrusted their affairs to him. The sense of rectitude he was taught to have has become his second nature, and he thinks it would be wrong to abandon his freely chosen obligations to his family and clients. He realizes that if he entered politics he would have to go against his present lawyerly self, to which he has been true for many years, and cultivate a future political self, which he toyed with but left behind after his college days when he chose law over politics. Yet he is also conscious of his growing dissatisfactions. He wants to do what is best for his country, family, clients, and himself, but he is confused about what that is.

The sources of his confusion are conflicts within his divided self. His present self, with which he is dissatisfied, prompts him to act one way, and a future self that he hopes would be free of dissatisfactions prompts him to act in another. These conflicts make him ambivalent, because he does not know whether he should be guided by the ideals of his present or his future self. He wants to do what is best but cannot decide whether it is better to remain as he is or better to try to become what he might be. He sees that his present self is good enough, but he also sees that the good enough is not enough. I now leave him temporarily in midthought.

The Lawyer's conflict is meant to illustrate a conflict that is present in many, but not all, lives. Saints and monsters do not have such conflicts because their present self is as close to their ideal as they can make it. Nor do people living in miserable circumstances have this kind of conflict. They are concerned with staying alive and coping with life-threatening problems; they have neither time nor energy to reflect on whether they should transform their present self into a better future one. Such conflicts are also absent from the lives of those who live in highly structured hierarchical societies. They were born into conventional positions and relationships whose possibilities and limits are defined by long-standing tradition, and how they should live was settled at birth. Few of us, living in contemporary Western societies, are saintly or monstrous; our conditions are rarely miserable; we have far more possibilities than we could try to realize; many of the limits on us are flexible; and our societies are characterized by much mobility and change. Conflicts and ambivalence in these circumstances are typical psychological states.

If we are confused in the way the Lawyer is, then we are ambivalent about how we want to live. Our present self motivates us to live in one way, and our desired future self in another. Our evaluations of the choices we might make conflict. We are undecided about what we should do, because we are unclear about what we want to do, and we are unclear about that, because our ideal of how we want to live is in a state of flux, as the Lawyer's is. To be ambivalent this way is not the result of stupidity or lack of thought. On the contrary, it is the result of a great deal of intelligent thinking, but the thinking makes us more, not less, ambivalent.

It would be a simple matter if the source of our conflict was that we failed to take into account relevant facts, but that is not it. Its source is that we do not know how to evaluate the facts whose relevance to how we want to live we acknowledge. Reflecting on our present self, with which we are dissatisfied, and the possible future self that we think would be better prompts conflicting evaluations of agreed-upon facts. And we could not just say that since we are dissatisfied with our present self and desire to change into a better future self, we should resolve the conflict in favor of the promptings of the future self. For that conflict resolution would have to be made by our present self, the only self we now have, and that one prompts us to resolve the conflict in precisely the opposite way. If it did not, we would not be ambivalent in the first place. We are ambivalent because we have conflicting attitudes toward changing how we are.

It is clear, I think, that conflicts of this kind stand in the way of living as we want. We are ambivalent because we do not know what we want. It is also clear, I think, that literature, history, and our personal experience testify to the frequency of such ambivalence in our present circumstances. According to Korsgaard's widely accepted ideal theory, whose inspiration, of course, is Kantian, we can resolve our conflict and overcome our ambivalence by becoming more autonomous.[3] I now turn to her defense of it.

Autonomy

Korsgaard thinks "there is only one principle of practical reason, the categorical imperative viewed as the law of autonomy, but there are different ways to fall away from autonomy and the different principles of practical reason really instruct us not to fall away from our autonomy in these different ways" (71–72). "My view" she writes, "is that action is self-constitution . . . [and] the essential characteristics of an agent are *efficacy* and *autonomy*. . . . An agent is *autonomous* when her movements are in some clear sense self-determined. . . . These two properties, efficacy and autonomy, correspond to Kant's two imperatives, hypothetical and categorical" (82–83). Following Kant, Korsgaard thinks that only autonomous actions are practically rational, morally good, and self-constitutive. Nonautonomous actions fail on all three of these counts.

Korsgaard would say that the Lawyer's trouble was that he did not act autonomously. Contrary to appearances, he did not have reasons for his actions and he failed to do what is morally right. He was not even an agent, because "it is essential to the concept of agency that an agent be unified." To qualify as an agent, I must see my action "as *my action*, I must see it as an expression of my self as a whole." The action "must result from my entire nature working as an integrated whole" (18–19). Korsgaard says to someone like the ambivalent Lawyer: "Stop dithering and bring your deliberation to an end: *Make up your mind*, or even better, *Pull yourself together*" (126). It is a mistake, according to her ideal theory, to think that the Lawyer is reasonable and morally right when he is affectionate and attentive to his family, faithfully serves the interests of his clients, governs his actions by unfailing rectitude, and agonizes over whether he ought to enter politics. His present and desired future self motivate him to act in conflicting ways, so he cannot act autonomously, cannot be guided by reasons, and cannot act morally.

What, then, is it to act autonomously? Korsgaard's answer is that it is to act on the basis of deliberation.

> To deliberate is to formulate a maxim, stating the complete package of considerations that together favor the performance of a certain action. . . . Your maxim, once formulated, embodies your proposed reason. You then test it by the categorical imperative, that is, you ask whether you can will it to be a universal law, in order to see whether it really is a reason. Universalizability is a condition on the form of reason, and if a consideration doesn't meet this condition, then it is not merely outweighed—rather, it is not a reason at all. (51)

Furthermore, "the work of practical deliberation is reunification, reconstitution: and the function of the principles that govern deliberation—the principles of practical reason—is the unification of the self." "The function of practical reason is to unify us into agents who can be the authors of our actions" (126).

I have quoted these passages at length because readers may find it incredible to suppose that Korsgaard really says that without a unified self and autonomy we cannot be human agents, cannot have reasons for what we do, and cannot do what is right. But that is what she says.

I do not see how the conclusion could be avoided that what she says is utterly implausible.

To begin with, it follows from Korsgaard's ideal theory that we act reasonably and do what is morally right when we keep an appointment, apologize for a tactless remark, pay the bill for what we bought, or signal before we turn the car we drive only if we have met the following conditions. We have deliberated, formed a maxim, stated to ourselves the complete package of relevant considerations, and tested the maxim by the categorical imperative, asking whether we would wish the maxim to become a universal law. If we do not meet these conditions, says Korsgaard, we fail to follow rational principles, because "rational principles [are] the principles that govern *self-conscious* self-determination" (106); we are self-determining beings only if "we choose our own maxims, the content of our principles. And the categorical and hypothetical imperatives are rules for doing this—rules for the construction of maxims" (108). Moreover, we also fail to act as human beings, because "a human being acts when she *self*-consciously determines herself to be the cause of a change in the world" (127). Human action "requires autonomy and autonomy requires universalizability" (180). Korsgaard's claim is that unless we self-consciously go through this mind-bogglingly complicated process, we can have no reason for action, we cannot do what is morally right, and, in fact, our actions cannot even qualify as human, since they are mere movements of the kinds animals perform.

Speaking for myself, I act from time to time, have reasons for my actions, and at least sometimes do what is morally right. Yet I have never gone through the process Korsgaard claims is necessary for action, for having reasons, and for doing what is right. Nor do I think that I am unique or deceiving myself. I think that what is true of me in this respect is true of the overwhelming majority of people, including the Lawyer, who do not cease to be human beings on account of having fallen short of the requirements of Korsgaard's ideal theory. In fact, I can think of no one in literature, history, or my personal experience who meets the requirements Korsgaard says are necessary for being human, having reasons, and doing what is right.

The implausibility of these requirements of Korsgaard's theory cannot be avoided by supposing that Korsgaard must mean that for reasonable and morally committed people, meeting the requirements she insists on has become habitual, so they do not have to go through them every time they take the necessary steps she says are required.

This would be a less unreasonable theory than Korsgaard's, but it is not hers. She repeatedly emphasizes that autonomy consists in self-conscious deliberation every time we act autonomously. If I act out of habit and without deliberation, I am not acting autonomously. If I act autonomously, "I must see it as an expression of my self as a whole" (18), autonomy involves acting according to "principles that govern *self-conscious* self-determination" (106), "to be autonomous or self-determined is to *choose* the principles that are definitive of your will" (108), and "a human being acts when she *self*-consciously determines herself to be the cause of a change in the world" (127).

The implausibility of this theory is even more glaring if we realize that autonomy as a moral ideal has emerged gradually and that it was "only from about the early eighteenth century that the effort to create a theory of morality as self-governance became conscious."[4] Before that time in Europe and in the rest of the world, the dominant moral ideal was obedience to divine or secular authority. It follows from Korsgaard's theory that all those proto-humans who lived before the eighteenth century in Europe and elsewhere were not full-fledged human beings, could not act on reasons, and could not do what was morally right. Since, according to Korsgaard's theory, living and acting with self-conscious deliberation, autonomously, and according to the categorical imperative is a universal requirement of practical reason and morality, no one before the emergence of autonomy was either reasonable or moral. Only someone blinded by a theory can believe this.

Let us suppose, however, if only for the sake of argument, that the Lawyer resolves to conform to Korsgaard's implausible requirements. He states to himself "the complete package of considerations" he needs to deliberate about in order "to formulate a maxim" that "embodies [his] proposed reason," then "test[s] it by the categorical imperative . . . in order to see whether it really is a reason," accepting that it will be a reason only if he can "will it to be a universal law." If he cannot will it, then his supposed reason "is not a reason at all" (51). There are two, to my mind decisive, reasons why he could not do what Korsgaard says he should.

First, being reasonable, the Lawyer has already thought a great deal about the complete package of considerations. But his thinking has yielded only a conflict between two incompatible courses of action he should follow. He still does not know whether he should continue with law or abandon it for politics. Both courses of action are open to him, and the complete package of considerations allows him to opt for either. That is why he is ambivalent. Korsgaard would tell him that "the function of the principles that govern deliberation—the principles of practical reason—is the unification of the self" (126).

The Lawyer would certainly like to unify his self and reach a decision, but he does not know how to do it, because his conflicting beliefs, emotions, and desires drive him in different directions. If he knew how to become unified, he would not have a conflict. He would resolve to live either according to his present or his future self. His self would then already be unified, he would not be ambivalent, and he would not need to struggle with formulating a maxim and testing it by the categorical imperative. Korsgaard's advice that he should do what he has again and again tried and failed to do is as useless as advising the sick to be healthy, the weak to be strong, or the stupid to be intelligent. And if the Lawyer, contrary to the facts, had a unified self and was not ambivalent, then he would not need to do what Korsgaard advises him to do. Consequently the whole rigmarole Korsgaard insists on going through as the key to following the requirements of her ideal theory is either useless or unnecessary.

Second, suppose the Lawyer unifies his self, resolves his conflict, and decides to continue with law. Does this mean that if his decision was based on deliberation guided by reason and morality, then he had to follow a universal maxim? What would this maxim be? It cannot just be that whenever anyone faces a choice between continuing to practice law and entering politics, he should choose the former. For if the lawyer was rich and had no need to earn a living, or had no family, or found the legal system corrupt, or his wife earned a lot of money, or he was unexpectedly appointed to replace a retiring legislator, or was given six months to live, or was psychoanalyzed and found that his conflict was the product of an overactive superego, or inherited a fortune from a distant relative who died intestate, and so on and on endlessly, then he may well have made a different decision.

The universal maxim cannot be formulated, because any proposed maxim would have to rule out possible exceptions in order to be universal. But then it would sink under the weight of a thousand qualifications. If it did exclude exceptions and was made precise enough to resolve the Lawyer's conflict, it would have to be so precise as to apply only to the Lawyer and only in his particular circumstances. It could then be said that reason and morality require anyone in those precise circumstances to act on that maxim, but if that maxim was as precise as it would then have to be, it would apply only to the Lawyer, because the precise circumstances of others would be different from his. It is a self-serving and highly misleading use of language to claim that a maxim that could apply only to one person in a particular circumstance is universal.

I conclude that Korsgaard's ideal theory, according to which autonomy is an overriding requirement of practical reason and morality, fails. My objections to the theory are not meant to deny that autonomy is good to seek and to have. They are rather meant to show that something has gone very wrong with the extravagant claims Korsgaard makes for what she understands as autonomy. Autonomy, in her sense, is not the key to overcoming the widespread ambivalence caused by the conflicting guidance of our divided self. Nor can autonomy be relied on to show that conflicts are not psychological obstacles to living as we want in our present circumstances. The Lawyer cannot overcome his conflict by becoming more autonomous, because the divided self that causes his conflicts about how he should live will make him conflicted also about acting on any autonomous decision he might arrive at.

Misguided Theorizing

These reasons against Korsgaard's ideal theory seem to me very strong, but those who are sympathetic to her Kantian approach may think that a suitably revised ideal theory, or perhaps a quite different ideal theory, could show that autonomy is the overriding ideal that is the key to overcoming the sort of familiar conflicts that the Lawyer and many of us have. I will now argue that this whole approach is mistaken. The reason against all ideal theories of autonomy proposed as possible ways of resolving our conflicts is not that they have possibly remediable defects, but that they are theories.

It is clearly right that if the Lawyer wants to resolve his conflict reasonably, he should deliberate further. But why should we suppose that his deliberation should abstract more and more from his character, circumstances, and context and bring him ever closer to formulating a universal and impersonal theory prescribing what anyone, everywhere, in all contexts ought always to do? The more he abstracts, the more he tries to act according to a universal and impersonal theory, the less relevant his deliberation becomes to himself. Contrary to any ideal theory of autonomy as the key to resolving conflicts, the Lawyer's deliberation should become more and more personal. It should lead him to consider more critically than he has hitherto done what has led to his conflict. He should redirect his deliberation away from considering which of the alternatives open to him he should opt for toward asking about the source of his conflict. Perhaps if he examined his evaluations of the importance of relevant facts, evaluations that reflect the conflicting ideals of his present and desired future self, he might find that some of them are mistaken, and that might help him to resolve his conflict.

Perhaps he should talk to his wife and children to find out whether his continued practice of law is really as important for them as he has been thinking. Perhaps his wife has for some time wanted to leave housewifery for a career. Perhaps his children have been aching to leave home and become independent. Perhaps they love him enough to accept less comfort and security if it enables him to do what he really wants. Perhaps he has exaggerated the extent to which they depend on him. Perhaps a career in politics would merely replace the drudgery of his law practice with the frustrations of a low-ranking junior politician. Perhaps his lifelong rectitude would be outraged by the inevitable compromises involved in political life. Perhaps what he imagines to be his boredom with his law practice is merely the familiar manifestation of a banal midlife crisis that assails some men, much as menopause assails some women. Perhaps what is happening to him is that he is unwilling to accept that the dreams of his college days were no more than dreams, and he should leave childish things behind.

Deliberating in this way will deepen his understanding of himself. It might lead him to consider seriously the possibility that he is in the grip of illusions about himself and his ideals and that they lead him to misperceive his situation, his family, and his own wants. But this deeper understanding would not consist in seeking and then acting according to any universal and impersonal theory. It would consist rather in finding out whether the ideals that guide both what he is and what he wants to become and his evaluations of the relevant facts are realistic, or whether either his present or future self is shot through with misperceptions that prevent him from seeing the facts reasonably.

In general, the efforts to understand our unavoidable conflicts between what we are and what we want to become can proceed in two directions. One is toward the future, trying to understand which of the available courses of action would be more likely to help us overcome our dissatisfactions with ourselves. The other is toward the past, trying to understand what has led to our present conflicts. We may come to understand that our conflicts are the result of unrealistic beliefs, emotions, and desires that we are reluctant to question, because doing so would threaten the illusions we nurture about ourselves. I have presented the Lawyer so far as trying to understand himself in the first way, looking toward the future. I am suggesting now that he might make progress toward coping with his conflict if he tried to understand himself also in the second way, looking toward the past.

It may be thought that I have just recommended relying on the universal and impersonal theory according to which we should cope with our conflicts by seeking deeper understanding of both our past and our desired future in order to evaluate the realism of our beliefs, emotions, and desires that guide how we should live. But this thought would be no better than sophistry. If we follow the recommendation I have made, we would be doing something that no one else could do, namely, seeking an unavoidably personal understanding of the ideals we hold and the life we want to have. The direction of such understanding is deeper into ourselves. Its aim is to eliminate mistaken beliefs, emotions, and desires that lead to or follow from our mistaken ideals and evaluations. If we succeed, we might—I do not say will—succeed in coping with our conflicts.

The alternative to relying on a theory, then, is the rather obvious one of focusing on our conflicts and trying to cope with them. This would be a simpler matter than it is if all it required was to identify what we want and do what we can to get it. Complications enter because the conflicts make us unclear about what we want, lead us to want incompatible things, and we may be wrong to suppose that what we want would make us less dissatisfied. Many of these complications are caused by conflicts between our present self, with which we are dissatisfied, and a possible future self we would like to have. Their conflicts make us ambivalent. This much is uncontroversial, I think. Basic disagreements emerge, however, between those who think the key to resolving these conflicts and overcoming our ambivalence is to rely on autonomy as an overriding ideal, and those, like myself, who think differently.

Ideal theorists think that autonomy rightly pursued involves abstracting from personal and particular considerations and evaluating our life and actions on the basis of their conformity to an ideal that reason requires everyone to follow regardless of individual differences. This cannot be a requirement of reason, because our lives and actions differ as a result of differences in upbringing, education, experiences, circumstances, and ideals. And even if we could do what is surely impossible: free ourselves from all personal and particular influences that have formed us and live according to a universal and impersonal ideal theory, there would still be no guarantee that we would stop having conflicts. For some of our conflicts are caused by the conflicting promptings of our present and future self and even if our dissatisfaction with the first and desire for the second may both be autonomous, it may leave us as ambivalent as we were when we were not autonomous. There is no reason why we could not be both autonomous and ambivalent at the same time.

This is not to say, of course, that we should not try to be more autonomous. I am not denying that more autonomy may make us less ambivalent about how we want to live. But it may have the opposite effect of making us more aware of our conflicts and ambivalence. Understanding the causes of our conflicts may make them more rather than less acute. Whatever its effect on us is, autonomy is not the universal and impersonal key to resolving our conflicts, but a particular, context-dependent ideal that many introspectively inclined people in contemporary civilized societies accept, provided they have sufficient comfort, security, leisure, education, and willingness to deliberate about how they should live. The claims made for it by Korsgaard and other ideal theorists are extravagant. It gives a bad name to reason to claim on its supposed authority that everyone must either live autonomously or fail to be reasonable. Autonomy is merely one fallible ideal that may, or may not, guide how we should live. Its pursuit is as likely as any other to go wrong because of our conflicting beliefs, emotions, and desires and the other ideals we accept.

If we reject the search for a universally and impersonally applicable ideal theory of autonomy as a requirement of reason, if we acknowledge that its pursuit, as the pursuit of any other ideal, may lead us astray because of the conflicts between what we are and what we want to become, then how can we avoid the resulting ambivalence? We cannot, because we cannot undo our dissatisfactions with our present self and our desire for a better future self. If we could, conflicts and ambivalence would not be psychological problems. What we can do is only to try to correct the mistakes we make about our beliefs, emotions, desires, and ideals. We cannot be certain that we will succeed, because the conflicts and ambivalence will affect also our efforts to identify the mistakes and correct them. But we can be certain that if we do not try, we will remain ambivalent about how to cope with our conflicts and dissatisfied with how we live.

The preceding criticisms of ideal theories may be thought to ally my view with moral particularism.[5] This would be partly true, partly false. According to Dancy's view, "a particularist conception is one which sees little if any role for moral principles. Particularists think that moral judgment can get along perfectly well without any appeal to principles, indeed that there is no essential link between being a full moral agent and having principles."[6] I agree. Dancy goes on: "There are two sorts of approach that a particularist can take in trying to make a persuasive case against any essential link between morality and principles. The first is to show that no suggested principles are anything like flexible enough to cover the job we require of them. Moral life, it can be said, is just too messy, and the situations we encounter differ from each other in subtle ways that no panoply of principles could ever manage to capture." This is my approach.[7] Dancy's own "is about how to understand the way in which reasons work, and deals largely with *theories* about reasons rather than with life," and he adds that "the issues discussed in [his] book are theoretical."[8]

My reason for preferring the first approach to the second is that while I think that an anti-theory theory of morality is certainly better than a pro-theory theory of morality, neither theory can do justice to the complexities of the conflicting beliefs, emotions, desires, and ideals of our divided self. Particular cases in morality necessarily take precedence over reasons and theories. That is why I begin each chapter with a particular case and go on to show with reference to it the inadequacy of an ideal theory that attempts to resolve the protagonist's conflicts. The adequacy of any theory of or in morality, whether an anti-theory or a pro-theory, depends on its capacity to account for the cases it was meant to explain. My aim is to show that not one of the ideal theories I discuss succeeds in doing that.

This is true also of Dancy's theory about reasons in morality. Reasons in morality must be about the real life of real people. It is a mistake, I think, to concentrate, as Dancy does, on theories about reasons rather than on life. For the adequacy of reasons must eventually be tested against particular cases we encounter in real life. We must probe reasons in this way, since we have no other, and we have to ask whether the reasons are good enough to cope with the conflicts we encounter in life. But there is no reason to think that reasons that are good enough in a particular case will be good enough in another case, since our self is divided and our beliefs, emotions, desires, and ideals are conflicting. It seems to me that the reasons against trying to construct an ideal theory of moral reasons are as strong as the reasons against trying to construct an ideal moral theory. And they are the same reasons: life is always more complex than theories about life, and the self is divided in more complex ways than can be dreamed of in any philosophy. What we, struggling with our conflicts, can do is to reflect on them in tranquility, if we can, and try to understand at least some of their complexities while resisting the urge of trying to fit them into some theory.

The Divided Self

We have a healthy, normal self oriented toward what we take to be the facts of our life. Sometimes the facts are so awful and they cause, or threaten to cause, traumas so bad as to make it seem preferable to construct an alternative self that falsifies the facts, in one of many possible ways, and thereby enable ourselves to cope with the awfulness of the facts that have either already befallen us or merely threaten to do so.[9] This is when psychiatrists and clinical psychologists treat the divided self as a more or less pathological condition.

I mention this only to say that this is not what I mean by a divided self. I mean by it that our healthy, normal self is divided. It is certainly oriented toward what we take to be the facts, but it is divided because we are ambivalent about how to evaluate much of what we take to be the facts. This is especially true of the facts that are relevant to living as we want. We have a conflict between two ways in which we want to live, which give us two ways of evaluating the relevant facts. This division characterizes the inner life of most of us in civilized circumstances. Our divided self can become pathological, of course, but in the usual course of events, the conflicts between its two parts are parts of many normal lives.

One part is formed by our genetic dispositions, upbringing, experiences, and preferences; the other by our need and aspiration to become better than we are. We feel the need and have the aspiration because few of us are satisfied with how we are. We want to be freer or more controlled, more forthright or more tactful, more courageous or less impulsive, more cautious or more adventurous than we presently are. And we evaluate our possibilities and actions either from the point of view of our present self or from that of a better future self we want to have, just as the Lawyer does.

Our present self is formed of our dispositions, habits, virtues and vices, desires and aversions, capacities and incapacities, talents and weaknesses, and the ideals we were taught to pursue. It guides how we live. But the self with which we enter adult life is typically unclear and unexamined. It may motivate us to act in ways we later find contrary to how we want to live. Most of us question the self with which we emerge from adolescence and experiment with other possibilities. We want to improve our present self, make it better, and we form some view of what a better self might be. Whatever it is, it will be unavoidably different from our present self. How different it would be and in what ways depends on how dissatisfied we are with our present self, what we think are the psychological sources of our dissatisfactions, and what we suppose our possibilities are. The better self will guide how we transform our less-than-satisfactory present self into a future self that, we hope, will be better. This will cause us unavoidable conflicts and make us ambivalent in two ways.

One is that we must act, or die, and however we act, it will be contrary either to how we live now or to how we want to live in the future. This has consequences we cannot reasonably want. For if we act contrary to the promptings of our present self, we will act contrary to some of our beliefs, emotions, and desires. If we act contrary to a better future self we want to have, then we will continue to live in a way with which we are dissatisfied. Both make us untrue to ourselves. No wonder we have a conflict and are ambivalent about choosing either of these unappealing possibilities.

The other reason why conflicts and ambivalence are part of our typical condition is that whatever we decide to do, the decision must be made by our present self, for that is the only self we have. But we think that our present self is flawed. Indeed, its flaws are the reasons why we try to transform it into a better future self. The transformation, however, has to be done by our present flawed self, some of whose dispositions, habits, character traits, and ideals we want to change. If we understand that the only way we can make the changes is to rely on the flawed self we want to change, then we will understand how difficult it would be to succeed. The only correction we can make may be sabotaged by the flaw we want to correct. And if it dawns on us further that this correction involves the extremely difficult task of acting contrary to some of the dispositions, habits, character traits, and ideals that make us what we are, then we will quite reasonably wonder whether it is worth making the great and disagreeable effort to overcome such conflicts. We will be ambivalent, therefore, about making it. The alternative to it will not seem disastrous, although not one that we would welcome. It is to put up with the dissatisfactions we have and accept that the ideal of a better future self will elude us. We will, of course, be ambivalent about that as well. And so our ambivalence will persist whatever we do, just as the Lawyer's will, no matter what he decides.

It is a characteristic thought in the present age among literate people that the way out of such conflicts and uncertainties is to understand better our present self, our dissatisfactions with it, the future self we want to have, and why we want it. This would no doubt be good to do, but it could not by itself change the fact that whichever self guides us, we will be untrue to something in us that we really care about. Understanding our conflicts need not help us to avoid them, as it need not help the Lawyer either.

This truth is hard to accept. Those who doubt it may concede that if the conflict between what we are and what we want to be is unresolved, we will be ambivalent about how we should live, and they may nevertheless insist that better understanding will enable us to resolve the conflict and overcome the ambivalence. They may think that we are ambivalent because we do not understand what we really want. Better understanding will allow us to discover what that is and motivate us to act accordingly, or so doubters may claim. In effect, they repeat what was a cliché even when in *Hamlet* Polonius repeats it to his son: "To thine own self be true." Countless people follow Polonius in mouthing these tired words.[10] The fact is, however, that being true to our self requires understanding what that self is, but that understanding is likely to show us only that our self is divided between what it is and what we want it to become. We have two ways of being true to ourselves, because our self is divided. And from our divided self there follow deep, genuine, but conflicting needs and aspirations. This is what better understanding is likely to make us realize.

Those who continue to think that better understanding is the key to living as we want may concede that our conflicts and ambivalence may remain, and still stress the necessity of finding some way of living that copes with them. They may say that this can be done more or less reasonably and that doing it more reasonably involves reaching the best decision we can in the circumstances. They may concede that we are fallible and may make the wrong decision but insist that we can do no better than weigh the relevant considerations as carefully as we can and act on them.

Unfortunately, this advice is of no help, because it fails to take account of the conflicts we face. One difficulty is that following this advice requires us to decide what considerations are relevant. We have many different beliefs, emotions, and desires, and they lead us to decide in many different and often conflicting ways. We also have many different ideals, evaluate what we might do from many different points of view, and aim to transform ourselves in many different respects. How do we decide which of them are relevant and which are not? It seems to me that the only nonarbitrary way of making that decision is to rely on the ideals that guide how we should live. What helps or hinders us to live according to them is relevant and what does not is irrelevant. This would tell us what we should or should not regard as relevant, if we were guided by only one ideal, but of course we are guided by many, and we are assailed by conflicts and ambivalence precisely because we cannot decide which ones we should rely on. We want to be true to our ideals, but the advice to consider all relevant facts and then decide as best as we can simply ignores the very conflict that the advice was meant to help us avoid.

To appreciate just how serious this problem is, consider the great variety of different ideals and evaluative points of view that normally guide how we should live. They may be aesthetic, moral, personal, political, religious, and so on. Our ideals are embedded in these evaluative points of view, and there are many of them. The ideals derived from one of them often conflict with those we derive from another. The ideals of either part of our divided self are likely to be derived from this great variety of often conflicting evaluative points of view. And even if we succeed in imposing some hierarchical order on them by one part of our divided self, it will conflict with the hierarchical order formed by the other part.

As if this was not a serious enough problem, it is exacerbated by another type of conflict embedded in our ideals. Few of us want to live exclusively in self-centered terms. We care about some people; for the causes we have made our own; for our country, culture, religion, profession, or political party; and perhaps even for humanity and some other forms of life. And the well-being of one thing we deeply care about often conflicts with the well-being of other things we also care about deeply. So, once again, we must impose some ranking on the relative importance of the many things we care about, but the ranking that would follow from one part of our divided self will be different from the ranking that will follow from the other part.

The advice to decide on the basis of all the relevant considerations glosses over this abundant variety of conflicting ideals and evaluative points of view. The advice is correct and useless: of course we should decide on the basis of all the relevant considerations, but wanting to do that depends on having decided what relative importance we should assign to them and how we should resolve their conflicts. Unfortunately, that is precisely the decision that the conflicts and the resulting ambivalence prevent us from making, just as it prevented the Lawyer.

This correct and useless advice is the same as the one the Duke of Wellington reportedly gave to someone who petitioned him for help: "You seem to have gotten yourself into a damned difficult situation and you must do your best to get out of it." The damned difficult situation that most of us have gotten ourselves into is that we "make for . . . [our]-selves pictures of ideal forms of life. Such pictures are various and may be in sharp opposition to each other; and the same individual may be captivated by different and sharply conflicting pictures."[11] Better understanding will perhaps tell us why we are ambivalent about the conflicting pictures we have formed, but it will not enable us to escape from being captivated by them.

Ambivalence and Understanding

I have so far left unquestioned the assumption that even if better understanding does not enable us to overcome our conflicts and ambivalence, there still are reasons to seek it. This is true, but it is also true that there are reasons against it. Consider our psychological state. We are dissatisfied with our present self because we have begun to suspect that the beliefs, emotions, and desires that lead us to live as we do may be mistaken. Perhaps we have been deceiving ourselves, ignored possibilities we should have pursued, or supposed that we lack capacities we in fact have. Perhaps we are wracked by deeply felt anger, jealousy, shame, envy, or self-pity, but these emotions are inauthentic because we have inflated vague fears into passionate convictions. Perhaps we are motivated to get a particular job, honor, house, recognition, love affair, or lifestyle only because we are dissatisfied with what we have. We often make such mistakes, and the reason for seeking better understanding of why we make them is to avoid making them in the future. That would make us less dissatisfied with how we live. This may indeed be gained from a better understanding. But better understanding may also open up dangerous possibilities about whose exploration it is reasonable to be hesitant.

Suppose we seek deeper understanding and ask ourselves why we left unquestioned our mistaken beliefs, emotions, and desires. The honest answer may bring us to understand that the source of our mistakes is that there is something wrong with the ideals that guide how we should live. Then we may begin to have reason to hesitate about proceeding further. For it is an alarming possibility that the ideals by which we live may be mistaken. If we are reasonable, we will think twice when confronted with this possibility.

It is, of course, good to be critical of our ideals. They are often mistaken, or we exaggerate the importance of some at the expense of others, or we just mindlessly accept some that we have been taught or manipulated to hold. We can and should examine our ideals and see whether we are dissatisfied with our present self because we live by mistaken, unimportant, or alien ideals. But their criticism and examination proceed, if they do, in the only way open to us: by evaluating the ideals in the light of other ideals we hold. The evaluation of anything must appeal to some ideal, and the only ideals to which we can appeal are those we at least tacitly recognize as such. Suppose, however, that we are serious about seeking deeper understanding, do not stop halfway, and take an additional step. We consider the possibility that may now occur to us that it is not just this or that ideal of ours that may be mistaken but all of them. That would be a devastating possibility because, if true, it would lead to the collapse of the evaluative dimension of our life, render untenable the distinctions we have been making between what is good and bad, better or worse, and destroy what we have supposed was the meaning and purpose of our life.

If we understand what is at stake and do not just heedlessly ask more and more questions about our ideals, we will have reason to proceed very cautiously about asking more and more questions. Such questioning can go on endlessly, like the four-year-old's why-questions. The possibility is ever-present that even our deepest, best-considered, and most sincerely and passionately held ideals may be mistaken. If we are reasonable, we eventually arrive at a point where we say to ourselves: for better or worse, these are the ideals I hold, this is how I should live, and I am willing to risk being mistaken. Having reached this point, we will realize that we have nothing else apart from our ideals to which we can appeal to accept, reject, change, or reevaluate the importance of any of the ideals by which we live. If we question all of our ideals, we cast ourselves adrift on a sea of uncertainty without an anchor or even a distant safe harbor. And that is a more radical questioning than most of us are willing to embark on. It is better, much better—we may say sotto voce—to put up with uncertainties about which of our ideals we should follow than to face the possibility of being left without any ideal that we could follow.

Yet, even if we reach this understanding, rare as it is likely to be, we may continue to suspect that something is wrong with our ideals if our dissatisfactions with how we live persist. And who, I ask again, is without some dissatisfactions? What do we do then? We still do not question all of our ideals. We say that we are dissatisfied because we have not tried hard enough to act according to our ideals. We blame our efforts, not the ideals that guide them. We say that we have not fully understood how demanding they are, or that we are too easily discouraged by temporary setbacks, or that the stupidity of a hostile world stands in our way. It is far safer to blame our efforts or the world than to blame the ideals we hold. For blaming our efforts leaves us the hope that we can overcome our dissatisfactions by trying harder, better, more intelligently. But if we blame our ideals, we endanger the very possibility that could guide any efforts we might make.

If we sense, usually only vaguely, that deeper understanding would bring us to this dangerous pass, we routinely abort it. We resolve instead to try harder; distract ourselves by work, athletic endeavors, drugs and alcohol, making money, shopping for bargains, seeking mindless entertainment, or watching pornography; or sink into a marriage that is only an unstable truce. And we often succeed in diverting ourselves by such tactics, as is apparent when we observe the many dissatisfied lives in affluent contemporary societies.

The danger from which we flee by such means is real, and it is a reason against seeking deeper understanding. No matter how strong this reason may be, however, it may nevertheless be reasonably overridden in serious crises. Life-changing experiences may bring us to question the ideals that have guided us in the past. Loss of religious faith, the collapse of our society, the murder of our family, epidemics, or extreme conditions created by natural disasters may be so wrenching as to shock us and make us question our familiar assumptions, habits, and ideals. But even if we are driven to radical questioning, it is unlikely to lead us to question all our ideals. Grief, terror, conversion, deprivation, disillusionment, revolution, and the like may change much, but when the dust settles, we are unlikely to have changed our culinary tastes, habits of hygiene, sense of beauty, sensitivity to temperatures, sympathy with or antipathy to other cultures, the pleasure we take in music, in learning a foreign language, or in vigorous exercise, and so forth. Even life-transforming experiences will leave unchanged many of the ideals that guide how we live. The deepest understanding would lead us to question all of our ideals and would leave us without anything to live for, except perhaps the satisfaction of basic physiological needs. It would deprive us of a recognizably human life and force us to stare into the abyss of a world without ideals. And that is something very few of us are willing to do.

I hope to have shown that alongside the obvious reasons for seeking deeper understanding than we have of our ideals there are also strong reasons against it and that these two sets of reasons conflict and make us ambivalent. Our ambivalence, however, does not alter the fact that we need better understanding in order to correct our mistaken ideals. But we need it as we sometimes need surgery or an emetic to enable us to remove an obstacle and restore us to a condition in which we can get on with life. What we do with our restored life is left just as much to the uncertain outcome of our conflicting and possibly mistaken ideals as it was before the obstacle was removed. Understanding, then, is not the key that will unlock a door to a life rich with satisfactions and no dissatisfactions. This is not because understanding is the wrong key, but because there is neither a key nor a door. Our condition is that we are prone to mistakes; our ideals are many, conflicting, and possibly mistaken; and we are therefore ambivalent.

It does not follow, and I do not believe, that ambivalence makes it impossible to live as we should, nor that it is unreasonable to try understand ourselves and our ideals better. But it does follow that the claims that have been and continue to be made for the importance of self-understanding are exaggerated. Better understanding often helps to correct the mistakes we make. What we gain from it, however, is unlikely to be an unmixed blessing. It may be good to understand our vices, weaknesses, failings, fears, and disappointments, but understanding them is just as likely to increase our dissatisfaction with ourselves as to decrease it.

It is a contemporary cultural phenomenon that countless literate and reflective people are enamored by Proust, psychoanalysis, stream-of-consciousness novels, biographies, and relentless self-examination. These cultural influences feed their passion for understanding themselves. But what such people like to do best need not be the best thing to do. Seeing need not be seeing through. It may be better to pursue ideals of goodness, beauty, and truth, which are not found inside our flawed self but outside of it in great works that go some way toward redeeming the human condition. The pursuit of these ideals, however, is not what this book is about. It is about psychological conflicts involved in living as we do. The equivocal benefits of understanding and the persistence of conflicts are among these problems. We need to recognize and face them, rather than to console ourselves with lullabies about autonomy. As the epigraph says, "he that knows not this, and is not armed to endure, is not fit to live in this world."[12]

4   Reflective Self-Evaluation

> That all men have one true purpose, and one only, that of rational self-
> direction . . . that the ends of all rational beings must of necessity fit into a
> single universal, harmonious pattern . . . that all conflict . . . is due solely
> to the clash of reason with the irrational or the insufficiently rational . . .
> and that such clashes are, in principle, avoidable, and for wholly rational
> beings impossible . . . that when all men have been made rational, they
> will obey the rational laws of their own nature, which are one and the
> same in them all . . . not one of the basic assumptions of this famous
> view is . . . true.
>
> ISAIAH BERLIN, "Two Concepts of Liberty"[1]

This chapter is about Harry G. Frankfurt's ideal theory of reflective self-evaluation (self-evaluation for short) as an overriding ideal that should guide how we live, resolve our conflicts, and overcome our ambivalence. There is a close connection between Frankfurt's ideal of self-evaluation and the Kantian ideal of autonomy, but there is also a crucial difference. The connection is that both self-evaluation and autonomy are species of self-governance that involve being governed by one's will, rather than by external influences of any kind. The crucial difference is that autonomy involves governing oneself in accordance with a universal rule, the categorical imperative, whereas self-evaluation consists in governing oneself by second-order self-evaluations.

There is a general agreement among defenders and critics that ideal theories are Kantian. Since Frankfurt's theory of self-evaluation is certainly not Kantian, the supposition is that it is not an ideal theory. I think this is a mistake. The most basic assumption on which all ideal theories rest is that there is an overriding ideal of how we should live and that we should always resolve conflicts between the overriding ideal and any other consideration in favor of the ideal. Ideal theories differ in what that overriding ideal is. Frankfurt's theory of self-evaluation is ideal because he thinks that the overriding ideal is self-evaluation. It is an overriding ideal because, as the passages I will cite explicitly claim, it is essential to being a person. Without it we are mere human organisms, lack free will, and fail to be responsible moral agents.

I think there are strong reasons why self-evaluation should not be accepted as an overriding ideal. I accept that it is a reasonable ideal of how we should live, but there are other reasonable ideals, and reason does not require that any of them should always and universally be overriding. In order to keep the discussion concrete, I begin with and will keep returning to the real life and conflicts of a real person. I will then consider how Frankfurt understands the ideal, what reasons he gives for it, and why these reasons fall far short of supporting his ideal theory.

The Dutiful Man

The Dutiful Man was born and raised on a dairy farm with close to a thousand acres of land. The farm has been in his family for three hundred years, and they always had about one hundred head of cattle. He is used to the farming life. It involves the hard work of twice daily milking, feeding the cattle during the winters when grazing is impossible, and maintaining the milking, bailing, and plowing machinery, without which the farm cannot function. The farm does not pay enough to sustain both his parents and himself, so he had to find some job. He trained as an electrician. To everyone's surprise, not least his own, he turned out to be very talented. He rapidly rose to a supervisory position in which he no longer did routine work. He designed complicated failsafe systems for hospitals and factories where much depended on getting it right. When computers revolutionized designing techniques, he took to them immediately, quickly trained himself to become an electronic systems analyst, and was much in demand.

He finished high school but had no further formal education. He rarely reads a book. He is not interested in politics or economics. He is not particularly religious. His knowledge of history and geography is rudimentary. He knows no foreign language. He is unconcerned with the visual arts, and music for him is pleasant background noise. He rarely has time to watch, listen to, or read the news. He is fully immersed in his life and cares very little about what happens outside of it. He is a decent, hardworking, conscientious, intelligent, poorly educated man.

He is married, his wife works, and they are raising two children. As the years pass, he is practicing his trade and his aging parents are finding the necessary work at the farm ever harder to do. The low price of milk and his parents' diminishing energy have been making it less and less possible to cover the cost of running the farm. Most days after work he helps with the tasks that have to be done. Even so, the farm is in poor shape. The old farmhouse needs paint, insulation, and other repairs, and the plumbing and the roof have to be replaced. The farm machinery is old and keeps breaking down, but they cannot afford to replace it. The cattle are not kept as clean as they should be. Things are let go.

He sees this and is dissatisfied with it. He takes pleasure in his job, but he is dissatisfied with it as well. Higher-ups in the company that employs him often alter his designs to make them more economical and thus less reliable. The people he supervises tend to do as little work for as much pay as possible. He dislikes having occasionally to do shoddy work, nor does he like the people below and above him who are self-serving and insufficiently concerned with quality. He minds this no less than the dilapidation of the farm. Nevertheless, he conscientiously does as well as he can both at the farm and at work, given limitations of time and energy.

As a result, he is often tired, does not have enough time for his wife and children, even less for himself, and he is sometimes irritable. He tries not to act on it, but his frustrations occasionally bubble up, and when he manages to hide them, he appears morose in his dealings with his parents, wife, children, and co-workers. His life is not easy, because he carries a heavy load. One result is that he is doing all that he does less well than he feels he should. But he also has many satisfactions derived from working on the farm; from the loving relationships with his parents, wife, and children; and from his skill as a systems analyst. He values the farming life that has been his family's for so many years; he does not want to withhold help from his aging parents who count on him. He also values working as a systems analyst, but he does not like supervising people who have to be cajoled into doing decent work, and he dislikes being forced by the demands of his employers to cut costs.

He feels strongly that it is his duty to do his job well, to help his parents maintain the farm, and to be a good son, husband, father, and supervisor. His sense of duty is not rigid but softened by his love of his family, of farming life, and of the work he does. The heavy load of duties he carries, however, takes up much of his time and energy. He wants more enjoyment in his life, more leisure for himself, and he misses what he lacks. His duties often conflict, require him to do more than he can, and he minds that he cannot do well all that he thinks he should.

Occasionally it fleetingly occurs to him to question how he lives, but he does not pursue the questions. He firmly believes that his duties are part of his life and that decency requires him to do the best he can to fulfill them. He knows that he could radically change his life and default on his duties, but he dismisses the possibility as unthinkable for himself. Acting on it would be incompatible with his self-respect, disloyal to the people he loves, and a betrayal of his skill, which he uses with pride and which enables him to earn a satisfactory living. His life is passing in this manner and it is a mixed bag of satisfactions and dissatisfactions. When the possibility of making a radical change comes into his head, perhaps in a moment of greater-than-usual frustration, he refuses to dwell on it, because he vaguely senses how damaging it would be to himself and to all those he loves to act on it. He is committed to living as he does, he is often uncertain about how to honor his conflicting responsibilities, he has many dissatisfactions and few satisfactions, but he nevertheless continues to carry on dutifully and does as well as he can.

Self-Evaluation

Bearing in mind the Dutiful Man, let us consider Frankfurt's well-known and influential ideal theory about living in full recognition of the importance of what we care about—a phrase that gives the title to what is perhaps his best known work.[2] Frankfurt focuses on self-evaluation, but it should be understood in what follows that it is reflective, not thoughtless. The focus of his later work is on love, as the most important of all that we care about. I will discuss it in chapter 5.

Frankfurt agrees with Plato's Socrates: the unexamined life is not worth living. Countless others have repeated it after him, and by now it is widely accepted without question. But it should be questioned, especially since Socrates forgot to mention that the examined life may not be worth living either. Why, then, stress the former but not the latter? Why is the unexamined life of simple, kind people not worth living? What about those hundreds of millions who were born into, lived, and died in highly structured, hierarchical societies, fulfilled the requirements of their station and its duties, enjoyed the perks, and unquestioningly obeyed the authorities to whom they were subject? Were all of their lives worthless? Why are the lives of artists, athletes, craftsmen, engineers, farmers, mechanics, nurses, and school teachers in our society not worth living if they are too busy with living to spend time examining how they live? What if the examination of one's life leads to self-loathing, despair, cynicism, boredom, or suicide? Do Socrates and his followers mean that examination is necessary, or sufficient, or merely important to make a life worth living? Is Socrates's dictum a generalization derived from observation of many different lives in many different contexts? Is it perhaps part of the definition of a worthwhile life? Is it merely a truth Socrates discovered about how he wanted to live?

Frankfurt's theory of self-evaluation is meant to explain why we should live an examined life and how we should go about it. We have first-order desires for specific objects, like lunch or a fancy car, and second-order desires for being a certain sort of person, such as incorruptible or powerful. We may or may not act on either kind of desire. But when we decide to act on a second-order desire, we have what Frankfurt calls a second-order volition. Self-evaluation involves "having second-order volitions," and they are "essential to being a person." A person has a second-order volition "when he wants a certain desire to be his will." Those who have first-order desires but no second-order volitions are wantons. Frankfurt says, "I shall use the term 'wanton' to refer to agents who have first-order desires but who are not persons because . . . they have no second-order volitions." A wanton "does not care about his will. His desires move him to do certain things, without its being true of him either that he wants to be moved by those desires or that he prefers to be moved by other desires" (*Importance*, 16). Self-evaluators have a second-order volition, make it their will, and thus identify themselves with it. "When a person identifies himself *decisively* with one of his first-order desires," then "the decisiveness of the commitment he has made means that he has decided that no further question about his second-order volition, at any higher order, remains to be asked" (21–22). Frankfurt repeats the same claim years later: "To be a person, as distinct from simply a human organism, requires a complex volitional structure of reflective self-evaluation. Human beings that lack this structure may be free of inherent volitional conflicts, but they are not persons" (*Necessity*, 103).

The importance of self-evaluation in Frankfurt's sense, therefore, is enormous. Personhood, free will, and moral responsibility all depend on it. They all presuppose the capacity to decide which of our first-order desires we want to be moved by. "There is a very close relationship between the capacity for forming second-order volitions and another capacity that is essential to persons — one that has often been considered a distinguishing mark of the human condition. It is only because a person has volitions of the second order that he is capable of enjoying and of lacking freedom of the will" (*Importance*, 19). "A person's will is free only if he is free to have the will he wants. This means that, with regard to any of his first-order desires, he is free either to make the desire his will or to make some other first-order desire his will instead" (24). And when he is free, he is also morally responsible for whatever decision he makes. "If someone does something because he wants to do it, and if he has no reservations about that desire but is wholeheartedly behind it, then — so far as his moral responsibility is concerned — it really does not matter how he got that way." Frankfurt adds, "The person's desires and attitudes have to be relatively well integrated into his general psychic condition. Otherwise they are not genuinely his, but merely disruptive intruders on his true nature" ("Replies," 27). Thus self-evaluation is necessary for being a person, free, and morally responsible. It is an ideal that is supposed to be a necessary condition of the pursuit of any other ideal we may have. That makes it an overriding ideal, and Frankfurt's theory of it an ideal theory.

Frankfurt's work has generated much controversy. Most of the participants in it accept the importance of self-evaluation to being a person. They are concerned with the implications of Frankfurt's view for the freedom of the will and moral responsibility.[3] My concern is different. It is to contest Frankfurt's ideal theory according to which self-evaluation is an overriding ideal and essential to being a person. I accept that self-evaluation is an important part, perhaps even an essential part, of the lives of many people, especially of analytically inclined academics. But I do not accept that what is true of them (and of myself as well) is true of the hundreds of millions of others who have been or are differently inclined and none the worse for that.

To begin with, what are we to say about the Dutiful Man in the light of Frankfurt's view? He has second-order volitions: to do well by his parents, wife, children, himself, and his job. But he has not identified decisively with any of them. His desires and attitudes are not well integrated in his general psychic condition. There is no doubt that his fragmented desires and attitudes create problems for him, because day in and day out they impose on him too many obligations. He is not reflective about his life. His will is scattered and prompts him to act in ways that are made incompatible by having unavoidably limited time and energy at his disposal. His feelings are a mixture of love for his family, job, and farming life and of frustration and chagrin caused by not being able to do all that he wants to do and thinks he should do. His self is divided among conflicting second-order volitions. According to Frankfurt's account, he is not a person, his will is not free, and he is not morally responsible, because his desires and attitudes are fragmented and he has not decisively identified with any of them. I ask: Is it credible that this Dutiful Man who voluntarily carries a heavy burden of responsibilities and does as well as he can by his family, job, and life really fails to be a person, free, and morally responsible?

Frankfurt acknowledges in a later work, inconsistently it seems to me, that there are persons like the Dutiful Man. He says it often happens that "a person is unable . . . to identify decisively either with one of the opposing tendencies of his will or with the other." Such a person "does not know which of these contending forces he would, in the end, prefer to prevail." In these cases, "the person is volitionally fragmented. His will is unstable and incoherent, moving him in contrary directions simultaneously or in a disorderly sequence. He suffers from a radically entrenched ambivalence" (Love, 92). Common experience bears this out: we all want many different things, and we all know that our wants sometimes conflict. The question is what we should do about it.

The answer, according to Frankfurt, is to become wholehearted. This "is a matter not of volitional strength but of whether the highest-order preferences concerning some volitional issue are *wholehearted*. It has to do with the possibility that there is no unequivocal answer to the question of what the person really wants, even though his desires do form a complex and extensive hierarchical structure." "The person's preferences concerning what he wants are not fully integrated, so that there is some *inconsistency* or *conflict* (perhaps not yet manifest) among them." This "kind of incoherence is *within* his volitional complex. In the absence of wholeheartedness, the person is not merely in conflict with forces 'outside' him; rather, he himself is divided" (*Importance*, 165).

The Dutiful Man should make up his mind about what he really wants. "A person who makes up his mind also seeks thereby to overcome or to supersede a condition of inner division and to make himself an integrated whole" (*Importance*, 174). "Wholeheartedness, as I am using the term," says Frankfurt, "does not consist in a feeling of enthusiasm, or of certainty, concerning a commitment" (175).

> In making up his mind a person establishes preferences concerning the resolution of conflicts among his desires or beliefs. Someone who makes a decision thereby performs an action, but the performance is not of a simple act that merely implements a first-order desire. It essentially involves reflexivity, including desires and volitions of a higher order. Thus, creatures who are incapable of this volitional reflexivity necessarily lack the capacity to make up their minds. They may desire and think and act, but they cannot decide. Insofar as we construe the making of decisions as the characteristic function of the faculty of volition, we must regard such creatures as lacking this faculty. (176)

And those who lack it lack a faculty essential to being a person.

This is made explicit by Frankfurt. "The essence of a person . . . is a matter of contingent volitional necessities by which the will of the person is as a matter of fact constrained. These constraints cannot be determined by conceptual or logical analysis. They are substantive rather than merely formal. They pertain to the purposes, the preferences, and the other personal characteristics that the individual cannot help having and that effectively determine the activities of his will" (*Necessity*, 138). And he goes on: "There is, I believe, a quite primitive human need to establish and to maintain volitional unity. Any threat to this unity— that is, any threat to the cohesion of the self—tends to alarm a person and to mobilize him for an attempt at 'self-preservation.'" A person who ignores this primitive need "is thereby acting voluntarily against the requirements of his own will. He is opposing ends and interests that are essential to his nature as a person. In other words, he is betraying himself. We are naturally averse to inflicting upon ourselves such drastic psychic injuries" (*Necessity*, 139). Those who lack this essential feature of being a person have not decisively identified themselves with one and only one second-order volition. They are not persons. Since few human beings come even close to being full-fledged self-evaluators, and since many of us typically lack volitional unity, contrary to appearance, very few of us are persons, and although we are supposed to be averse to it, we nevertheless inflict on ourselves "drastic psychic injuries."

It seems to me that Frankfurt has fallen into the error that Hume identified more than two hundred years earlier: "When a philosopher has once laid hold of a favourite principle, he extends the same principle over the whole creation, and reduces to it every phaenomenon, though by the most violent and absurd reasoning. Our own mind being narrow and contracted, we cannot extend our conception to the variety and extent of nature; but imagine, that she is as much bounded in her operations, as we are in our speculation."[4] Frankfurt elevates self-evaluation into an overriding ideal that few among the living or the dead have or could have met. Since we fail, we oppose our essential interests, betray ourselves by voluntarily acting against the requirements of our own will, and inflict drastic psychic injuries on ourselves. If we consider that we ourselves and perhaps most of those we know personally or from psychology, history, and literature fail in this way, then Jeremiah's judgment of humanity will seem upbeat compared to what is implied by Frankfurt's overriding ideal. He has constructed an ideal theory, laden with technical terms, one of whose consequences is that most human beings are not persons. I will now consider the contrary possibility: that his ideal theory fails as an account of how we should all live.

Real Lives and Ideal Theory

If we are untouched by Frankfurt's theory, the Dutiful Man will seem to us to be living a decent life, doing as well as he can, given his upbringing, education, circumstances, and preferences. He certainly has dissatisfactions that he would no doubt prefer not to have, but that is true of all but the most fortunate among us. We who are not among the most fortunate have conflicts and are ambivalent about how to deal with them. Managing such conflicts and living with ambivalence are normally thought of as signs of maturity. As we are buffeted by life and its and our uncertainties, some of us learn a measure of what Keats aptly called negative capability: accepting the messiness of life and that we cannot have all we want, not even if we want it wholeheartedly. We can, of course, scorn such acquiescence, dwell on our dissatisfactions, and inveigh against the human condition, but that will add useless passions to our dissatisfactions and make matters worse than they might otherwise be. Frankfurt will have none of this accepting attitude. His overwrought judgment of anyone who does not opt to pursue the ideal of self-evaluation and prefers to live as the Dutiful Man is living — cultivating negative capability and putting up with dissatisfactions, conflicts, and ambivalence — is not simply that he errs on the side of prudence, but that he fails to be a person, is "voluntarily acting against the requirement of his own will," is "opposing ends and interests that are essential to his nature as a person," and is inflicting "drastic psychic injuries" on himself (*Necessity*, 139).

Consider for a moment: if you observed the Dutiful Man in the ordinary course of life, would you think that he was acting against his will, against his essential nature as a person, and that he was suffering from drastic psychic injuries? Would you have the slightest doubt that he is a person, that at least sometimes he is acting freely and responsibly? And if, unlikely as it is, you judged him as you should according to Frankfurt's ideal theory, would you be willing to make the same judgment of the many human beings, including in all likelihood yourself, who live in the relevant respects pretty much as the Dutiful Man does?

If Frankfurt's ideal theory were a description of what it is to be a person, it would be glaringly at odds with how being a person is normally regarded by virtually everyone in everyday life. The theory would transform "person" into a technical term that drew its stipulated meaning from the theory. Frankfurt then would need to give reasons for adopting this unusual usage and the theory from which it drew its meaning. Whatever those reasons might be, they could not be derived from the ordinary understanding of what it is to be a person, since that understanding is very different from what it is in the theory. The required reasons would have to show why it is reasonable to describe persons as Frankfurt does rather than as we ordinarily describe them. I have looked hard, but I could not find any such reason in Frankfurt's writings. I think Frankfurt intends the theory to persuade those who understand it to say Yes, that is how we are. I do not think the theory manages to do this. Nor do I think Frankfurt would be much concerned with this, because his theory is not meant to be a description of what it is to be a real person.

The theory is meant, rather, to be a description of an ideal that we should follow in order to become the kind of person Frankfurt thinks we should be. If we follow Frankfurt's prescription, we will develop a second-order volition, commit ourselves to it decisively and whole-heartedly, evaluate the choices and actions open to us in the light of this pivotal second-order volition, and thus become self-evaluators. If his theory were understood in this way, Frankfurt could readily acknowledge that many, or even most, real lives fall short of the ideal that according to his theory is overriding. The theory would then explain that the reason why there are so many dissatisfactions in our lives is that we fail to live according to the theory as we should, just as the Dutiful Man is failing. And if we fail, we are neither persons nor morally responsible.

The source of these dissatisfactions is ambivalence. "A person is ambivalent, then, only if he is indecisive concerning whether to be for or against a certain psychic position. Now this kind of indecisiveness is as irrational, in its way, as holding contradictory beliefs. The disunity of an ambivalent person's will prevents him from effectively pursuing and satisfactorily attaining his goals. Like conflict within reason, volitional conflict leads to self-betrayal and self-defeat" (*Necessity*, 99). To avoid this irrational state of disunity of will and ambivalence, we should impose a volitional structure on our desires. This involves "identification with some desire" and having "a higher-order desire by which the first desire is endorsed," and that higher order desire must be one "with which the person is *satisfied*" (*Necessity*, 105).

Consider, then, what the Dutiful Man and many of us whose psychological conditions are like his would have to do follow Frankfurt's ideal. We would have to endorse our first-order desire by a higher-order desire with which we are satisfied; it would have to become our second-order volition; and we would have to identify ourselves wholeheartedly with the second-order volition. If we did all this, we would indeed have a guide to deciding which of our lower-order desires we should try to satisfy. But of course, part of our and the Dutiful Man's typical psychological condition is that we have wholeheartedly identified ourselves with several of our higher-order volitions, and they conflict. The Dutiful Man did this with the higher-order volition to be a good father, son, husband, and system designer, with fulfilling what he regarded as his duties, with wanting to have an enjoyable life, with respecting himself, and so forth. And most of us are like him in having several higher-order volitions with which we have wholeheartedly identified. We want to meet our moral obligations, support our political cause, have a loving marriage, seek to enjoy the good things in life, do our job well, raise responsible children, relax in agreeable ways, and so on. If we become self-evaluators, we will understand better our various second-order volitions, but there is no reason to suppose that this would make us less ambivalent. It is much more likely to reinforce the ambivalence we already have as a result of the conflicting second-order volitions with which we have wholeheartedly identified ourselves.

Frankfurt's likely response would be that if we want to be persons, free, and responsible, we should become better self-evaluators, rank the relative importance we attribute to our desires, and act accordingly. The Dutiful Man should make up his mind whether farming or systems analysis is more important to him, whether his love of his parents, wife, or children is the deepest, whether he desires more doing all he thinks he should or having more leisure and less fatigue, and then he will be able to overcome his ambivalence. This advice, however, is useless, because it ignores his psychological condition. He cannot do what Frankfurt says he should, because the desires that matter to him conflict, and he is uncertain about which of them matter to him more than the others. That is what makes him ambivalent. To advise him that he should make up his mind is as helpful as advising people who have lost their way to find it.

Suppose, nevertheless, that we follow Frankfurt's advice and assign priority to one of our desires. This would generate new dissatisfactions without putting an end to old ones. For our wholehearted identification with whatever the overriding desire is will be inevitably conjoined with frustration over the ones that have been overridden. The stifled desires would not disappear but remain, suppressed and frustrated. And since living and acting according to the stifled desires was an important part of how we wanted to live, stifling them would be no less dissatisfying than the ambivalence was that the imposition of priority was meant to overcome. If the Dutiful Man gave up farming for systems analysis, devoted himself to his wife at the expense of his parents and children, or chose more leisure over fulfilling his many duties, he would be no less dissatisfied with his life than he was in his ambivalent prior condition. For if he neglected his beloved parents, children, or family farm, he knows he would cause grievous injury and lose his self-respect, and this he would not do. Our psychological condition is that the more dissatisfied ambivalence makes us, the more dissatisfied we would be if we resolved our conflicts by imposing a priority, any priority, on our desires and volitions.

It remains to be observed that for most of us, conflicts among our desires and acts of will are the rule, not the exception. Our aesthetic, economic, legal, moral, personal, political, prudential, religious, and other commitments routinely prompt us to act in incompatible ways, because our time and energy are limited. Although Frankfurt recognizes that wholeheartedness is difficult and must be struggled for, his defense of the ideal of self-evaluation nevertheless fails, because the cost of the struggle is the unavoidable dissatisfaction caused by violating some of our wholehearted commitments. Such dissatisfactions are unavoidable consequences of our many and conflicting commitments and psychological limits. No amount of self-evaluation can overcome these conflicts without making us bear the cost of violating one of our wholehearted commitments. In the light of this, ambivalence about pursuing the ideal of self-evaluation is neither unreasonable nor unnatural. And the threat that self-evaluation will call into question all the important commitments by which we want to live makes ambivalence about self-evaluation reasonable and natural. Nevertheless, countless people find, contrary to Frankfurt's denial, that their unexamined life, although often ambivalent, is worth living. If in doubt, ask them, rather than apply Frankfurt's theory to them.

What, then, should the Dutiful Man do? He should continue to do pretty much what he has been doing: try to balance as well as he can his conflicting duties and desires. Whenever they conflict in a particular situation, he should figure out what is the least unsatisfactory way of coping with their conflicts. Doing this is not another name for self-evaluation, but ordinary commonsensical thinking about how to juggle all we have to do in our particular circumstances. It does not require anything as momentous as wholeheartedness, self-evaluation, and decisive identification with one and only one second-order volition. It requires the Dutiful Man to decide whether on a particular day repairing the milking machinery is more or less urgent than helping his daughter with an arithmetic assignment, or whether learning about a supposedly better software program for improved systems analysis can wait until he and his wife discuss her plan to change jobs. The best way of coping with conflicts often involves no more than temporizing in a particular context, rather than trying to resolve the conflict once and for all.

If our commitments are many and conflicting, then there is nothing we can do to eliminate all possible conflicts among them. For any overall conflict-resolution would have the unavoidable consequence of denying the importance of one of the conflicting commitments. But if each of the conflicting commitments is important for living as we want, then a once-and-for-all conflict resolution would doom us, if we accepted it, to act contrary to how we want to live. This makes ambivalence a psychological obstacle and the reluctance to follow Frankfurt's overriding ideal natural and reasonable.

Contingency

I turn now to another problem with Frankfurt's ideal theory. He writes that self-evaluation "is a matter of contingent volitional necessities by which the will of the person is as a matter of fact constrained" (*Necessity*, 138). But if the ideal of self-evaluation is combined with the recognition that the volitional necessities that self-evaluation reveals are contingent, then the ideal is subverted. Self-evaluation may bring us to understand what our volitional necessities are. If we recognize that they are contingent, that we feel bound by them perhaps only because we have been indoctrinated or manipulated in the course of our upbringing or by some religious or ideological dogma, then the question of why we should feel bound by them, now that we understand their origin, naturally arises and needs to be answered. We will not agree with Frankfurt that our wholehearted volitional necessities "are absolute and unconditional" (*Taking & Getting*, 45). Self-evaluation may lead us to question them. And answering the question becomes especially pressing if we are compelled by the contingent volitional necessity we feel to fulfill onerous obligations that others around us find difficult to understand, such as commitment to a corrupt political cause or to an indefensible religious dogma. Self-evaluation will lead us to realize that feeling bound by a volitional necessity is not a sufficient reason to remain bound to it. Frankfurt denies this. He says: "What counts is our current effort to define and manage ourselves, and not the story of how we come to be in the situation with which we are now attempting to cope" (*Taking & Getting*, 7).

Self-evaluation, as Frankfurt understands it, is reflective, and if it leads us to understand that we feel bound by a volitional necessity as a result of contingent influences to which we have been subjected beyond our control, then, if we are reasonable, we will want to know why, now that we have the control we earlier lacked, we should continue to feel bound by it. If we are reasonable self-evaluators, rather than dogmatic self-affirmers who unquestioningly endorse their own desires simply because they are theirs, then our hold on the volitional necessities we feel bound by will be weakened, rather than strengthened, contrary to what, according to Frankfurt's theory, self-evaluation would do.

Frankfurt considers and rejects this appeal to reason. He says that "for normative guidance in understanding what we should want or what we should do, there can be no authority superior to the welcome necessities of our own nature." And "a rational acquiescence to this authority requires a clear self-understanding and a wholehearted acceptance of the essential requirements and boundaries of our will. This amounts to finding a mature confidence, which is not vulnerable to destruction of the self's integrity by familiar varieties of hyperrationalistic skepticism" (*Taking & Getting*, 51). But why would our mature confidence not be vulnerable to doubts that self-evaluation may cause us to have? Why might we not repudiate the necessities of our nature, especially when they conflict? Why could self-evaluation not lead us to conclude that the requirements and boundaries of our will often shift and sometimes should?

Furthermore, if self-evaluation unfolds as Frankfurt says it should, it will not only allow us to discover which of our commitments should become volitionally necessary, but also, by the same token, show us what we should not regard as volitionally necessary. If we discover, as Frankfurt says we would, that the contingencies of our upbringing, education, and experiences, rather than the intrinsic merits of our commitments, make us regard them as volitionally necessary, then, if we are reasonable, the commitment will seem to us much less compelling.

If the Dutiful Man discovers that his sense of duty is the remnant of the faith his ancestors based on a literal reading of the Bible, a faith he does not share, then he will feel less keenly the volitional necessity that compels him to be dutiful. He will see that what he thinks is right is what he inherited from his ancestors. And then, if he is reasonable, he will think differently as a result of the discovery that self-evaluation led him to make about the contingency of his beliefs. Self-evaluation will make him less wholehearted, less compelled by volitional necessity than he was before he embarked on self-evaluation.

Suppose, then, that he understands that his sense of duty has a religious origin and he is not religious. He may still conclude that doing his duty is the right thing to do. He will have found a reason for continuing to live as he has been doing. That reason, however, will not come from better self-evaluation, but from a better understanding of why it is right to do his duty. So although self-evaluation may lead us to understand what volitional necessities we feel bound by, it is neither necessary nor sufficient for continuing to make us feel bound by them. It is not necessary because we may feel bound by volitional necessities even if we do not understand why we feel bound by them. And it is not sufficient because we may understand why we feel bound by them and then repudiate our commitments to them.

If we are indeed self-evaluators, we will see our commitments as contingent products of our contingent circumstances. Since they are contingent, they might have been different, and, if they had been, we would hold different commitments to different volitional necessities. We will understand that our commitments are conditional on influences to which we have been subject but cannot control. When our conditional commitments conflict, as they will, our situation will be the same as the Dutiful Man's, no matter how proficient we become at self-evaluation. If our commitments and volitional necessities are contingent, as Frankfurt believes, then self-evaluation may make us more, not less, ambivalent, which is the opposite of what he believes.

Oddly enough, Isaiah Berlin, having very different concerns, arrives at a view remarkably similar to Frankfurt's but no less mistaken. Berlin quotes Schumpeter with deep approval: "'To realise the relative validity of one's convictions,' said an admirable writer of our time, 'and yet stand for them unflinchingly, is what distinguishes a civilised man from a barbarian.'"[5] But neither Schumpeter nor Berlin has explained why it is reasonable to stand unflinchingly for convictions that we recognize as only relatively valid, or why doing this would be a mark of being civilized rather than dogmatic.

In an influential essay, John McDowell denies that understanding the contingency of our commitments leads to ambivalence. He discusses how a sensitive man views a situation. He is not "balancing reasons for and against." "The view of a situation that he arrives at by exercising his sensitivity is one in which some aspect of the situation is seen [by him] as constituting a reason for acting in some way; this reason is apprehended, not as outweighing or overriding any reason for acting in other ways . . . but as silencing them."[6] McDowell asks about the source of the confidence that could silence any contrary view of the situation. He answers by citing Stanley Cavell: confidence is a matter of "interest and feeling, modes of response, senses of humor and of significance and of fulfilment, of what is outrageous, of what is similar to what else, what a rebuke, what forgiveness . . . all the whirl of organism Wittgenstein calls 'forms of life.'"[7] The sensitive man's confidence, McDowell thinks, derives from his immersion in a form of life so deep as to silence contrary considerations. He has no conflicting commitments, and he is not ambivalent about what he should do. He simply sees the situation in a certain light and acts accordingly. McDowell and Cavell think that if we are immersed in a form of life, we will encounter no conflicts, no incompatible commitments, no ambivalence, and we will have no need to become self-evaluators. As we have seen, however, although the Dutiful Man was certainly immersed in his form of life, he did encounter many conflicts. Contrary considerations about what he should do were not silenced.

Consider what would happen if, for one reason or another, the sensitive man of McDowell and Cavell happens to become a self-evaluator and reflects on his immersion in his form of life. According to Cavell, he would come to understand that "human speech and activity, sanity and community, rest upon nothing more, but nothing less, than this. It is a vision as simple as it is difficult, and as difficult as it is (and because it is) terrifying."[8] McDowell's comment is that "the terror of which Cavell speaks at the end of this marvellous passage is a sort of vertigo, induced by the thought that there is nothing but shared forms of life to keep us, as it were, on the rails. We are inclined to think that is an insufficient foundation for conviction."[9] And McDowell says that this "should not induce vertigo at all. We cannot be whole-heartedly engaged in the relevant parts of the 'whirl of organism,' and at the same time achieve the detachment necessary in order to query whether our unexamined view of what we are doing is illusory. The cure for vertigo, then, is to give up the idea that philosophical thought, about the sorts of practice in question, should be undertaken at some external standpoint, outside our immersion in our familiar forms of life."[10]

Assume that this is true and we give up the idea that there is an external standpoint. Why should we think, with McDowell, that we should engage in our activities and seek the necessary detachment "at the same time"? McDowell gives no answer, and I doubt that a convincing one could be given. Why could not self-evaluation subsequent to various activities lead us to understand the contingency of our form of life? This need not make us fall into the vertiginous terror of which Cavell somewhat melodramatically speaks. It may merely make us ambivalent about our commitments whose contingency we come to understand. Self-evaluation, then, will not permit us to silence our understanding that it is a mere coincidence of a number of causal processes that we have the form of life, commitments, and volitional necessities we have, and that the best we can say in favor of them is that they happen to be ours.

If there is no external standpoint, we can talk about the strength of our commitments but not about their rightness or wrongness. We cannot, then, overcome the ambivalence to which self-evaluation leads once we understand the contingency of our commitments and volitional necessities. Nor can we silence our ambivalence. We would just understand the contingency of our condition and realize how quixotic it is or would be to be wholeheartedly committed to volitional necessities whose contingency self-evaluation makes us understand. If self-evaluation is incompatible with silencing, then it may not eliminate but reinforce our ambivalence, contrary to what Frankfurt claims on behalf of his ideal of self-evaluation.

In the light of this, it is perhaps obvious that there are good reasons why the Dutiful Man should not accept self-evaluation as an overriding ideal, why he should cope with his conflicting duties case by case, and why he should not question his form of life. There are good reasons also for continuing to proceed the way he has been doing. But he is not aware of these reasons. He is guided by unexamined decency, love, a sense of duty, and the many demands of a busy life. They have served him better than he would have been served by self-evaluation that casts doubt on much of what he quite reasonably values.

Justification

It is a basic psychological fact that we have choices about whether to become self-evaluators or wantons; whether to be self-evaluators in some areas of life, say finances, but not in others, like sex; whether we are self-evaluators consistently after we begin or only sporadically; whether our self-evaluation is honest and critical or full of self-deception and fantasy; whether we take to heart what our self-evaluation reveals or relegate it to the margin of our attention; and so forth. Frankfurt's view is that the more and better self-evaluators we are, the more free and responsible we become, the closer and closer we come to the ideal of knowing what we care about most deeply and commit ourselves to living that way wholeheartedly. And as we approximate the ideal, we become persons.

If this ideal is reasonable, it needs to be justified. Why should we pursue it? Why should we try to live according to it? It is not enough to say that some of us care about it, since we all care about many different things, and we often care about stupid, trivial, destructive, or vicious things. Why should we think that we should care about some things more than about others? Why should we care more about becoming self-evaluators than, say, about becoming secure, prudent, respected, good at our job, tranquil, or a great chess player? Why should we trust what we wholeheartedly care about now and about our present volitional necessities, when we remember how foolish we were in the past about our wholehearted concerns and about the volitional necessities we felt? Why should we care about pursuing the ideal of self-evaluation? Why not recognize instead, as the practical approach does, that there are various other reasonable possibilities?

We may opt instead to pursue no ideal at all and just coast along on as even keel as we can manage. Or we may opt to live a life of service and humility in which we subordinate what we care about to God's will, or to helping the poor, or to vanquishing the foe. Or we may opt to pursue intense pleasures regardless of consequences; or to pursue adventure, risk-taking, challenging limits, beauty, or justice. And we may opt for these other ideals consciously ignoring how doing so might affect our own interests. It is not an acceptable justification of the ideal Frankfurt favors to say that whatever other ideal we may opt to pursue presupposes Frankfurt's because we devote our life to it only if we care about it wholeheartedly. For that would make Frankfurt's ideal into the utterly trivial one from which no one could possibly deviate, not even wantons, since they could be said to care about being wantons. If the ideal of self-evaluation is to avoid triviality, it must be specific, and Frankfurt makes it so.

Self-evaluation is the specific ideal "of separating from the immediate content and flow of our own consciousness and introducing a sort of division within our minds. This elementary maneuver establishes an inward-directed monitoring oversight. It puts in place an elementary reflexive structure, which enables us to focus attention directly upon ourselves" (*Taking & Getting*, 4). The question I am asking, then, is what is the justification for making this into an ideal that should override any other ideal that might conflict with it? I grant that it is an ideal, but what needs to be justified is that it is or should be an overriding ideal.

Having a justification matters because, as Frankfurt recognizes, what we find when we "focus attention directly upon ourselves" may generate "a profound threat to our well-being. The inner division that we introduce impairs our capacity for untroubled spontaneity." And it "exposes us to psychological and spiritual disorders that are nearly impossible to avoid. These are not only painful; they can be seriously disabling." It "frequently leaves us chagrined and distressed by what we see, as well as bewildered and insecure concerning who we are" (*Taking & Getting*, 4–5). Why, then, should we pursue the overriding ideal of self-evaluation and run the risk of "a profound threat to our well-being"?

Frankfurt's answer is that self-evaluation may also lead us to "the foundational structure for several particularly cherished features of our humanity. It accounts for the very fact that we possess such a thing as practical reason; it equips us to enjoy a significant freedom in the exercise of our will; and it creates for us the possibility of going beyond simply wanting various things, and coming instead to care about them, to regard them as important to ourselves" (*Taking and Getting*, 5). With this we have reached the most basic assumption on which Frankfurt's entire work rests, and it is, of course, an assumption that needs to be justified. Frankfurt elaborates it again and again, shows how it works out in practical reasoning, the freedom of the will, and moral responsibility, but this does not amount to a justification of the assumption that without self-evaluation none of these "cherished features of humanity" would be possible. I have looked as carefully as I can, but I have not found in Frankfurt's work a justification for the assumption that the Dutiful Man and the countless others like him who are not self-evaluators fail to be persons, have no free will, are not morally responsible, and lack practical reason.

Let us suppose, however, that Frankfurt has provided the required justification and I have just stupidly missed it. Even in that case there would remain a crucial question. Suppose we are reasonable and see the world, life, and the available choices as Frankfurt sees them. We then see "when we focus attention directly upon ourselves" both the possibility of "the profound threat to our well-being" and "the cherished features of humanity" that the cultivation of our capacity for self-evaluation makes possible. It seems to me that it cannot be justified to claim that reason requires us to cultivate our capacity for self-evaluation. Reason may allow it, but it also allows us to remain ambivalent whether we should cultivate this capacity in the hope of developing further cherished features of our humanity or whether we should cautiously avoid the profound threat to our well-being that its cultivation represents.

Surely, reason allows us to get on with our life, not to evaluate it all that much, maintain our marriage, raise our children, do our job, and enjoy the small pleasures we may find, and do all this as well as we can without much self-evaluation. No defensible view of reason would disallow us to be careful, prudent, and cautious in dealing with profound threats to our well-being by not cultivating those capacities of ours that we rightly suspect might lead to the profound threats that Frankfurt acknowledges. Reason allows us not to live in the way that Frankfurt implausibly stipulates would make us persons, free, and morally responsible. Reason allows us to say—accepting his stipulation for the sake of argument—that if the cultivation of these cherished features of our humanity presents profound threats to our well-being, then we do not want to cultivate them. Frankfurt proposed self-evaluation as an overriding ideal for resolving our conflicts and overcoming our ambivalence. But it now transpires that even if we accept all that Frankfurt claims, our conflicts and ambivalence may remain. And as I have just shown, we can appeal to Frankfurt's own argument to make that acceptable to reason.

This, however, is not all that can be said against the case Frankfurt makes in defense of his overriding ideal of self-evaluation. Let us ignore that living with conflicts and ambivalence may be a reasonable alternative to cultivating self-evaluation, and let us suppose that the volitional necessity we are wholeheartedly committed to trying to approximate is to be a full-fledged self-evaluator. Surely, it makes a difference to Frankfurt's recommended ideal just what the volitional necessity is to which we wholeheartedly commit ourselves. If self-evaluation leads us to care most deeply about what is utterly trivial (collecting canceled streetcar tickets), irrational (squaring the circle), vicious (ridding the world of infidels), self-destructive (doing without sleep), pathetic (trying to communicate with the dead), quixotic (writing without using the letter *e*), stupid (trying to grow a third arm), then it cannot be reasonably regarded as an ideal whose cultivation makes us persons, free, and responsible.

In a way, Frankfurt recognizes this, but in another he does not. He says, on the one hand, "The fact that what a person cares about is a personal matter does not entail that *anything* goes. It may still be possible to distinguish between things that are worth caring about to one degree or another and things that are not" (*Importance*, 91). And "the critical question cannot be whether the object is sufficiently important to the person to warrant his caring about it. It must instead be whether the person is justified in *making* the thing important to him by caring about it" (*Importance*, 93). And "when the importance of a certain thing to a person is due to the fact that he cares about it, however, that fact plainly cannot provide a useful measure of the extent to which his caring about it is justified" (*Importance*, 93). These passages seem to me to be right.

Yet, Frankfurt also says, on the other hand, that "the only way to justify doing this is in terms of the importance of the activity of caring itself." Caring matters "because it serves to connect us actively to our lives in ways in which we are creative of ourselves and which expose us to distinctive possibilities for necessity and for freedom" (*Importance*, 93). Frankfurt then asks: "What makes it more suitable, then, for a person to make one object rather than another important to himself?" And he answers: "It seems it must be the fact that it is *possible* for him to care about one and not about the other, or to care about the one in a way which is more important to him than the way in which it is possible for him to care about the other" (*Importance*, 94). Frankfurt's view is, then, that caring about what one regards as important to care about is all the justification we need and can have. These passages seem to me to be very wrong indeed.

In chapter 5, I consider Frankfurt's development and extended treatment of this view by connecting the importance of what we care about with love. I conclude this chapter with Frankfurt's own words: "The pan-rationalist fantasy of demonstrating—from the ground up—how we have most reason to live is incoherent and must be abandoned" (*Love*, 28). This is precisely what a practical approach stresses, and what I am arguing for throughout the book. But surely abandoning the pan-rationalist fantasy need not lead to accepting that caring about trivial, irrational, vicious, self-destructive, pathetic, quixotic, stupid things can be cherished features of our humanity and that caring about such matters makes it worth our while to overcome our ambivalence about risking profound threats to our well-being. Nor does it lead to agreeing with Frankfurt that we should embrace his own pan-rationalist fantasy that "to be a person, as distinct from simply a human organism, requires a complex volitional structure of reflective self-evaluation" (*Necessity*, 103).

5   Unconditional Love

When you shall these unlucky deeds relate,
Speak of me as I am; nothing extenuate,
Nor set down aught in malice; then you must speak
Of one that lov'd not wisely but too well.

WILLIAM SHAKESPEARE, *Othello*[1]

"September 1, 1939" is the title of W. H. Auden's poem. It refers to the day Germany invaded Poland and the Second World War began. A much-cited line from it has brought tears to many an eye: "We must love one another or die." Auden does not mention that we must die even if we do not love one another, nor that although we should love the lovable and perhaps, compassionately, the pitiable, it is perverse to love fanatical ideologues, religious maniacs, ethnic cleansers, mass murderers, and sadistic torturers. Auden's line is an unintended illustration of the sentimentality of unconditional love. It clouds our judgment by falsifying the facts to fit our overwrought feelings. One would expect philosophers to resist the blandishment of such effusions, but many of them follow Rousseau's lamentable example and succumb to it. Life would not be worth living without love, but that does not make love an unconditional ideal that should override whatever consideration might conflict with it.

Yet, in his later work Frankfurt has extended his earlier ideal theory of reflective self-evaluation into the claims that "the authority of practical reason is less fundamental than that of love," that love is "absolute and unconditional,"[2] and that love is "a terminal value" (*Love*, 55). These, and other claims I will cite later, make clear that the importance Frankfurt attributes to love is far more than a personal preference. It is at the core of his ideal theory of how we should live and the key to overcoming our conflicts and ambivalence. No one can reasonably deny that love is important. But we can love unwisely and too well, as Shakespeare says and shows, as does the story which I will now tell.

The Father

The Father was one of his parents' many children. He was raised in a rough neighborhood by rough parents who had to work long hours to support the family. They had neither time nor energy to give him the love he needed and craved. He had to make do as well as he could in the midst of none-too-loving brothers, sisters, and neighborhood children. The older ones vented their aggression and frustration on the younger and weaker ones. He learned to fight, rely on himself, take his lumps, and be tough. He finished school, took a job, found an opportunity, started a business, and eventually became successful and affluent through intelligence, hard and disciplined work, and relying on no one but himself.

His experiences led him to form a view of the world not far removed from a Hobbesian state of nature. He believed that the strong are motivated by self-interest and the weak have to endure the consequences. He proved himself strong and was proud of it, but he still craved love and yearned to find someone trustworthy enough for him to love. He eventually met a woman whom he could love and who loved him, and they have been happily married for many years. They have two boys and a girl. He loves his wife, but that is dwarfed by the love he feels for his children. He sees them as helpless, trusting, warm, cuddly, innocent things who depend on him for love and protection, and he gives them all he can give, and what he, as a child, never had. He is happy, because he has found what he lacked all his life: he loves and is loved. He sees the life he and his wife have made together as a haven, for themselves and the children, from the harsh realities of the world. It is their family against the world, and it is up to him to make them as secure as possible. Outside the family he becomes an even fiercer competitor than he was before, because he now has to protect not only himself but also his family. He is fierce also inside the family, but he is fierce in loving his children. That is by far what he cares about most in life.

As the children are growing up basking in his love, he comes to believe that they are not ready to face the harsh realities of the world, and he fears for them. He sees that he must teach them the facts of life, toughen them up, make them ready to protect themselves when he is not there any more to do it for them, and prepare them for life outside the secure cocoon he and his wife have created for them. After much reflection he concludes that he must become much less indulgent toward his children, spoil them no more, and set demanding tasks for them. He believes that their well-being depends on learning to be disciplined, just as he learned it. He regards their interests as his own and endeavors to teach them by setting a personal example and requiring them to work hard to stifle their easygoing ways and soft emotions so that they will prevail in the hard competitions they will have to face. He loves his children as much as ever, but he is convinced that the best way of expressing that love is to teach them not to rely on it.

The children yearn for their previous carefree existence, when they felt that the Father was the center of their universe, but he is resolved to wean them from it, although he himself longs to indulge them as he did before. But love, as he understands it, demands that he should not do what both he and the children long for. The love of his children, his dominant motive, leads him in conflicting directions: one is to continue to express as palpably as before the love he has for them, and the other is to become as hard and demanding a taskmaster as he thinks the well-being of his beloved children requires him to be. He is at first ambivalent about how to resolve the conflict. But his will is as strong as it has been since his own childhood. He stifles the expressions of his love he longs to give and resolves to adopt the second way, regardless of how hard he finds it.

The children of course realize that a dramatic change has occurred in their lives. They feel that they must have done something terrible that made the Father stop loving them, but they do not know what it was. They desperately try to win back what they see as their loss of his love. The girl does her best to live up to the Father's increasingly greater demands. She succeeds and is rewarded by the Father's praise and carefully modulated expressions of love. The two boys are disoriented, resent the change in their lives, want things to be as they were before, and rebel against the demanding tasks the Father sets for them. The Father, however, insists and shows his disapproval of them, in sharp contrast with his approval of his daughter. And of course, the boys resent that too, and the loving harmony of the family is poisoned by the spreading of bad feelings. The Father believes that he is acting in the best interest of the children, and he does not allow himself to weaken, because that would be contrary to the most important thing he cares about: the love he has for his children and their well-being. Although he resolved his conflict and overcame his ambivalence, neither disappears; they are only stifled. By great effort he acts as if they did not exist, and he does what he thinks he ought to do for the sake of his children.

His wife understands what is happening, but she is helpless in the face of it. She loves and is loyal to her husband and loves the children no less. She tries to talk her husband out of what he is doing, tries to tell him that the children need to feel his love and that the world is not the jungle he takes it to be. But he thinks she is naive about the world and that he is acting in the best interest of the children. She does all she can to be extra loving to the children, but the children need to feel their Father's love, and that she cannot give them. She sees that nothing she could do would change the situation. She has not changed, but the family has, and she sees but cannot help the bad feelings that are becoming entrenched as time passes.

The two sons grow up miserably, although they show it in different ways. One becomes depressed, withdrawn, passive, listless, and loses interest in life. The other keeps challenging his Father by taking ever more dangerous risks and by one outrageous act of rebellion after another. In their different but uncomprehending ways, both boys hope to regain what they believe they have lost. But the Father is firm and strong, and they are disappointed again and again. The sons become deeply frustrated adults. The daughter continues to revel in the Father's love and approval. For that, however, she pays the price of having no will of her own. The Father's love for all the children is as strong as ever, but it is precisely its strength that keeps him from giving them what he knows they want and need, what he longs to give. He is embittered by the estrangement of his sons and saddened by the realization that his daughter lacks the will to be her own person. The Father's love has gone very wrong. The fact that emerges from this story, as it does from *Othello*, is that both the Father and the children would have been better off if the Father had loved them less but more wisely.

Love

Frankfurt has proposed an ideal theory about love as the overriding ideal that we should care about above all else, one that is the key to coping with our psychological conflicts and resolving our ambivalence. He writes that "the commands of love derive from the essential nature of a person's will; a person who voluntarily disobeys those commands is thereby acting voluntarily against the requirements of his own will. He is opposing ends and interests that are essential to his nature as a person. In other words, he is betraying himself" (*Necessity*, 139). Frankfurt lists four conceptually necessary conditions of love. "First, it consists most basically in a disinterested concern for the well-being or flourishing of the person who is loved." "Second, love is unlike other modes of disinterested concern for people — such as charity — in that it is ineluctably personal." "Third, the lover identifies with the beloved: that is, he takes the interest of his beloved as his own." "Finally, loving entails constraints upon the will. It is not simply up to us what we love and what we do not love. Love is not a matter of choice but is determined by conditions that are outside our immediate voluntary control" (*Love*, 79–80).

Let us now see Frankfurt's ideal theory in the light of the ordinary understanding of love. We might begin with two obvious questions. Love is usually thought to be a spontaneous emotion. If it has to be willed, then it seems contrived, something we make ourselves feel, rather than just feel, often in spite of ourselves. So the first question is, Why should an emotion that we must will ourselves to have be essential to our nature as a person? The other question is, Why should we think that if the commands of love are indeed among the requirements of the will, then they cannot go wrong by being unreasonable, destructive, inconsistent, and contrary to our interests, or be mistaken in other ways?

Frankfurt's answer is that both of these questions rest on the mistaken assumption that the commands of love could conflict with the requirements of the will or reason. There can be no conflict between loving and willing. "The necessities of love, which drive our conduct and which circumscribe our options, are necessities of our will" (42). According to Frankfurt, saying that love is a matter of will is not to state a causal relation: willing is not the cause, and loving is not the effect. Love is the form and direction of the lover's will. "Love commits us to significant requirements and limitations. These are boundaries that delineate the substance and structure of our wills" (43).

Nor can there be a conflict between love and reason. "Reason and love play critical roles in determining what we think and how we are moved to conduct ourselves. They provide us with decisive motivations, and also with rigorous constraints" (1). However, "the authority of practical reason is less fundamental than that of love. In fact, I believe," writes Frankfurt, "its authority is grounded in and derives from the authority of love" (3). If it seems to us that the requirements of our love and reason conflict, then either what we have is not true love but something we mistake for it, or we are mistaken about what we take to be a requirement of reason. If our love is true, we derive from it the reasons that guide our actions. If this is right, then the Father must have derived from love the reasons that guided his actions toward the children. And he certainly believed that, but should we also believe it?

We should ask, If love cannot conflict with either the will or reason, then what has gone wrong with the Father's actions? Who could reasonably believe that there was no conflict between the Father's love and will or that, since he derived the reasons that guided his actions toward his children from his love for them, what he willed and what he had reason to do were the same? Might our will not be misdirected even if our love dictates it? Might we not have reasons against doing what our love dictates? Frankfurt is committed to denying both possibilities. Would he, then, also deny that there was something very wrong with the Father's actions toward his children? And if he concedes the obvious and acknowledges that something did go wrong, then what was it, if the fault lay neither with the Father's will nor with his reasons? These are, I think, serious problems for the large claims Frankfurt makes for the overriding importance of love in life. No one can reasonably deny that love is an important part of life. But why should we think that its importance is always greater than the importance of whatever conflicts with it? Perhaps if we understand better what Frankfurt means by love, we will agree with his claims about its overriding importance.

What, then, is love, according to Frankfurt? "Love is a particular mode of caring. It is an involuntary, nonutilitarian, rigidly focused and—as in any mode of caring—self-affirming concern for the existence of and the good of what is loved" (40). "Love entails two volitional necessities. First a person cannot help loving what he loves; and second, he therefore cannot help taking the expectation that an action would benefit his beloved as a powerful and often decisively preemptive reason for performing that action" (42). Love, according to Frankfurt, "profoundly shapes our personal identities and the ways in which we experience our lives" (43). "Lovers do not waver or hold back. Their love, I shall assume is always wholehearted, uninhibited, and clear." There is nothing within a lover that would "undermine his love, or that gives him any interest in freeing himself from it." Love is "absolute and unconditional" (44–45).

Consider: do you know any real, as opposed to fictional, person who loves like that? do you love like that yourself? do we lose our identity when we stop loving someone? how could love be absolute and unconditional when pride, jealousy, honor, anger, ambition, and countless other motives may, and often do, defeat it? Nevertheless, and contrary to these considerations, as the passages I have cited show, Frankfurt does make these claims for love — on the one hand.

On the other hand, he takes them back. He writes: "So far as love is concerned, people tend to be so endlessly ambivalent and conflicted that it generally cannot be asserted entirely without caveat either that they do love something or that they don't. Frequently, the best that can be said is that part of them loves it and part of them does not" (44). He goes on, "There is also the fact that we often do not understand ourselves very well. It is not easy for people to know what they really care about or what they truly love. Our motives and dispositions are notoriously uncertain and opaque, and we often get ourselves wrong" (49). And "the inner lives of human beings are obscure, not only to others but to themselves as well. People are elusive. We tend to be rather poorly informed about our own attitudes and desires, and about where our commitments truly lie. It is useful to keep in mind, then, that a person may care about something a great deal without realizing that he cares about it. It is also possible that someone really does not in the slightest care about certain things, even though he sincerely believes that he considers these things to be extremely important to him" (Love, 21).

In an earlier work, Frankfurt writes, on the one hand, "how is it that things may come to have for us a terminal value that is independent of their usefulness for pursuing further goals? In what acceptable way can our need for final ends be met? It is love, I believe, that meets this need." On the other hand, he adds that practical reason is "concerned with setting our final ends. It accomplishes it by identifying what it is we love. This may require significant investigation and analysis" (Love,

55). In that case, however, love presupposes practical reason, and it cannot be that "the authority of practical reason is less fundamental than that of love. In fact, I believe," writes Frankfurt, "its authority is grounded in and derives from the authority of love" (3).

Can Frankfurt avoid what seems like blatant inconsistency between the claims that the authority of love is unconditional, that practical reason presupposes it, that we cannot help loving what we love, and the claims that we are as ambivalent and fallible about love as we are about our beliefs and other emotions? I can think of only one way of avoiding the inconsistency: by distinguishing between love as an unconditional ideal and love as it actually is. The first set of Frankfurt's claims is about love as an unconditional ideal that we should aim at, and the second set is about love as it is, given our conflicts and ambivalence. Frankfurt could argue, then, that we should aim at love as an overriding and unconditional ideal, because it would help us overcome our conflicts and ambivalence that often permeate our actual loves. If this is the right interpretation, then Frankfurt owes us an explanation of why we should aim at such an overriding and unconditional ideal of love, given his understanding of what love is. There are several reasons that follow from Frankfurt's account of love that make it impossible for him to provide the needed explanation.

First, "what we love is shaped by the universal exigencies of human life, together with those other needs and interests that derive more particularly from the features of individual character and experience" (*Love*, 47). Whether we love something is "determined for us by biological and other natural conditions, concerning which we have nothing much to say" (*Love*, 48). "We cannot directly and freely determine what we love and what we do not love" (*Love*, 63). And then comes the crucial acknowledgment, "We are often helplessly driven by the necessities that love entails. These necessities may lead us to invest ourselves unwisely. Love may engage us in volitional commitments from which we are unable to withdraw and through which our interests may be severely harmed" (*Love*, 63).

Given the acknowledgment that our love may be unwise and may severely harm us, why should we aim at it as an overriding ideal? Why should we strive to be "helplessly driven by the necessities love entails," rather than rely on will and reason to restrain us from loving unwisely and too well? And if it is not up to us what we do and do not love, then it is utterly pointless to postulate love as an ideal that we should aim at, since it is not up to us whether we can or do aim at it. Love is "involuntary, in that it is not under the immediate control of the will. We cannot love—or stop loving—merely by deciding to do so" (41). Frankfurt's account of love, then, is a description of a possible psychological state that we cannot make an effort to get into or get out of once we are in it. If love is the ground on which practical reasons rest, then all those who are not in the very odd involuntary state that Frankfurt calls love will be lacking practical reason.

Second, Frankfurt says that "what a person really needs to know, in order to know how to live, is what to care about and how to measure the relative importance to him of the various things about which he cares. These are the deepest, as well as the most immediate, normative concerns of our active lives" (28). Frankfurt recognizes that we may care about "personal projects," "individuals and groups," "such ideals as being steadfastly loyal to a family tradition, or selflessly pursuing mathematical truth, or devoting oneself to some type of connoisseurship" (*Importance*, 81). And he writes that "as for the notion of what a person cares about, it coincides in part with the notion of something with reference to which the person guides himself in what he does with his life and in his conduct" (*Importance*, 82). I find no reason in Frankfurt why we could not enlarge this list to include other things we care about and regard as very important to how we live and act, such as career, comfort, fear, health, honor, justice, revenge, security, wealth, and so on. And, as he says, "what a person really needs to know, in order to know how to live, is what to care about and how to measure the relative importance to him of the various things about which he cares" (28).

What reason do we have to think that in measuring the relative importance of all the important things we care about, love will always come on top? Why should we not sometimes care more about duty, honor, faith, loyalty, safety, and so forth than about love? Why should our commitments to independence, justice, or comfort not balance our commitments to love? We often leave our beloved behind and march off to fight battles, or systematically subordinate the love we genuinely feel to a creative life or to the pursuit of truth. Many of us simply do not proceed as Frankfurt says we do or that we should. And when we do not, our will may be engaged and we may have reasons to proceed as we do. I repeat, Frankfurt cannot reasonably say that if we do not live as he thinks we should, then we should change how we live and start loving. If love is indeed involuntary, then we cannot choose to aim at it. It is a fact of life that love and many other things we regard as important and care about routinely conflict, that we are often uncertain about how to resolve their conflicts, and that the uncertainty makes us ambivalent. I do not think that Frankfurt has given any reason to suppose that the ideal of love is not as subject to conflicts and ambivalence as any other ideal we may care about.

Problems

Suppose that we are in the grip of a volitional necessity that meets what Frankfurt says are the conditions of love: we have a nontransferable, disinterested concern for the well-being of a person whose interests we make our own, and it imposes requirements and limits on how we act. How do we know that our psychological state is love, rather than pity, conscientiousness, sympathy, the comfortable familiarity of shared memories, infatuation, loyalty, or something similar? The natural answer is that we know it because we feel it. This answer, however, is not available to Frankfurt, because he thinks "it is not essential to love that it be accompanied by any particular feelings or thoughts. The heart of the matter is not affective or cognitive, but strictly volitional" (42). Note how extraordinary is the view that love need not be a feeling or that we can love a person or a cause even without thinking that he, she, or it is in some sense lovable.

Yet Frankfurt also says, far more plausibly, that "the fact that someone cares about a certain thing is constituted by a complex set of cognitive, affective, and volitional dispositions and states" (*Importance*, 85) and that "being concerned for the true interests of his beloved surely requires that the lover also be moved by a more elementary desire to identify those interests correctly. In order to obey the commands of love, one must first understand what it is that love commands" (*Love*, 88). If these claims are right, then love is not just a volitional matter, but also an affective and cognitive one. And surely it may happen that the affective and cognitive components of love conflict with its volitional component and require correcting or redirecting it. We may discover that our emotions and will move us in different directions or we may come to believe that we should not care as deeply about someone as we in fact do. This will loosen the supposed volitional necessity of love and shows that it is neither overriding nor unconditional.

Furthermore, it is not just that the cognitive, affective, and volitional components of what Frankfurt calls love may prompt us to act in incompatible ways. Regardless of whether they conflict, each may be mistaken. Frankfurt acknowledges this, even if only in a footnote: "People cannot reliably discover what they love merely by introspection; nor is what they love generally unmistakable in their behavior. Love is a complex configuration of the will, which may be difficult both for the lover and for others to discern" (*Love*, 55, note 9). Also, "consider a man who tells a woman that his love for her is what gives meaning and value to his life. . . . It is possible that, although he believes he is telling the truth about himself, he doesn't really know what he is talking about" (*Love*, 60). And Frankfurt grants "the possibility that people may sometimes be divided within themselves in such a way that it is impossible to give categorical and univocal answer to questions concerning what they love and what they do not love" (*Love*, 91). Given his acknowledgment of these possibilities, it becomes undeniable that what Frankfurt calls love neither is nor should be the overriding ideal he thinks it should be. It is as contingent and fallible as any other cognitive, affective, or volitional component of our psychology.

Love may involve false beliefs, excessive or misunderstood emotions, and misguided desires. Consider the Father's love in the light of these possible ways of going wrong. Love of his children is the deepest emotion he has. But that does not mean that its cognitive, affective, and volitional components could not be mistaken. I start with cognitive ones. His love involves the belief, formed on the basis of his experiences, that the world is a harsh, competitive place in which people do what they think they must in order to pursue their self-interest. The world in some places, times, and contexts is like that, and we can understand that he was led by his experiences to believe that the world is like that everywhere. But, understandable or not, the belief is false. There is also kindness, generosity, sympathy, and affection in the world. The Father's belief is based on facts that confirm it and ignores facts that are contrary to it. But it is this false belief that leads him to want to prepare his children for the harsh realities he thinks they will inevitably encounter. So withholding the expression of his love and imposing the hard discipline on his children that damages them rest on a misunderstanding of the world.

The affective component of his love suffers from a similar defect. The Father sees his children as helpless, innocent, and vulnerable. They were no doubt like that as infants, but they are growing up, fight with each other as brothers and sisters do, and are often angry, selfish, competitive, envious, and jealous. They are no longer as pure and cuddly as they once were. They are beginning to develop their character and form a tougher self than the Father allows himself to see. They are not without resources to cope with adversities and challenges, although they still rely on the continuing support of their parents. It is just this support of which the misguided volitional component of the Father's love deprives the children. He wants to toughen them up, but what they need is the continued loving support they could rely on in the past and the sense of security, as they grow up, that they are always welcome in the safe haven their parents have created. The volitional necessity that the Father is moved by accomplishes the precise opposite of what he intends and what the children need.

Another problem is that even if none of the components of love is mistaken, the volitional necessity that follows from loving one person may conflict with a no less strong volitional necessity that follows from loving another person or with loving justice, a creative life, a cause, or safety, or with a sense of duty, honor, or curiosity. Frankfurt recognizes that "people may sometimes be divided within themselves in such a way that it is impossible to give categorical and univocal answer to questions concerning what they love and what they do not love." In such a case, "the person is ambivalent" (Love, 91). This, of course, is one of my main objections to Frankfurt's ideal theory of love. But Frankfurt thinks the objection can be met.

It is possible, he writes, "for a conflict of this sort to be resolved, so that the person is freed of his ambivalence." "Resolution requires only that the person become finally and unequivocally clear as to which side of the conflict *he* is on." "As soon as he has definitely established where he himself stands, his will is no longer divided and his conflicts and ambivalence therefore disappear. He has placed himself wholeheartedly behind one of his conflicting impulses, and not at all behind the other" (Love, 91). Of course, *if* we can deliberately establish which side of the conflict we are on, then our problem is solved. But the problem is that we are often on both sides. The "resolution" Frankfurt proposes is to ignore the problem. His proposal is that when we have a conflict and are ambivalent about how to resolve it, we should wholeheartedly opt for one component of our divided will. In other words, we should do what we do not know how to do. If we could resolve our conflict and overcome our ambivalence, then of course we should and would, and we would not need Frankfurt to tell us to do it. Our problem is that we do not know how to do what we know perfectly well we should do.

Frankfurt acknowledges that "perhaps we care about worldly success and also about peace of mind, and then it comes to our attention that pursuing the one tends to interfere with attaining the other." But "as we learn more about what each is and what it entails, it will become clear that one arouses in us a more substantial interest and concern than the other" (49). We may indeed become clear, but we may not. We may want both, can have at most only one, and cannot make up our mind which it should be. What stands in the way of making as clear-cut a decision as Frankfurt thinks better understanding will enable us to make need not be that we cannot decide which we love more. It may be that even if we have decided that, on balance, we love one somewhat more than the other, we will not stop loving the less important one. And then we will be ambivalent about losing it, even if we might thereby gain the other. Remember the choice Sophie had to make; remember the choices tragedies are about.

Frankfurt does not seem to remember them:

> The wholehearted lover cannot help being wholehearted. His wholeheartedness is no more subject to the immediate control of his will than is loving itself. There may be steps that would cause his love to falter and to fade; but someone whose love is genuinely wholehearted cannot bring himself to take those steps. He cannot deliberately try to stop himself from loving. His wholeheartedness means, by definition, that he has no reservations or conflicts that would move him to initiate or to support such an attempt. There is nothing within him that tends to undermine his love, or that gives him any interest in freeing himself from it. (45)

This may be true if, but only if, we love only one thing, love it unconditionally, and do not seriously care about anything else. Then we may not be ambivalent about the volitional necessity that it imposes on us. But only fanatics love only one thing so wholeheartedly as to exclude them from loving or caring about anything else wholeheartedly. It is an obvious psychological fact that we may wholeheartedly love our children, parents, husbands or wives, friends, country, cause, house, job, and comfort, not to mention ourselves. If we love more than one thing wholeheartedly, then we may not be able to make ourselves take the steps that would cause our love for one of them to falter and fade. It is no use saying, as Frankfurt does, that if such conflicts occur, then, "by definition," both loves could not be wholehearted. A familiar psychological conflict cannot be resolved by defining it out of existence. In many lives, conflicting loves will cause ambivalence, and that is just one of the facts that a practical approach to love acknowledges and Frankfurt's ideal theory is committed to denying.

Yet a further problem with the supposed wholeheartedness of love is that our love of one thing may conflict not just with our love of some other thing. There are other emotions that may impose on us volitional necessities as stringent as love does. We may be no less wholehearted in our hatred or fear than we are in our love. Frankfurt says that love is a particular mode of caring. But hatred and fear are other particular modes of caring, and these modes may conflict in two ways. One is that we may love and fear, or love and hate, the same person. According to some psychologists, many of us simultaneously love and hate our parents. Many Christians simultaneously love and fear God. Many women endure battering because they simultaneously love, hate, and fear the person who abuses them. Another way modes of caring may conflict is that we wholeheartedly love, hate, and fear different persons and these emotions prompt us to act in incompatible ways. We may hate and fear a tyrant and love our family, but we cannot act on both because acting on the first endangers the second, and acting on the second preempts acting on the first. Such conflicts cannot be finessed by saying that hatred and fear are irrational emotions, because exactly the same can be said of love.

The existence of modes of caring other than love raises for Frankfurt's celebration of love the question of why, if "the commands of love derive from the essential nature of a person's will" (*Necessity*, 139), the same may not be true of the commands of hate or fear? He cannot say that following the commands of love is justified, but following the commands of hate or fear is not. For he answers the question of "what makes it more suitable, then, for a person to make one object rather than another important to himself?" by saying that "it seems that it must be the fact that it is *possible* for him to care about the one and not about the other, or to care about the one in a way which is more important to him than the way in which it is possible for him to care about the other" (*Importance*, 94). Whether we should care as much about someone as we do, then, is simply a question of whether it is possible for us to care as much as we do. But that possibility holds equally for love, hate, and fear.

In an effort to avoid the whole question of the justification of love, Frankfurt asks rhetorically, "Why should we not be happy to fight for what we wholeheartedly love, even when there are no good arguments to show that it is correct for us to love it rather than to love other things instead?" (*Love*, 31). But of course the same may be asked about fighting against what we hate or fear. And fighting against them may be incompatible with fighting for what we love. It is a mistake to suppose that just so long as we are wholehearted, we will not be ambivalent. We routinely remain ambivalent, because we are often wholehearted about incompatible courses of action. It is psychologically difficult to hold contrary beliefs simultaneously, but it is a psychological commonplace that we simultaneously have contrary emotions. Frankfurt thinks that by emphasizing the importance of love, he has found the key to overcoming conflicts and ambivalence. But his emphasis is arbitrary, because hatred and fear are also important, and all three emotions often coexist, conflict, and make us ambivalent about how we should act.

Sentimentalism

I have been arguing that Frankfurt's ideal theory of love is mistaken because, while of course love is important, it is unreasonable to suppose, as Frankfurt does, that it is so important as always to override any other ideal, or, indeed, another love, that conflicts with it. Nothing is always, in all contexts, at all times, for all people more important than something that may conflict with it. To think otherwise, to suppose that a theory could be constructed about an ideal to which we should adhere no matter what emergencies, conflicts, or changes may occur in the future, is the dangerous illusion to which ideal theorists remain committed, regardless of the multitude of failed attempts to provide the promised theory.

We are as fallible about what we love as we are about any one of our other beliefs, emotions, and desires. It is therefore a mistake to do as Frankfurt says a true lover should, which is to guide "himself away from being critically affected by anything—in the outside world or within himself—which might divert him or dissuade him from following that course [i.e., the one dictated by love] or from caring as much as he does about following it" (*Importance*, 87). True lovers want to love wisely and well, for both their own and their beloved's sake, and that depends on allowing themselves to be critically affected by internal and external facts that bear on the reliability of their beliefs, emotions, and desires regarding themselves and their beloved. They would want to know, for instance, whether their love is reciprocated, whether their beloved is dead or alive, or, if it is a cause they love, whether it is just, defeated, or corrupt. Frankfurt's ideal of love focuses on the overriding importance of loving and explicitly rejects questions about its appropriateness. The name for the mistake that permeates Frankfurt's ideal theory of love is sentimentality.

The relevant part of the *OED* definition of sentimentalism is "1. The sentimental habit of mind; the disposition to attribute undue importance to sentimental considerations, or be governed by sentiment in opposition to reason; the tendency to excessive indulgence in or insincere display of sentiment." I do not think that what Frankfurt calls love is insincere, but I do think it suffers from the other defects.

The *OED* definition is of sentimentalism as a psychological tendency. There is also a philosophical understanding of the term, from which the psychological one should be distinguished. The sentimentalism of Frankfurt's account is at best a cousin twice removed of the philosophical understanding of it, according to which sentiment is the basis of morality. I set aside the question of whether the moral-sense school and the claim of its defenders that morality is based on sympathy, compassion, or, indeed, love is defensible. It is sentimentalism in the psychological sense that is relevant to Frankfurt's ideal of love.

In that sense, sentimentalism is excessive indulgence in sentiment. The sentiment in the present case is love. Sentimentalism is always a mistake, regardless of what the sentiment is. The mistake is a quasimoral one, similar to crudity, insensitivity, obscenity, tactlessness, and vulgarity—on the borderline between morality and good taste.[3] One outstanding literary representation of sentimentalism is Goethe's Werther; another is what Jane Austen calls sensibility, which she rightly contrasts with sense. And I stress: The sentimentalist mistake is not stressing the importance of love—love is important—but claiming for it excessive importance, or an overriding one, as Frankfurt does. The mistake is the claim that love must be "wholehearted, uninhibited, and clear," that it must be "absolute and unconditional" (44–45), and that the authority of practical reason "is grounded in and derives from the authority of love" (3).

Sentimentalism is to love what fantasy is to imagination, obsession to discipline, and recklessness to courage. Sentimentalism is always a fault, usually a self-indulgent one. It falsifies facts not just by unwittingly misrepresenting them, but by colluding in their misrepresentation. Sentimentalists interpose a veil of emotion between themselves and the world. They prevent themselves from seeing the facts as they are in order to make them appear as they would like them to be.

Why do sentimentalists do this? "Because it serves to connect us actively to our lives in ways which are creative of ourselves and which expose us to distinctive possibilities for necessity and for freedom" (*Importance*, 93). What matters is the creative power of loving, which, make no mistake, is the lover's self-creative power, not the beloved's. Frankfurt is explicit: "The justification for caring about something rests upon the importance of caring itself, rather than being derivative from the antecedent importance of its object." Note what this means: what matters is the caring, not what we care about. But if this is true, Frankfurt asks, "what makes it more suitable, then, for a person to make one object rather than another important to himself? It seems it must be the fact that it is *possible* for him to care about one and not about the other." "The person does not care about the object because its worthiness commands that he do so." He cares about "the worthiness of the activity of caring" (*Importance*, 94).

As Savile rightly says, someone whose

> love is sentimental will tend to resist the correction of the thought on which his emotion rests, and this very recalcitrance suggests that what holds the thought in place is not a desire for the truth and knowledge but something else—a desire that can be satisfied by seeing the object in a false light. . . . What the sentimentalist seeks is the occurrence of certain enjoyable emotions. And since no emotion can be felt except as supported by a certain thought about its object, an appropriate thought has to be entertained for the sake of the pleasure. . . . What is desired is not so much a gratifying feeling as a gratifying image of the self that is sustained by the fabricated emotion.[4]

What is important, according this extraordinary view, is the loving, not the object the lover loves. It is irrelevant to loving whether the beloved is worthy of love, or whether the lover has a realistic view of the beloved. The only reason that follows from Frankfurt's account of why love is directed outward is that it needs an object, any object, that it is possible for the lover to love. Presumably, any but the most despicable person would do, or indeed any cause, no matter how indefensible it may be, provided the lover finds it possible to love it. According to Frankfurt's ideal, if fanatics find it possible to love the Great Leader or the cause that involves the murder of those who resist it, then it is fine for them to love him or it, because it gives them something to care about and provides them with volitional continuity and a direction to their agency.

This is such an outrageous view that it may be doubted that Frankfurt actually holds it. And he does indeed say, "The fact that what a person cares about is a personal matter does not entail that *anything goes*. It may still be possible to distinguish between things that are worth caring about to one degree or another and things that are not." How, then, do we draw the distinction? Frankfurt's answer is: "Caring about something *makes* that thing important to the person who cares about it" (*Importance*, 94). So what is worth caring about is what we can make ourselves care about, regardless of whether it is vicious, stupid, destructive, trivial, or changing from day to day. It is scarcely believable that a good philosopher like Frankfurt could actually hold such a view. But as the passages I have cited show, he does.

Why is the fact that we love whatever we love so important? Because it is "indispensably foundational as an activity that connects and binds us to ourselves. It is through caring that we provide ourselves with volitional continuity, and in that way constitute and participate in our own agency" (*Love*, 17). Lovers love because they care about themselves. "No attempt to deal with the problem of what we have good reason to care about . . . can possibly succeed. Efforts to conduct a rational inquiry into the matter will inevitably be defeated and turned back upon themselves" (*Love*, 24). "What we love necessarily *acquires* value for us *because* we love it. The lover does invariably and necessarily perceive the beloved as valuable, but the value he sees it possess is a value that derives from and that depends upon his love" (*Love*, 39). Love requires caring for the beloved for the beloved's sake, but that the lover cares in that way is for the lover's sake. If the lover rejoices in the well-being of the beloved, it is because the lover's volitional continuity and agency depend on being able to rejoice in it. The well-being of the beloved is merely what enables the lover to have good feelings about himself.

What Frankfurt has succeeded in formulating is not an ideal theory of love but a demonstration of one way in which love can be corrupted by turning it into sentimentalist excess. He explains that sentimental lovers cultivate their own excess in order to convince themselves that they are the person they want to be. They want to be loving, so they make a person or a cause the object they can love and then convince themselves that they are in the grip of a powerful emotion that commands them absolutely and unconditionally, one that is so powerful as to override any belief, emotion, or desire that may conflict with it.

This account may actually be a correct description of some people. Their emotion may be as powerful as Frankfurt's ideal requires; however, it is not the emotion of love, but of self-regard. They want, as we all do, to feel good about themselves, and they contrive to do so by deceiving themselves about what they feel. In doing this, they may well be sincere. Successful self-deception must be sincere, or it fails to deceive. But lovers may not have managed to convince themselves totally by the emotion they have cultivated, so they contrive to make it powerful enough to overcome any trace of doubt, and that involves making the emotion Frankfurt calls love so excessive as to override any lingering doubt they may have. Frankfurt is taken in by the fakery. He is correct in seeing that people's perfervid emotions may take this form, but that does not make it a good, let alone ideal, form to take.

Let us return to the Father in the light of this discussion of sentimentalist excess. I have argued that his love and the way it prompts him to treat his children have gone wrong because they were based on false beliefs about the world and about what the children's well-being required. We can now see perhaps why the Father held these false beliefs in the face of readily available contrary evidence. His wife had a more realistic view of the world and of the requirements of their children's well-being. She tried but could not convince her husband that his beliefs were mistaken and ruinous for the family's happiness, including the Father's own. The Father listened and rejected his wife's views because he thought they were based on naïveté about the world from whose harshness he had managed to protect his wife and children.

The Father could not have succeeded in making a good life for himself and the family if he had not been an intelligent man. Why, then, did he not see what was there to be seen, what his wife saw, and why did he not accept what she pointed out to him patiently and lovingly? He did not see it because his love was corrupted by sentimentalism. He did just what Frankfurt describes: he cared about caring. The children were the objects toward which he directed his caring, and their individuality did not make much difference to him. His understanding both of the world and of his children was filtered through and falsified by his caring, which was the most important thing in his life. It was essential to his view of himself as one who has prevailed in the hostile world, has made a loving haven in which his family is protected, and can afford to be loving and loved. He was in love with loving all that, and that love was the falsifying veil that obscured the facts. He could have lifted it, but he did not because his view of himself and pride in his achievements stood in the way. Not to have loved as he loved would have undermined that view of himself, his self-respect, and his achievements. He ignored the facts that were contrary to his view of himself as an achieving, protective, and loving person by using his powerful will to reinforce his view of himself. He made his love excessive because feeling good about himself depended on it. He did not allow facts to stand in his way. The result was the sentimental excess that led him to love unwisely and too much.

Love within Reason

I want to avoid a possible way of misunderstanding my criticisms of Frankfurt's ideal theory of self-evaluation and love. They are directed neither against self-evaluation nor against love, but against the exaggeration of the importance of either one. Each is important for us. Self-evaluation can make our life better by helping us cope with our psychological conflicts and ambivalence. And love can immeasurably enrich our life. But even if we are as reasonable as we can be as self-evaluators and lovers, we can only cope with our conflicts and ambivalence. We cannot overcome them, because our efforts to cope with them are also vulnerable to the forever conflicting beliefs, emotions, and desires to which we are genuinely committed.

We are going to remain ambivalent about self-evaluation because we sense the danger of going too far with it. We may find much that we dislike and that may undermine our confidence in our ability to cope with the adversities of which few lives are free. Self-evaluation may alienate us from what is ultimately the only resource we have. For the same reason, we should be cautious also about loving. Frankfurt's celebration of love is sentimental because it exaggerates the importance of one of our emotions at the expense of our reasonable beliefs, contrary emotions, and desires to form a realistic view of ourselves, our loves, and the problems we face. Of course, it is important for us to love, but only within reason. The claims of reason, however, are as fallible and riddled with conflicts and ambivalence as any other claim we might make.

I have offered specific criticisms of Frankfurt's ideal theory of self-evaluation and love, but there is a general criticism that applies equally to all ideal theories that focus on one of our many ideals and assign overriding importance to it. The ideal may be any one of those familiar from the long history of ideal theories: it may be goodwill, sympathy, fellow feeling, practical reason, self-interest, self-knowledge, reflection, love, compassion, justice, the sense of duty, the common good, and so forth. But whatever the ideal is, its defenders argue that when we encounter conflicts and are ambivalent about what to do, then we should rely on the ideal to which we have assigned overriding importance. That should be our ultimate guide to how we live and act.

There are three quite general reasons against relying on such an ideal. One is that we may assign overriding importance to the wrong ideal. We need some reason for regarding it as more important than anything else we care about. The search for such an overriding ideal has gone on for thousands of years. Yet no ideal has been found that could reasonably be claimed to be overriding regardless of the nature of our conflicts; of changes in our understanding, experiences, and preferences; and of the great variety of contexts and conditions in which we find ourselves. I think the ideal has not been found because it does not exist.

The second reason is that when we are searching for an overriding ideal but have not yet found it, we continue to search because we face conflicts and need some reasonable way of coping with them. If we had a reasonable way, we would not need to search. But the conflicts we have between our beliefs, emotions, desires, and evaluative points of view, on the one hand, and the ideals we derive from them, on the other, will make our search for an overriding ideal liable to the very conflicts we are trying to overcome. If we discontinue the search by putting an end to the recurring conflicts, then the decision to regard one of the various conflicting ideals as overriding will be arbitrary. If we continue the search for an overriding ideal, then of course, we have not yet found it. In neither case will we have found an ideal that we can reasonably accept as overriding.

The third reason is that even if, impossible as it is, we have arrived at an ideal we can reasonably suppose to be overriding, it will not enable us to overcome our conflicts. We will know then that we should resolve the conflicts as the overriding ideal guides us to do, but we will not stop caring about whatever it is that we override. Resolving the conflict in favor of one of our conflicting beliefs, emotions, desires, evaluative points of view, or ideals involves the unavoidable violation of a commitment we have made to the ideal we have overridden. And if the conflict is serious because we value what we are committed to, then the resolution of the conflict will force us to violate something we deeply care about. If we did not, the conflict would not be serious. This conflict resolution will depend, then, on having to face a further conflict between three ways of resolving the original conflict. One is to rely on whatever the overriding ideal is. Another is to try to find some balance or compromise between our conflicting commitments, so that we can avoid violating our commitment to something that we deeply value. The third is to put up with conflict and try to live with it. There are reasons both for and against each of these conflict resolutions. So, even if there were an overriding ideal, reason would only allow but not require us to follow it. The joint persuasive force of these three reasons against continuing the search for an ideal theory as a way of overcoming our conflicts and ambivalence seems to me very strong.

6   Strong Evaluation

> In our life of uncertainties, where no one system or formula can explain
> everything—where even a word is at best, in Bacon's phrase, a "wager of
> thought"—what is needed is an imaginative openness of mind and height-
> ened receptivity to reality in its full and diverse concreteness. This, how-
> ever, involves negating one's ego. . . . To be dissatisfied with such insights
> as one may attain through this openness, to reject them unless they can be
> wrenched into a part of a systematic structure of one's own making, is an
> egoistic assertion of one's own identity.
>
> WALTER JACKSON BATE, "Negative Capability"[1]

It is an acute observation that "every culture seems, as it advances
toward maturity, to produce its own determining debate over the ideas
that preoccupy it: salvation, the order of nature, money, power, sex,
the machine, and the like. The debate, indeed, may be said to *be* the
culture, at least on its loftiest levels; for a culture achieves identity not
so much through the ascendancy of one particular set of convictions
as through the emergence of its peculiar and distinctive dialogue."[2] In
our culture—the Western, affluent, democratic one we have had for
the past hundred years or so—part of the distinctive dialogue is what
Isaiah Berlin has described, making use of Archilocus's fable, as between hedgehogs who know one big thing and foxes who know many
small ones. Hedgehogs believe, as Bate puts it in the epigraph, that
everything can be wrenched into a systematic structure of their own
making.[3] Hedgehogs are ideal theorists who believe that we should all
live according to an overriding ideal and rely on it to resolve our con-

flicts and ambivalence. Foxes believe that in our life of uncertainties, no system or formula can explain everything. They deny that there can be an ideal theory, or an ideal that reason requires everyone to accept as always overriding, or a way of overcoming once and for all our conflicts and ambivalence. Foxes are likely to favor a practical approach.

Charles Taylor makes no bones about which side he is on. He says in the introduction to a book of his essays that they "are the work of a monomaniac; or perhaps better, what Isaiah Berlin has called a hedgehog."[4] The overriding ideal of Taylor's ideal theory is strong evaluation. He develops this ideal by drawing on Frankfurt's ideal of self-evaluation (discussed in chapter 4), but Taylor goes beyond it in a crucial way. I argue in this chapter that Taylor's ideal theory is indefensible. I begin with a story about a woman and then discuss Taylor's ideal theory with reference to her.

The Nurse

The Nurse is a highly trained, very skillful surgical nurse, known as an OR (operating room) Nurse, much in demand by surgeons. She is single, in her early thirties, and intensely alive. She has numerous carefree sexual relationships, and her partners remain her friends even after she and they pass on to other partners. She shares a house with an airline stewardess, with whom she often travels to foreign places that happen to attract them. She is in excellent health, runs daily, eats prudently, and generally looks after herself. She is also a movie buff, fond of old films but also attentive to new ones. She is well paid and, because of her recognized skills, allowed to work longer hours one week and be free the next. She has much free time, which she fills with activities she values and enjoys. The Nurse's life is full, and she lives with verve and pleasure. She has conflicts and she is often ambivalent about how to resolve them. But she is an outstanding example of how the conflicts of a life need not be bad and how ambivalence may result from an embarrassment of riches. For her conflicts are caused by her hesitations about which of several enjoyable activities she should choose. She lets her moods dictate her choices.

She is normally intelligent but quite unreflective. All her life is on the surface. It does not cross her mind to ask and try to answer serious questions about religion, politics, morality, the meaning of life, or the justification of her various activities. She is genuinely likable and she is liked, even if rather grudgingly and perhaps enviously by those who are less fortunate than she is. But she takes little notice of such unpleasantness. It has been a long time since she read a book, although she occasionally leafs through a magazine or two and sometimes watches the news headlines on her computer, especially when she hears that something newsworthy has happened at some place she and her housemate have visited. Her parents are still working, she has a brother and a sister who are married and have children, and she sometimes spends holidays with them, although they all live at some distance from the hospital where she works.

If asked how she would change her life if she could, she would say that she would like to get a raise, go to bed with an actor she has found particularly sexy, and that the surgeon she most likes to assist be less peremptory and more appreciative of her skillful assistance. She would like to enlarge her DVD collection with some rare films, improve her running speed and distance, and perhaps live for a while in one of the places she has visited and particularly liked. But these wishes are not urges, and she does not normally think about them much. They are just how she would answer the question if asked about what she would like that she does not have.

Cynics may say that her life is too good to be true and may suspect that she has repressed much, that there are bound to be dark secrets below the cheery surface, periods of depression, self-doubt, and childhood traumas, but the cynics would be wrong. The appearances, in this case, are not deceptive. Her life really is to her liking, she is satisfied with it, and there is no hidden depth disguised by a brave and false face she presents to the public. The face she turns to the world is her real face.

The Nurse is a fox, if there ever was one. She is committed to no overriding ideal. All her many commitments to various ideals are flexible, and if they conflict, as they often do, she resolves their conflicts as her momentary inclinations prompt her. She rarely thinks about the long-term consequences of living as she does. Certainly, she wants to remain in good health, be appreciated for her skill, continue to enjoy carefree sex, take precautions to avoid AIDS, have fun with friends, go on exploring shops in foreign countries, and she prudently does what is needed to satisfy these desires. Let us now think about the Nurse in the light of what Charles Taylor says about strong evaluation.[5]

Strong Evaluation

Taylor distinguishes between weak and strong evaluation. In "weak evaluation, we are concerned with outcomes," in "strong evaluation, with the quality of our motivation" (*Agency*, 16). "In weak evaluation, for something to be judged good it is sufficient that it be desired, whereas in strong evaluation there is also a use of 'good' or some other evaluative term for which being desired is not sufficient; indeed some desires or desired consummations can be judged as bad, base, ignoble, trivial, superficial, unworthy, and so on" (18). "When in weak evaluation one desired alternative is set aside, it is only on grounds of its contingent incompatibility with a more desired alternative" (18–19). In strong evaluation, "some desired consummation may be eschewed not because it is incompatible with another . . . but rather because it is base" (19). "What is important is that strong evaluation is concerned with the qualitative *worth* of different desires" (16).

Taylor explicitly acknowledges (*Agency*, 15–21) that his distinction between weak and strong evaluation is a development of Frankfurt's distinction between first- and second-order desires, and of his claim that we should all evaluate our first-order desires by our second-order desires and volitions. Taylor's strong evaluation goes beyond self-evaluation by requiring that second-order desires and volition be directed toward the good, rather than the bad, base, or ignoble. Strong evaluation "is a question about what our motivation really is, how we should truly characterize the meaning things have for us" (22). The question is about "self-interpretations," which "partly shape the meanings things have for us." That question, however, is not merely about what second-order desires and volitions we should have, as Frankfurt has it, but also about "which is more valid, more faithful to reality." "To be in error here is thus not just to make a misdescription"; it is "distorting the reality concerned" (22). For a strong evaluator, what is "desirable is not only defined for him by what he desires, or what he desires plus a calculation of consequences; it is also defined by a qualitative characterization of desires as higher and lower, noble and base" (23).

Frankfurt thinks that self-evaluation involves the qualitative characterization of our desires based on what we really care about. In this sense, self-evaluation is subjective. Taylor thinks that strong evaluation is objective, not a matter of what we care about most, but what we ought to care about most. Strong evaluations "involve discriminations of right and wrong, better or worse, higher or lower, which are not rendered valid by our own desires, inclinations, or choices, but rather stand independently of these and offer standards by which they can be judged." These are "standards, independent of my own tastes and desires, which I ought to acknowledge" (*Self*, 4). How do we discover these standards? What is their source? Why ought we to acknowledge them?

Taylor's answer emerges from his discussion of romantic expressivism (*Self*, chapter 21). He agrees that it is true, as Frankfurt says, that we begin with "an inner impulse or conviction which tells us of the importance of our natural fulfilment." Taylor, however, thinks that it is not merely a subjective impulse or conviction, but "the voice of nature within us" (369–70). "My claim," writes Taylor, "is that the idea of nature as an intrinsic source goes along with an expressive view of human life. Fulfilling my nature means espousing the inner élan, the voice or impulse. And this makes what was hidden manifest for both myself and others. But this manifestation also helps to define what is to be realized" (374–75). Taylor's view is, then, that "if nature is an intrinsic source, then each of us has to follow what is within" (376). Human nature is part of nature and provides the standard by which we can distinguish between good and bad. We can do so by listening to our inner voice, and thereby we listen to nature. Strong evaluation is based on what we hear when we listen attentively and well to the voice of the good that is intrinsic to our nature.

Strong evaluation satisfies our "craving for being in contact with or being rightly placed in relation to the good." It "can be more or less satisfied in our lives"; however, it is not just "a matter of more or less but a question of yes or no. And this is the form in which it most deeply affects and challenges us. The yes/no question concerns not how near or far we are from what we see as the good, but rather the direction of our lives, towards or away from it, or the source of our motivations in regard to it" (*Self*, 45). Taylor goes on: "We cannot do without an orientation to the good, and since we cannot be indifferent to our place relative to this good, and since this place is something that must always change and become, the issue of the direction of our life must arise for us" (47). "This sense of my life as having a direction towards what I am not yet" gives unity to how we live and act. This is captured by seeing our life "as a quest" (48) for the good.

Make no mistake, Taylor's ideal theory that regards strong evaluation as an overriding ideal, is committed to a metaphysical theory about the nature of reality. According to it, the good is part of scheme of things, and since we too are part of it, the good is also part of us. Strong evaluation involves identifying the part of our nature that is good and motivates us to live according to it. But living according to the good is not just something we might do. We are driven to it by our craving—craving!—for the good. "This craving for being in contact with or being rightly placed in relation to the good can be more or less satisfied in our lives." Conflicts and ambivalence occur when we are less motivated by the good than we should be. We then hesitate to follow the direction in which we crave to move by the good that is implicit in our nature. The direction of our life toward the good we crave is the source of our commitment to the overriding ideal of strong evaluation and the source of the identity, worth, and meaning of our life. The extent to which we are not strong evaluators, we lack these benefits, and as a result, our lives are full of conflicts and ambivalence and we do not know how to cope with them.

"The capacity for strong evaluation," writes Taylor, "is essential to our notion of the human subject; that without it an agent would lack a kind of depth we consider essential to humanity." "In fact the human beings we are and live with are all strong evaluators" (*Agency*, 28). "Strong evaluation is something inescapable in our conception of the agent and his experience, and this because it is bound up with our notion of the self" (33). Our self is our identity, which is "defined by certain evaluations which are inseparable from ourselves as agents" (34). And "the notion of identity refers to certain evaluations which are essential because they are the indispensable horizon or foundation out of which we reflect and evaluate as persons." "To lose this horizon, or not to have found it, is indeed a terrifying experience of disaggregation and loss. This is why we can speak of an 'identity-crisis' when we have lost our grip on who we are. A self decides and acts out of certain fundamental evaluations" (35). But strong evaluation enables us not merely to have a self, an identity, but also, as we have seen, to base our evaluations on "the qualitative *worth* of different desires" (16), on the "characterization of desires and higher and lower, noble and base" (23), on standards "independent of my own tastes and desires" and ones that "I ought to acknowledge" (*Self*, 4). Not to do so dooms us to lack a standard to which we could appeal to resolve our conflicts, and to have nothing that could save us from a lifetime of ambivalence.

The source of the qualitative distinctions of strong evaluators is the framework that provides the vocabulary that makes strong evaluations possible. There are many frameworks, but, as Taylor emphasizes (*Self*, chapter 1), they are inescapable. We do not begin with a clear, articulate sense of what is important, worthwhile, meaningful. The inner voice through which nature speaks to each one of us is at first inchoate and inarticulate. As we mature we learn to become more articulate and to express our deep sense of what is good, noble, worth living for in terms we adopt from the vocabulary of one framework or another. Without a framework we could not make sense of what we desire, value, and find worthwhile. That is why frameworks are inescapable. "A framework incorporates a crucial set of qualitative distinctions. To think, feel, judge within such a framework is to function with the sense that some action, or mode of life, or mode of feeling is incomparably higher than the others readily available to us" (19).

The vocabulary of our framework enables us to see "a mode of feeling or living as deeper, a style of life as more admirable, a given demand as making an absolute claim against other merely relative ones." And this "connects up," Taylor says, "with what I have been calling 'strong evaluations': the fact that these goods and ends stand independent of our desires, inclinations, or choices, that they represent standards by which these desires and choices are judged" (*Self*, 20). Our framework, therefore, does not only provide us with the means to articulate how we should live, but also with a standard by which we can justify or criticize the particular evaluations we make. Strong evaluations can go wrong, but they can also be corrected by ourselves or other participants in the same framework. The correction involves comparing and contrasting the qualitative evaluations we make with those that according to the standards of the framework we should make.

"Our evaluations are not chosen. On the contrary they are articulations of our sense of what is worthy, or higher, or more integrated, or more fulfilling," and "as *articulations*, they offer . . . purchase for the concept of responsibility" (*Agency*, 35). "Our evaluations are articulations of insights which are frequently partial, clouded and uncertain. But they are all the more open to challenge when we reflect that these insights are often distorted by our imperfections of character." "Responsibility falls to us in the sense that it is always possible that fresh insight might alter my evaluations and hence myself for the better. So that within the limits of my capacity to change myself by fresh insight . . . I am responsible in the full direct, 'modern' sense for my evaluations" (39). Because we can change ourselves in this way, "we can be called responsible for ourselves; and because it is within limits always up to us to do it, even when we do not . . . we can be called responsible for ourselves, whether we undertake this radical evaluation or not" (42). Thus Taylor's view is, "The capacity for what I have called strong evaluation is an essential feature of a person. I think that this has helped to cast light on the sense in which we ascribe reflection, will and also responsibility to human agents" (43). And "in fact the human beings we are and live with are all strong evaluators" (28).

Doubts

Having read hundreds of pages of Taylor's work, I am left amazed at its high-flown metaphysical speculation expressed in the tone of a patient teacher who explains to students the facts of life. Taylor simply declares that the good is intrinsic to the scheme of things and to our nature, that the good speaks to us with a voice to which we should pay attention in order to articulate what we inchoately sense is part of our nature. For these pronouncements no reasons are given. It is a remarkable feature of Taylor's ideal theory that he nowhere says what the good is that is implicit in everyone's nature, what our inner voice tells us about it, and what it is that we all crave. Taylor writes as if the history of ideas he reconstructs were not full of deep disagreements about the nature of the good that all of us are supposed to crave. We are to take Taylor's word for the truth of these most basic assumptions that have been questioned again and again throughout the ages since Plato first articulated them.

Taylor is a fine and learned historian of ideas. His erudite reconstructions in *Sources of the Self* of the history of ideas about the self, however, do not come close to providing an adequate reason for accepting any of the ideas he discusses. He simply appropriates part of the history of these ideas for his own purposes and then proceeds as if he has given some reason for believing the reconstructed claims about these ideas. It is true that many people have held the ideas Taylor reconstructs, but many people have also held absurd, pernicious, fantastic, and other mistaken ideas. Taylor owes an answer to the question of why his metaphysical speculations about the self are not among the mistaken ones. I have found no such answer in the many pages of his works.

Stripped of the rhetoric, what Taylor is saying is that if we hear the inner voice in which the goodness inherent in the scheme of things speaks to each one of us, then we will know how reason requires us to live. If we do not hear what the inner voice tells us, it is because we have not been listening attentively enough. And if what we hear tells us to live in pernicious ways, then we have misinterpreted what the inner voice tells us. This is indeed monomania. It is an ideal theory that leaves no room for doubt, no chink through which criticism could enter, and any reason that might be given against it will be interpreted as confirmation of Taylor's view that we have been insufficiently attentive.

All of it is an arbitrary construction that would not mislead those who understand it. But it is worse than arbitrary, because it leads the ideal theorists who accept it to dictate how others should live. They regard resistance to it as at once irrational, immoral, and detrimental to those who resist it. For the dictates of their ideal theory are for the good of those who resist them, the good that is articulated by their own inner voice, if only they would listen to it. Since they do not listen, ideal theorists will tell them what they would hear if they did listen, or listen better. I find it impossible to understand how someone could propose such an ideal theory knowing, as Taylor must, the awful crimes that have been perpetrated throughout history in the name of such claims about a supposed inner voice.

If we leave these metaphysical speculations aside and come back to reality, we may think about real lives, such as that of the Nurse, who is not a strong evaluator, given Taylor's account. (Frankfurt would call her a wanton.) It follows from Taylor's account that since the Nurse is not a strong evaluator, she is not a human being, does not have a self, and lacks identity because she does not evaluate her desires by standards that are independent of her tastes and desires. Who could believe that the Nurse lacks a self, that she is undergoing an identity-crisis, and that she has a terrifying experience of disaggregation and loss? The Nurse certainly lacks depth, but what Taylor claims is that what she lacks is "a kind of depth we consider essential to humanity" (*Agency*, 28). Who are the "we" who consider that kind of depth essential? If shallowness is a disqualification for humanity, then hundreds of millions of apparently human beings fail to be human, lack a self, and possess no identity. Why must shallowness lead to terrifying loss rather than to avoiding deep questions whose answers are not readily available? On what grounds does Taylor claim that the lives of countless people like the Nurse who do not live according to his ideal theory lack a sense of what is good?

Furthermore, the Nurse is certainly not unique in living as she does. Although she is more fortunate than the countless others who seek the satisfactions of their desires without evaluating them by a standard that is independent of their desires, a standard they must—note the *must*—accept. Why must they? The vast majority of human beings live and act as they do in order to satisfy their desires, some of which are reasonable, moral, and prudent, and others not. They do not evaluate their desires by any other standard than their conscience; the likely consequences of satisfying them, among which are possible legal sanctions and the moral disapproval of others whose judgment matters to them; their estimate of the cost of satisfying their desires in time, energy, and money; and the effect the satisfaction of one of their desires has on the satisfaction of the others.

Talk about desires should not mislead by taking desires, as Taylor does in his various examples, to be some kind of physical pleasure, like food or sex. Desires may be for salvation, justice, happiness, love, respect, appreciation, continued creativity, or solving difficult problems. There is nothing demeaning, less than fully human, disaggregating, damaging, or incoherent in being committed to satisfying such desires without appealing to an overriding ideal that enables us to be the strong evaluators that Taylor incredibly says we all in fact are.

I am not denying that there may be standards independent of our desires by which our desires can be evaluated, nor that some people may in fact be strong evaluators and actually live as Taylor says that all must who are human beings, have a self and an identity. What I am denying is that "the human beings we are and live with are all strong evaluators" (*Agency*, 28). Where does that leave the Nurse and all the other proto-humans who live as she does?

I accept that Taylor's book is a learned reconstruction of some of the historical influences that formed the contemporary Western world, but it does not ask the questions that a philosopher should ask: are these influences reasonable? are they for the better or for the worse? should we embrace or resist them? What Taylor does instead is to take his reconstruction as setting a standard by which we must—must!—evaluate how we live and act. By that standard, if we fail, we lack a self and an identity, we are not human beings, and we are undergoing the terrifying experience of something he calls disaggregation, suffer debilitating loss, and fail to be responsible for ourselves.

Taylor is right to characterize his book as the work of a monomaniacal hedgehog who knows one big thing. But hedgehogs only believe they know whatever their big thing is. This would make their certainties no worse than farcical, if it were not for the harm monomaniacs often cause to those who do not share their supposed certainties. The great danger of monomania is attested to by the millions of victims of fanatical ideologues, religious dogmatists, murderous revolutionaries bent on ridding the world of their suspected opponents, and other true believers who follow their inner voice, their élan, and aim to transform the lives of others so as to make them conform to their standard that is vouchsafed by whatever their inner voice tells them. They cause immense harm to others.

I do not think Taylor has caused any harm. But I do think that one consequence of views like his is that they can and often have led to monumental suffering partly because their defenders forget how often ideal theories and the best intentions formed by those who follow them go dreadfully wrong. The inner voice we hear is fallible and hence unreliable, because it is often the result of fantasy, self-deception, unreason, and base instincts, and it often leads to the horrors familiar from the past and the present. As Bernard Williams rightly says, "there are areas of philosophy which might be supposed to have a special commitment to not forgetting or lying about the [world's] horrors, among them moral philosophy. No one with sense asks it to think about them all the time, but, in addressing what it claims to be our most serious concerns, it would do better if it did not make them disappear."[6] Taylor takes no notice of the horrors. He writes as if they did not exist, as if there were no ways of living and acting reasonably and morally apart from being a strong evaluator. The reconstruction Taylor offers and the strong evaluation he takes to be essential for being human ignore the dark side of human lives, the untold number of stupid wars, awful crimes, irrational follies, and unspeakable atrocities that abound in the past and the present. He does not acknowledge that those who perpetrate them are human beings and, by his account, strong evaluators.

Lastly, even if all that Taylor says were correct, strong evaluation would not be a way of overcoming our conflicts and ambivalence. For a strong evaluator must face unavoidable conflicts that are intrinsic to strong evaluation. Strong evaluation is the evaluation of our desires, and it involves the judgment that some of our desires are bad, ignoble, or objectionable in other ways. But the adversely judged desires are our desires, and we are not neutral judges of them. We want to satisfy them, even if we admonish ourselves not to do so. These admonishments, however, are acknowledged by Taylor to be unavoidably uncertain because they are our interpretations of our inarticulate, inchoate urges. We interpret them in terms of whatever happens to be our framework and its standards. The vocabulary of all frameworks is imprecise, their standards are various, and permissible exceptions are many and contestable. As Taylor says of strong evaluators, "they are aware of their own uncertainties, of how far they are from being able to recognize a definitive formulation with ultimate confidence" (*Self*, 17).

Taylor thus acknowledges that our interpretations are uncertain. When we juxtapose them to the insistent promptings of the desires we want to satisfy, then of course we will face a conflict between wanting to satisfy the desires and the admonishment not to satisfy them. And we will be ambivalent about whether we should suppress the desires that we want to satisfy or accept the uncertain interpretation that condemns them. Being a strong evaluator does not mean that we will act on our strong evaluation. We will often have reasons against acting on it, reasons that are derived from the desires themselves and from the recognition of the uncertainty of our interpretations. Therefore, even if we all were strong evaluators, our conflicts and ambivalence would remain.

Capacity or Activity?

I turn now to two ambiguities in Taylor's account of the ideal theory of strong evaluation. They are not merely infelicities of formulations, but fundamental difficulties that would follow if the ambiguities were avoided. The first of these ambiguities is whether strong evaluation is a capacity that all human beings are supposed to have, or an activity that all human beings actually engage in. Taylor sometimes writes as if it were a capacity: "To be a strong evaluator is thus to be capable of reflection" (*Agency*, 25) and "The capacity for strong evaluation is essential to our notion of the human subject" (28). At other times, he writes as if it were an activity that involves the exercise of the capacity: a subject "who deploys a language of evaluative contrasts ranging over desires, we might call a strong evaluator" (23), and "in fact the human beings we are and live with are all strong evaluators" (28). The result is that we do not know whether strong evaluation is a capacity or an activity. This ambiguity runs through Taylor's work.

The problem is not merely unclarity that Taylor could avoid by saying what he means. For the ambiguity glosses over a serious problem that becomes obvious if we ask why we should think that strong evaluation is essential to being human. If we point out that many people, like the Nurse, are human beings who are not strong evaluators, then Taylor can reply that she is a strong evaluator because she has the capacity for it. If we ask why we should think that all human beings have the capacity, then Taylor can reply that they have it because at least sometimes they act on it. And if we ask for evidence of that, then Taylor replies: "It may be left entirely to us, observers, historians, philosophers, anthropologists, to try to formulate explicitly what goods, qualities, or ends are here discriminated. It is this level of inarticulacy, at which we often function, that I try to describe when I speak of the 'sense' of a qualitative distinction" (*Self*, 21). But, of course, many observers deny that the actions must reflect the capacity for strong evaluation. These are observers whom Taylor criticizes for being unable to recognize the essential importance of strong evaluation, such as naturalists, utilitarians, Nietzscheans, existentialists, to which may be added observers who think, as I do, that many human beings are only weak evaluators. So the "evidence" Taylor offers is the "observation" made by those who agree with him, while he ignores the contrary observation of those who disagree with him. By this method just about anything can be made to look reasonable.

The problem, however, is still deeper. Regardless of whether strong evaluation is said to be a capacity or an activity, no one who thinks about it could suppose that it is essential to being human. Suppose that it is an activity. Who could believe that since time immemorial all human beings—including hunters and gatherers; those born into and living in slavery and condemned to a short life of brutal labor; preliterate or illiterate people eking out a subsistence living; hundreds of millions of long-suffering Chinese, Russian, Indian peasants throughout history; troglodytes on various continents; marauding armies of Hunnish, Mongolian, and Viking brutes; and so on—lived lives informed by strong evaluation that led them to reflect on their desires for food, rest, sex, booty, and the blood of their enemies? Who could believe that throughout human history all human beings pondered whether their desires were favorably or unfavorably evaluated by the standard of their framework and in the vocabulary in terms of which they supposedly articulated their strong evaluations? Surely, the vast majority of human beings throughout history had their desires, acted on them, and, understandably enough, that was that.

It might be thought that Taylor has in mind the activity of strong evaluation only of those who live in civilized societies, above the subsistence level, and have some education. This would be a less implausible view, but it is not Taylor's, because he holds that strong evaluation is essential to being human, not just to those who live in a civilized society. It is absurd to suppose that all human beings who ever lived must at least sometimes have engaged in the activity of strong evaluation.

Let us suppose, then, that Taylor's assumption is that strong evaluation is a capacity that all human beings have, regardless of whether they ever act on it. The first question that cries out for asking is how he could know this about all the dead and the living billions. It is no good saying that he knows it because the capacity for strong evaluation is part of human nature, since that is precisely the assumption for which he needs to give reasons. I have found no such reason in his voluminous writings, and I looked hard.

If we set this problem aside and assume that strong evaluation is a capacity that all human beings have, we still need some reason for thinking that having a life that is meaningful, worth living, and guided by an overriding ideal depends on the mere possession of a capacity? How could a capacity be efficacious if we do not act on it? If the fine things whose importance Taylor rightly stresses depend on some one thing, it must surely be more than a mere capacity. At a minimum, they must depend on the occasional exercise of that capacity. But that, of course, is to abandon the view that strong evaluation is a mere capacity rather than an activity.

And why should we think that the sense of direction, worth, and meaning we may have must be derived from strong evaluation, whether it be a capacity or an activity? I acknowledge that they may be derived from it, but Taylor's claim is that they must be, that without strong evaluation we lack these important things, and we are not human beings. Why could they not be derived from our upbringing that we have accepted without question or reflection? Or from the similarly unconsidered and unreflective acceptance of the teachings of some charismatic figure? Why could we not be like the lilies of the field and derive them from the simple joy of living? Taylor says that we could not derive them from naturalism, utilitarianism, radical choice, or merely weak evaluation. But I have found no convincing reason in Taylor's writing why direction, worth, and meaning could not have sources other than strong evaluation, such as, for example, tradition, authority, creativity, a judicious mixture of lower and higher pleasures, and so forth. I conclude that Taylor's view about strong evaluation as essential to being human and having a sense of direction, worth, and meaning is indefensible. Taylor seems to have started with the description of a way of life he rightly finds possible and important and then inflated its importance to being the way we must all live or else forfeit our humanity, doom ourselves to a life that lacks direction, meaning, worth, and a standard for distinguishing between what is good and bad.

The implausibility of Taylor's description of strong evaluation, regardless of whether he thinks of it as a capacity or an activity, can perhaps be avoided if we do not treat it as a description of how people actually are, but as a description of an ideal of how they ought to be. Even if only a few human beings are strong evaluators, Taylor, then, may be taken to propose it as an ideal that all human beings ought to try at least to approximate.

Fact or Ideal?

This brings us to a second ambiguity in Taylor's account: is it an account of strong evaluation as the description of a fact that characterizes all human beings or of an ideal that all human beings ought to try to approximate?

If his account is no more than a description of how human beings are, then it is indefensible for the reasons I have given. But if it is meant as an ideal, then the failure of many human beings to live according to it is not an objection to it. In fact, it may be a reason for stressing the importance of trying to approximate it. Doing so, according to this understanding of Taylor's account, is the way to give our life direction, worth, and meaning that it would otherwise lack. Is strong evaluation defensible as an ideal thus understood? It is not, for reasons I will now give.

If strong evaluation were proposed by Taylor as one possible ideal among others, it would be unobjectionable. If some people want to adopt it, try to live according to it, and see what happens, then it will be an experiment in living. I agree with Mill that the more such experiments are conducted, provided they do not harm others, the more we learn about human possibilities and limits. The problem is that Taylor does not propose strong evaluation as one ideal among many. He proposes it as an overriding ideal that all human beings either follow or doom themselves to a worthless, meaningless life that lacks a clear distinction between what is good and bad. That is the one big thing that Taylor insists on. "Our self-understanding essentially incorporates our seeing ourselves against a background of what I have called 'strong evaluation'" (*Agency*, 3). "My claim is that this is not a contingent fact about human agents, but is essential to what we would understand and recognize as full, normal human agency" (3). What Taylor claims is that we must either be strong evaluators or fail to be full, normal human beings.

I think that strong evaluation is not necessary for a full, normal human being; it is a contingent fact that some people are or aim to be strong evaluators and that others can and do live full, normal lives that have direction, worth, and meaning without being or aiming to become strong evaluators. Taylor spends much time explaining what strong evaluation is and no time explaining why those with whom he disagrees because they are naturalists, utilitarians, or existentialists, and who according to him fail to be strong evaluators, do not cease to be human beings. Perhaps Taylor is much too polite to say such harsh things about people with whom he disagrees, but the judgment follows from his view even if he does not say it.

The problem is that Taylor's explanation of the ideal and his few critical remarks about theories that are inconsistent with it come nowhere close to reasons for believing that strong evaluation is necessary for being human, for having direction, worth, and meaning. Taylor provides at most only a reason for believing that one way of being a full, normal human being is at least to try to become a strong evaluator. The fact that there are other ways of being fully, normally human is a conclusive reason for rejecting Taylor's claim that strong evaluation is necessary for being a full, normal human being. I have already discussed some of these other ways, and I will now come back to them once more.

Consider once again the Nurse. She is fully engaged with her life, enjoys it, harms no one, has an important job, does it skillfully and well, and contributes to the treatment of many sick people. She is liked and appreciated, has many interests, friends, and lovers, visits many places in the world, and lives a healthy, comfortable existence. It is true that she is superficial, poorly educated, unreflective, has no intellectual interest, and is ignorant of the fine arts. But she does not miss them, and her ignorance does not detract from her contentment. I do not see how it could be reasonably claimed that she should not be content with her life, that she is not a full, normal human being, that her life has no direction, worth, and meaning, and that she cannot tell the difference between what is good and bad.

Suppose, however, that she becomes reflective. She does not just try to satisfy her desires but asks all the searching questions about them that Taylor says we all should. Suppose further that she undertakes the arduous task of reading Taylor's works, understands them, and thinks about them seriously. Why would it make her less than a full, normal human being if she decides not to become a strong evaluator? She might say to herself that an examination of her motives bores her to death. She might decide that it would be imprudent, time-consuming, and much too self-centered to embark on this soul-searching and that she would rather go on living just as she was before she started to reflect. Would it be unreasonable, less than fully human, and in some sense abnormal if that was what she decided and acted on? She has made for herself, perhaps by brute luck, a life she likes, and she is living it successfully. In the scenario just presented, she would be not only not a strong evaluator, but someone who deliberately and thoughtfully had rejected the ideal of becoming one. It would be absurd to claim, as consistency requires Taylor to do, that she would not be a human being, that her life would lack direction, worth, and meaning. It follows that it cannot be necessary for human beings to pursue the ideal of being a strong evaluator.

There is another reason for rejecting strong evaluation as an ideal that all human beings ought to pursue. Consider the ordinary, more or less typical, undramatic lives of countless people in the Western world. They are married and have children. Perhaps both husband and wife work in civil service, or in a business, factory, school or university, hospital, or a law or medical office. They have a middle-class income, but they are not rich. They have had more than a high school education, but they are not researchers or engaged in a creative endeavor. They have hobbies, friends, and acquaintances, visit their more remote family members, plan for their annual vacation, go shopping, and watch television. They have preferences, ideals, and commitments, but none of them is overriding. They do their best to live according to them, but when they conflict, or they face some emergency or crisis, or when they have to make a difficult choice, they are not dogmatic about how to cope. If in their judgment circumstances warrant it, they temporarily suspend one commitment or another that they normally hold. Perhaps they are somewhat religious, or involved in some organization that promotes political, benevolent, artistic, or sporting interests. Their lives are full and they are rarely bored and not particularly reflective about whether they live as they should. They know that better housing, higher income, livelier sex, longer vacations would improve their lives, but their unsatisfied needs are not urgent. They do not need to examine their lives and nothing in their existence prompts them to do so. They neither are nor aim to be strong evaluators.

Suppose, however, that something unexpected and disturbing happens to them: serious illness, grief, blatant injustice, their house burns down, someone they love and trust betrays them, or they lose their job. This may provoke them into considering their life and how they want it to go in the future. They may realize that they have not been reflective, or reflective enough, and that puts them on the road toward better, deeper reflection, toward considering whether to embark on strong evaluation, although, of course, they would not know, not having read Taylor, that that was what they were considering. If they take that first step, it is likely to be followed by the second step of asking whether they really want or should want to continue that process toward an uncertain, unknown, and possibly dangerous end. They may realize that if they do continue to pursue the ideal of strong evaluation, it may lead them to condemn how they have been and how they by and large like living. It may lead them to think that they have been much too supine, unimaginative, and intellectually lazy, settling for familiar comforts rather than exploring the possibilities of life. If they reach that point, they have to decide whether they want to continue going that way or do what they can to return to their familiar life that the crisis has interrupted.

It is a consequence of Taylor's view that unless they decide to pursue the ideal of strong evaluation and take the risks that go with it, they will not be full, normal human beings, and their life will lack direction, worth, and meaning. They should decide how they really want to live, make an overriding commitment to living that way, and subordinate their other commitments to it. I think this is an unacceptable consequence. Certainly, they may decide to do what according to Taylor's view they must, but, no less certainly, they may reasonably decide against it. They may say to themselves that their pre-crisis life was good enough, that good enough is enough, and that it would be imprudent to aim at an unknown result that strong evaluation may yield. Only monomania could lead one to say of them that this decision disqualifies them from being human, that it deprives their lives of direction, worth, and meaning, and that they must make an overriding commitment to pursuing a possibly dangerous course of action.

I conclude, first, that there is no reason to accept Taylor's view of strong evaluation, understood as a description essential to being human; and second, that there is no reason either to accept Taylor's account if strong evaluation is understood as an overriding ideal that reason requires all human beings to pursue. I accept that there are some people who fit the description and pursue the ideal, but I do not accept that everyone ought to do so or face the dire consequences that Taylor's ideal theory indefensibly implies.

Loss

The arguments I have so far offered against Taylor's view took the form of showing the inadequacy of the reasons Taylor gives for accepting strong evaluation as an overriding ideal. I will now show that, even if there are reasons for strong evaluation, there are also reasons against it, and the reasons against it may outweigh the reasons for it.

Strong evaluation is proposed as a way of resolving our conflicts and overcoming our ambivalence about how to act. Taylor's proposal is that we should listen to our inner voice that directs us toward the good and make an overriding commitment to live and act as that voice tells us we should. I will not repeat the reasons I have already given against the idea that nature speaks, we hear its voice, and if we interpret it correctly, it tells us how we should live. I will proceed instead by questioning the assumptions that this supposed inner voice gives us one ideal, rather than many, that if we listen to it, we will make an overriding commitment to it, and that we will interpret what the voice tells us in whatever terms our framework happens to provide.

It is obvious, I think, that we are typically committed to a variety of ideals: moral, political, religious, aesthetic, economic, personal, scientific, historical, and so forth. These ideals and our commitments to them often conflict, and we are often ambivalent about how to resolve their conflicts. Even if some sense could be given to our possession of an inner voice, there is no reason to think that the voice would always favor one of our numerous ideals and speak always in terms of one of the many frameworks in which we participate. Participation in each of these frameworks involves often-conflicting commitments to various ideals and ways of evaluating their relative importance. It is a simple mistake to use the standards of one framework to resolve conflicts that occur between commitments and ideals of another framework. But this is just what strong evaluation is intended to do, by claiming that we should make an overriding commitment to some one ideal. It is unreasonable to try to resolve aesthetic conflicts in economic terms, scientific conflicts in moral terms, personal conflicts in political terms, and so forth.

According to Taylor's ideal theory, being human, giving direction, worth, and meaning to our life, requires that we recognize one of the variety of ideals of the frameworks in which we participate as overriding. Only then can we reasonably resolve the unavoidable conflicts and overcome our ambivalence about which of these ideals should guide how we live. The crucial point for Taylor is that being human and living a life that has direction, worth, and meaning depend on commitment to an overriding ideal. We may have many other commitments, but if they conflict, then we can rely on our overriding ideal to resolve their conflicts. If we have not made such a commitment, our life will lack direction, worth, and meaning. Taylor's ideal of strong evaluation is that reason requires us to make such a commitment.

I think he is wrong about this. Reason perhaps allows us to make an overriding commitment, but it does not require it. There is at least one other possibility that reason allows. It is to follow the practical approach and cope with a conflict that we have in a particular context by relying on one of our numerous commitments to override the conflicting one, but recognize that in another context the reverse may be reasonable. We can thus have many commitments without supposing that any of them is always overriding in all contexts. If reason allows both ways of coping with our conflicts, then the question arises why we should opt for the one favored by Taylor and other ideal theorists, rather than for the one favored by the practical approach.

Taylor would say, of course, that we should opt for the one favored by his ideal theory because the direction, worth, and meaning of our life depend on it. Why would someone opt for the practical approach? Because Taylor's ideal theory would lead to an unacceptable loss that would impoverish our life, stifle some of our reasonable beliefs, emotions, and desires, and require us to sacrifice much on which the direction, meaning, and worth of our life depend. It is quite true that if we make a commitment to an overriding ideal, we have a clear guide to how we should live. It is also true, however, that by accepting an overriding ideal we override a variety of ideals to which we are also committed. We may not want to do that, and it may be reasonable to opt for an alternative. And a practical approach is a reasonable alternative.

I acknowledge that there are reasons for both alternatives. What I want to insist on is that neither alternative can eliminate our conflicts and ambivalence. Either one can only help us to try to cope with them in their different ways. When ideal theorists deal with conflicts by suppressing one of the conflicting ideals, they will not make the conflict disappear, nor will they make the resulting loss less keenly felt. They will have made a decision, but the loss they have thereby accepted will continue to make them ambivalent about their decision, even if they are convinced that it was the right one and would make it again if they had to.

When defenders of the practical approach deal with a conflict by making a context-dependent decision that leaves open the possibility that if the context changes they might make a different decision, they, like ideal theorists, will not have eliminated the conflict but merely proposed a temporary expedient for coping with it. They will have the same ambivalence about incurring the temporary loss as ideal theorists have about incurring the permanent loss. The ineliminability of conflicts and ambivalence is a good, though not conclusive, reason for thinking that our conflicts and ambivalence are unavoidable parts of life.

The reason for rejecting Taylor's ideal theory is not that it is forbidden by reason to be guided by an overriding ideal. Nor am I saying that the practical alternative to Taylor's is required by reason and that reason forbids committing ourselves to an overriding ideal. The reason for rejecting Taylor's ideal theory is that it rests on the metaphysical fantasy of an inner voice that tells us how we should live, a voice that only strong evaluators hear and follow, and that therefore only strong evaluators can be full, normal human beings whose life has direction, worth, and meaning. The fantasy is dangerous because it involves the imposition of a way of life on people who reasonably prefer another way of life. No thoughtful person can be indifferent to the horrors that have followed throughout human history from the mentality of ideal theorists.

It is natural to ask what might have led Taylor, who is firm in his condemnation of the horrors, nevertheless to propose a view that easily leads to them. My conjecture is that he found a particular way of life involving commitment to a particular overriding ideal very appealing. And then he did what people do who are addicted to theorizing about how everyone should live: made it a requirement for everyone to live the way he found attractive or else be condemned for a variety of grave faults. Our lamentable history is strewn with the mangled corpses of those who have been thus condemned, not by Taylor of course, but by other, less benign people who have considered themselves entitled to legislate for humanity.

I close with the fine words of Adam Smith: "The care of the universal happiness of all rational and sensible beings is the business of God, and not man. To man is allotted a much humbler department, but one much more suitable to the weakness of his powers, and to the narrowness of his comprehension—the care of his own happiness, of that of his family, his friends, his country."[7]

7   Narrative Unity

> Neither in the social order, nor in the experience of an individual, is a
> state of conflict the sign of vice, or defect, or a malfunctioning. It is not
> a deviation from the normal state of a city or of a nation, and it is not a de-
> viation from the normal course of a person's experience. To follow through
> the ethical implications of these propositions about the normality of con-
> flict, these Heracleitean truths, a kind of moral conversion is needed,
> a new way of looking at all the virtues.
>
> STUART HAMPSHIRE, *Justice Is Conflict*[1]

In this chapter I continue the discussion of whether there is an overriding ideal that guides how we should live, resolves our conflicts, and
overcomes our ambivalence. I discuss Alasdair MacIntyre's ideal theory
according to which the overriding ideal should be the unity of our self
(unity for short). MacIntyre thinks that unity is achieved by constructing a narrative of our life.[2] There are numerous other contemporary
ideal theorists who favor the same approach, allowing for some differences, but I will concentrate on MacIntyre's defense of it. There is also
a minority of critics who deny that reason requires us to construct a
narrative of our life.[3] I think that their doubts are justified. I begin with
a story about a man whom I call the Civil Servant.

The Civil Servant

The Civil Servant is approaching fifty, married, and has two children. His wife also works, and their children are grown and gone. Their marriage has become a habitual arrangement that continues because neither he nor his wife cares enough about other matters to get a divorce. They have enough money for their needs; they recently paid off the mortgage; their house is adequate; and it is in a tolerably secure neighborhood. He became a civil servant after graduating from college. He does his jobs without enthusiasm, no better or worse than he might. His work has become routine, and he follows it without much thought or effort. He is a conventional man who plods along well-trodden grooves as a husband, parent, employee, neighbor, and citizen. Retirement is many years away, but he does not look forward to it, because he is not sure what he might do with all the free time it will give him. After work, he watches TV, reads the local newspaper, follows the ups and downs of the team he is a fan of, washes the car more frequently than necessary, and sometimes goes out for a beer with a neighbor, a colleague, or a distant cousin.

Perhaps because of the approaching milestone of his fiftieth birthday, he is thinking about his life. He sees it passing. He wonders where all the past years have gone and what he has to look forward to in the years to come. The answer he gives himself is that the future is likely to be as uneventful as the past was. He is neither satisfied nor particularly dissatisfied with his life. He is often bored, but so are most people around him, and he has accepted that as a natural state. He has no serious interest in religion, politics, history, literature, or the arts; he has never traveled outside the country; and although he has had a few casual extramarital sexual encounters, he does not seek to repeat them. He sees that his life is not fulfilling, but he does not know how to relieve its drabness. He knows, of course, that he could change jobs, get involved in politics, be active in one church or another, do volunteer work, divorce and try to find someone who will bring joy to his life, learn about gourmet cooking, take up billiards, sell his house and use the money to gamble, speculate on the stock market, or start a business of his own. But he sees also that he is not all that dissatisfied with what he has and that he does not care deeply enough about any of these or other possibilities to risk making radical changes. So time goes on in this boring, conventional, and uneventful way.

If he were asked, or if he asked himself, whether his life has meaning or purpose, he would not know what answer to give. He certainly does not want to die, get some ghastly disease, be left without a livelihood, be injured in a car accident, or get into a serious fight with his wife, children, or colleagues. As to caring about something inspiring, uplifting, interesting, or of more than passing concern, he can think of no such thing. So he carries on his various activities with a mixture of mild satisfaction and dissatisfaction that makes him ambivalent about everything except avoiding trouble. His life is neither good nor bad; he is not enjoying it, but neither is he sufficiently frustrated to want to change it; he does not know how to make it better. Nor does he know whether the lives of others around him are like his, or whether they have some secret that he has not discovered. No one he knows seems to ask such questions, and he does not know anyone who could or would answer the questions he has or would have if he pursued the thoughts prompted by his approaching fiftieth birthday.

Looking at the Civil Servant from the outside, we see a life in the doldrums, pervaded by ill-considered beliefs, insipid emotions, feeble wants, and a reluctance to explore alternative possibilities. His life has no center, no unifying theme; his concerns are scattered; there are no positive aims he values above the boring routines he has for many years followed. He is guided by utterly conventional and unexamined concerns. He inhabits his life without coming anywhere close to wholeheartedly living it. His faint ideals have been formed by unquestioned upbringing, experiences, and influences. We see a man who is the servant, not the master, of his life. This is the view that we, from the outside, form, not the inside one he himself has of his life. His own view is a mixture of boredom with what he has, uncertainty about what he would like to have, and disinterest in evaluating his past, present, and future. He is timid, lazy, and unimaginative.

The Civil Servant has not reached a point at which he could have more than momentary conflicts in his life. Serious conflicts would require him to care more than he does about what he takes to be the possibilities open to him. His life shows that the absence of serious conflicts may indicate a failure, rather than an achievement. He does not like how his life is going, but his dislike of it is not acute enough to compel him to do anything about it. His life is one of many without the redeeming influence of an inspiring teacher, a great talent yet to be discovered and developed, a ruling passion under the placid surface, or the opportunity to say a heroic yes or no to some life-transforming possibility. His life is as it seems to be, and what is below its surface is much the same as what is on it. There is no fairy tale awaiting to be told about it.

According to the narrative ideal, what is missing from the Civil Servant's life is a narrative in terms of which he could give his life a direction and change it from boring to interesting. A narrative is supposed to give his life the unity it now lacks. It would provide a standard by which he could evaluate the possibilities open to him or seek new ones. It would get him out of the doldrums in which he has been languishing. What would such a narrative be?

The Narrative Ideal

I start with some general claims about narratives. Bruner writes, "The heart of my argument is this: eventually the culturally shaped cognitive and linguistic processes that guide the self-telling of life narratives achieve the power to structure perceptual experience, to organize memory, to segment and purpose-build the very 'events' of a life. In the end, we *become* the autobiographical narratives by which we 'tell about' our lives."[4] According to MacIntyre, "the unity of a human life is the unity of a narrative quest."[5] Schechtman explains that "selves, on this view, are beings who *lead* their lives rather than merely having a history, and leading a life is taken inherently to involve understanding one's life as a narrative and enacting the narrative one sees as one's life."[6] And Taylor claims that it is a "basic condition of making sense of ourselves, that we grasp our lives in a *narrative*." This is "not an optional extra." "Our lives exist also in this space of questions, which only a coherent narrative can answer. In order to have a sense of who we are, we have to have a notion of how we have become, and of where we are going."[7] Ideal theorists defending the narrative ideal, then, claim that understanding our life in terms of a narrative is essential to giving it unity and direction, and that without a narrative our the life will be as unsatisfactory as the Civil Servant's is.

I now turn to the details of MacIntyre's ideal theory that explains and defends the narrative ideal. Central to it is the "self whose unity resides in the unity of a narrative which links birth to life to death as narrative beginning to middle to end" (205). MacIntyre claims that "narrative history of a certain kind turns out to be the basic and essential genre for the characterization of human actions" (208); "we all live out narratives in our lives and . . . we understand our lives in terms of narratives" (212); "personal identity is just that identity presupposed by the unity of the character which the unity of a narrative requires" (218); and "to ask 'What is the good for me?' is to ask how best I might live out that unity and bring it [the narrative] to completion" (218).

What about lives like the Civil Servant's that are permeated with indecision, boredom, drudgery and are passively inhabited rather than actively lived? Such lives must have unity if "we all live out narratives in our lives"? Can the Civil Servant be plausibly characterized as engaged in a narrative quest? Consistency requires MacIntyre to give an affirmative answer, which is more than a little implausible. But he claims even more. Not only does the unity and direction of all lives depend on a narrative; so does also the intelligibility of our actions, our accountability, and our knowledge of good and bad.[8] It is no exaggeration to say, then, as Taylor does, that it is an "inescapable feature of human life . . . that we grasp our lives in a *narrative*" and that unless we do so, we cannot make sense of our life.[9]

If we understand narratives in the sense ideal theorists intend, we will recognize that they are quite different from the more usual narratives given by novelists, historians, prosecutors, or social workers. Narratives of a life are formed by us as we live the life we narrate. They reconstruct a pattern that is meant to be true of our life, makes us conscious of it, and guides us to continue, discontinue, or alter the pattern. Narratives therefore are not just descriptive, but also interpretive, evaluative, action-guiding, and reflexive accounts we give to ourselves of how we do and should live.

If narratives thus understood were inescapable features of all human lives, if we were all engaged in a quest for what we regard as good, then how could narratives go wrong? How could it be that "quests sometimes fail, are frustrated, abandoned or dissipated into distractions," and how could it be that "human lives may in all these ways fail" (219)? If they fail, do narratives cease to be inescapable features of human lives? Do those with a failed narrative fail to live a human life? Could a narrative in terms of which we pursue what we take to be a worthwhile ideal not be mistaken? Could we not be wrong about the ideal that is supposedly the object of our quest? I repeat MacIntyre's answer: "The only criteria for success and failure in a human life as a whole are the criteria of success or failure in a narrated or to be narrated quest" (219). Are we to suppose, then, that there is no reasonable external criticism possible of the quests of ideologues, religious fanatics, and other true believers of various stripes? Not quite.

Narratives have two components: the intentions of the subject and the cultural pattern in terms of which the intentions are formed and articulated. "We cannot, that is to say, characterize behavior independently of the settings which make the intentions intelligible both to agents themselves and to others" (206). What are these settings? They may be institutions, milieus, practices, and the like.[10] A narrative requires that we place the agent's intentions "in a causal and temporal order with reference to their role in his or her history; and we also place them with reference to their role in the history of the setting or settings to which they belong" (208). MacIntyre stresses that intentions may be short- or long-term and that shorter-term ones "can only be made intelligible by reference to some longer-term intentions" (207). But the intentions inevitably "make reference to settings." "There is no such thing as 'behavior' to be identified prior to and independently of intentions, beliefs and settings" (208). MacIntyre does not make much of it here, but it is obvious that institutions, milieus, and practices are conventional, rule-governed, and have standards of appropriateness. Consequently the success or failure of our lives is not just a matter of the intentions we happen to have, but also the conformity of our intentions to the standards of appropriateness of the cultural pattern in terms of which they must be made intelligible. But this is not the only ground on which success or failure can be judged.

A second feature of narratives is "a certain teleological character" (215).[11] The success or failure of intentions, quests, and lives, then, can be judged on the basis of their intended aim. "If the narrative of our individual and social lives is to continue intelligibly . . . it is always both the case that there are constraints on how the story can continue *and* that within those constraints there are indefinitely many ways that it can continue" (216). I note here, and return to it later, that this still leaves MacIntyre's account without an external standard by which the individual and social components of narratives can be jointly evaluated. Surely, it must be a possible criticism of a narrative that its aim is irrational or immoral, and that it should not be pursued at all, or not in the way dictated by rules, conventions, or standards implicit in the narrative. I have looked in vain for MacIntyre's acknowledgment of this possibility.

Nevertheless, the case MacIntyre makes has its attractions. Imagine people like the Civil Servant, whose life lacks unity. They go through the motions, but their heart is not in it. They have no lasting overall aim. They have intentions—human life is impossible without them— but their intentions are neither firm nor coherent, their aims are largely short-term, and the longer-term ones, if any, are passive, aiming to avoid what is clearly bad rather than seeking anything they recognize as good. Acquiring a narrative that starts them off on a quest for some ideal would give their life unity and direction. It would make them accountable and their action intelligible. It would alleviate their boredom, give them positive longer-term intentions, and enable them to be clear about what they want to get out of life.

Furthermore, as MacIntyre stresses, a narrative provides the story of our life up to the present and of its intended future. It allows us to make sense of the countless facts in our past, distinguish between significant and insignificant ones, and explain what makes them one or the other. Narratives give coherence to our life and a sense of how what we did or did not do fitted into it, what we should be proud or ashamed of, and whether and why the important choices we have made were good or bad.

We have the testimony of many people whose aimless or unsatisfactory lives have been changed for the better, often much better, by forming a narrative of their lives derived from a political ideology, religious faith, psychoanalysis, or some other ideal theory. Such people may be aptly describable as having found a new lease on life or having been born again. And that, MacIntyre and other defenders of the narrative ideal might say, is just what would transform the Civil Servants unsatisfactory life into a more satisfactory one by giving it unity and direction.

I acknowledge that a narrative may have this beneficial effect. However, the claims made for narratives are the much stronger ones that narratives *will* have this effect, and that unless we are guided by a narrative, our life will lack unity and direction, our actions will not be intelligible, and we will not be accountable for them. That is why reason requires us to construct a narrative of our life. I think these stronger claims are false.

To begin with, the narrative we construct may have pernicious effects both on ourselves and on others, if the ideology, faith, or ideal theory from which they are derived is pernicious. We know from bitter experience that many of these all-embracing ideal theories have awful consequences that no reasonable person could accept. We would be better off living an unsatisfactory life than with a narrative derived from some vicious ideal theory. Whether it is reasonable to be guided by a narrative surely depends in part on the content of the narrative.

Notice also that the narrative ideal is contemporary. I know of no one in the history of ideas who claimed, as MacIntyre and other defenders of the narrative ideal do, that the unity and direction of life, the intelligibility of actions, accountability, and knowledge of good and bad depend on having formed and being guided by a narrative. Perhaps some notable historical figures, like Socrates, Augustine, and Montaigne, have lived as MacIntyre thinks we all should. But surely billions of others in the past, before the narrative ideal came to be formulated, have not followed a not-yet-existing ideal. In the preceding dark ages, only a few precocious constructors of narratives could have enjoyed the enormous benefits the narrative ideal promises. The dead multitudes who lived before our enlightened epoch were doomed to unsatisfactory lives. No reasonable person could believe this. Even if, unlikely as it is, an unexamined life is not worth living, an examined life need not take a narrative form.

It may be said in defense of the narrative ideal that it has in fact existed throughout history, even though it was not named as such. What is contemporary is the naming of it, not the ideal itself. This is conceivable, but neither MacIntyre nor other defenders of the narrative ideal provide the necessary historical evidence for it. They proceed as if it has been true throughout history, across different epochs, cultures, and contexts that the unity and direction of all lives, the intelligibility of actions, accountability, and knowledge of the good always and for everyone depended on a narrative. How could MacIntyre, or indeed anyone, possibly know that? What reason could we have for believing it? And, oddly enough, MacIntyre gives good reasons for doubting the timeless universal requirement of living according to the narrative ideal, by stressing the historicity of traditions, conventions, and practices. There is good reason to doubt that the narrative ideal has been the key to living as we all should in all the many changing and very different historical contexts.

Several reasons for the narrative ideal are derived from unclarity about how narratives are to be understood. The sorely needed clarification will show that the claims for the ideal are grossly inflated. A narrative may make some lives better, others worse, and unity, direction, accountability, intelligibility, and knowledge of the good can be achieved in other ways than by forming a narrative. We may acquire these benefits, for instance, by unreflectively and inarticulately following a way of life into which we have been born and whose conventional practices we follow in the company of many others who do the same. We need not share the reflective mentality whose necessity is presupposed by defenders of the narrative ideal. Billions throughout history lived and are still living in this way. It is absurd to suppose that they could not have had, or now have, satisfactory lives.

Criticism

Part of the truth of the narrative ideal is that a chronological description can be constructed of all lives. We were born at some point, into some context, passed and are passing through various stages of life, had specific experiences, worked at specific jobs, got married and had children, or not, fell ill and with luck recovered, and so forth. Such descriptions have an unavoidably temporal dimension: first we did this and then that; this happened to us first and then that. If this were all that defenders of the narrative ideal meant, then it would be trivially true that "we all live out narratives in our lives" (211). But they must mean more, because a chronological description can be given also of material objects, nonhuman lives, and human lives that lack the good things that supposedly only a narrative could provide. Furthermore, many of the facts that form these temporal sequences are utterly trivial and without any interest. If a narrative is to provide the benefits ideal theorists claim for it, it must recognize that some of the countless chronologically describable facts are significant and others are not. A nontrivial narrative must distinguish between significant and insignificant facts, between, say, putting one foot before the other in taking a routine walk and having a foot amputated. And the distinction must be drawn by interpreting and evaluating the facts on the basis of whether they do or do not affect how we want to or should live.

How are such interpretations and evaluations arrived at, according to defenders of the narrative ideal? Their generally agreed answer is that the narratives we form interpret and evaluate the significance of facts in terms of the cultural patterns in our social context. These patterns are called by Bruner "culturally shaped cognitive and linguistic processes";[12] by MacIntyre "social settings";[13] and by Taylor "the language and culture" that "constitute the individual."[14]

Reading a book, for instance, is a describable fact. A reader and a book have a specifiable spatial and temporal location; the book has a title, length, weight, and subject matter; and these and a multitude of other facts are as objective, factual, and verifiable or falsifiable as any other fact. The significance of the book, however, is quite another matter. It may be religious, if the book is the Bible, or political, if it is the *Mein Kampf*, or educational, if it is a textbook, or horticultural, if it is about hybridizing orchids, and so forth. However, it is not the content of the book alone that makes it significant. Its significance also depends on whether we have a religious, political, educational, or horticultural commitment. Reading a book may have no significance for us if reading it just helps to pass the time while waiting for our turn in an office, or if we have no interest in what the book is about. So the interpretation of a fact depends on the combination of a cultural pattern and our participation in it. Both have a history, including a roughly datable beginning, and a sequence; and our participation is made more or less appropriate by the aims, conventions, or standards implicit in the cultural pattern.

According to defenders of the narrative ideal, interpretations must take a narrative form in order to make facts intelligible. As MacIntyre puts the point: "Narrative history of a certain kind turns out to be the basic and essential genre for the characterization of human action" (208). We can say, therefore, that narratives are both descriptive and interpretive. But facts made intelligible by interpretations may still be insignificant unless it is explained why what we have done was worth doing. Narratives, therefore, must also be evaluative and explain why we find some facts significant and others not. The explanation is that significant facts make our life better or worse by strengthening or weakening the unity and direction of our life, the control we have of our actions and hence of our accountability for them, and these facts provide a standard by which we can evaluate what is good or bad. Narratives do not merely characterize our life, but guide how we live by enabling us to evaluate our past, present, and intended future choices and actions. Narratives, therefore, must be understood as combining description, interpretation, and evaluation. Each is supposed to be necessary, and they are jointly sufficient for making our life better, resolving conflicts we have, overcoming our ambivalence about what we should do, and thereby give unity to our life.

I think these claims are mistaken. Consider first the claim that without having a narrative of our life, we cannot decide what facts are significant. It is true that we derive the significance of some facts from a narrative. We can explain in this way the significance of a chance meeting with a charismatic person, of being stuck alone in an elevator, or of a news report that touched us deeply. Such facts may prompt us to reconsider how we live, and we may be able to give a narrative account of why they have this significance. But it is not true that the significance of all facts derives from a narrative. Numerous facts carry with them their own significance. Such facts are that we pass from childhood to youth, from there to early and late middle age, and eventually become old; that we are male or female, form or fail to form various intimate relationships, have good health or suffer from serious illness, have or lack the unimpaired use of our limbs and senses, like or dislike the work we do; are rich, poor, or in-between; and do or do not have children.

No reasonable narrative of a life can omit recognizing the significance of some basic facts of human physiology and psychology. Given human nature, these facts are more basic than the intentions we may form and the cultural patterns in which we may participate. It is such basic facts that make it possible for us to have some at least minimal understanding of other human beings across very different epochs, cultural patterns, and aims in life. It is therefore not true that unless we have constructed a narrative of our life we cannot identify some facts as significant. There is no reason, for instance, to suppose that the Civil Servant must have constructed a narrative in order to recognize that approaching the milestone of his fiftieth birthday, being bored much of the time, or having a stale marriage are significant facts in his life.

Consider next the implications of the claim that our actions will be unintelligible unless we fit them into a narrative and derive from it an interpretation of the significance of what we do or might do. MacIntyre stresses that human actions cannot be understood independently of the prevailing cultural patterns, the historically continuous but forever changing institutions, practices, and milieus in which we participate (206–7). He says that it is a "conceptual commonplace" that "one and the same segment of human behavior may be correctly characterized in a number of different ways. To the question 'What is he doing?' the answer may with equal truth and appropriateness be 'Digging,' 'Gardening,' 'Taking exercise,' 'Preparing for winter' or 'Pleasing his wife'" (206).

This is true, and what follows from it is that the same action may be correctly interpreted in terms of a number of different cultural patterns in our context. They may be economic, medical, moral, political, prudential, or religious; conservative, existentialist, liberal, Marxist, psychoanalytic, or Thomist; aesthetic, cynical, optimistic, pessimistic, skeptical, stoic, and so forth. There is a large variety of readily available cultural patterns in whose terms even moderately intelligent and not particularly well-educated people can interpret the significance of the facts in many different ways. And, of course, interpreting a particular fact in terms of one of these cultural patterns carries with it no commitment to interpreting other facts in the same terms.

Most of us routinely interpret in quite different terms the significance of our parenthood and political allegiance; work and friendship; medical and financial problems; the obligations of marriage and citizenship; the importance of sex and wealth; and so forth. Furthermore, our interpretations change as the years pass. We change our minds about what we think is worth spending time and energy on; about the relative importance of the various cultural patterns in which we participate; and about what we regard with detachment, compassion, despair, indignation, or laughter. The kinds of things toward which we have any attitude at all also changes. Aging, adversity, success and failure, happiness and grief, poverty and prosperity inform the seasons of our lives and lead us to deepen or revise the relative priority of the various points of view from which we interpret the significance of the facts and our responses to them.

Interpretation must be one of the aims of the narrative ideal. But the multiplicity of cultural patterns on which we routinely rely for interpreting the significance of the facts is a virtual guarantee that our interpretations will often conflict. Our conflicts are not normally the result of lacking an interpretation, but of having many. Defenders of the narrative ideal misdiagnose the source of our conflicts. They think that the conflicts indicate that we lack a narrative in terms of which we can interpret how we live and act. And then they go on to claim that we can resolve our conflicts only by forming a narrative. There are several reasons why this is a mistake. First, the Civil Servant has no serious conflicts not because he has formed a narrative, but because he does not care about anything all that much. He is just going with the flow and sometimes favors one possibility, sometimes another, without bothering to interpret and evaluate the significance of much of what he is doing.

Second, those of us who are unlike the Civil Servant in having serious concerns do have conflicts, but not because we have not formed a narrative, but because we have done so. It is from our narrative that we derive our many conflicting interpretations and evaluations of the significance of the facts. Without the narrative we would not have the conflicts. We would merely amble along in life in the desultory way the Civil Servant is doing. So the idea that narratives will help us resolve our conflicts is the opposite of the truth. Narratives produce many of the conflicts we would not have if we had not formed a narrative.

Third, defenders of the narrative ideal will say that the way to avoid conflicts is by forming a narrative that commits us to regard one cultural pattern as overriding. We then subordinate to it the other cultural patterns in which we participate and in terms of which we interpret the significance of facts. Such a narrative, however, requires us to subordinate much of what we value to one of the cultural patterns. And that would make us systematically untrue to a large part of how we in fact evaluate the possibilities open to us. Think of the impoverishment of ideological and religious fanatics who interpret art, science, literature, personal relations, sex, illness, history, and so forth predominantly from a particular political or religious point of view. Only a few fanatics would be willing to do this. They may thereby further the cause to which they are so single-mindedly committed, but it will not make their lives better, which is what narratives are supposed to do.

It seems to me that a reasonable response to this way of coping with conflicts would be to conclude that the impoverishment to which it dooms us would make it preferable to put up with conflicts. I am not saying that we must respond in this way, only that we may do so. Defenders of the narrative ideal, however, are committed to the much stronger and indefensible claim that unless we construct such an impoverishing narrative, our life will have no unity and direction, we will not be accountable for what we do, cannot know what is good for us, and will be lacking an essential requirement of living a human life.

Problems about the evaluations involved in narratives compound these problems of the narrative ideal. Description and interpretation are supposed to be necessary but not sufficient for understanding the significance of the facts. Narratives are supposed also to evaluate the facts on the basis of their contribution to making our life better. I accept that a narrative may make our life better, but defenders of the narrative ideal ignore the obvious possibility that it may make our life worse. Since we cannot know ahead of time whether a narrative will lead to this unwanted result, a prudent aversion to taking unnecessary risks might make it reasonable to put up with our conflicts rather than risk constructing a narrative that could make our life worse.

A narrative may lead us to condemn our life by making us realize that, judged by its own standards, we have been dishonest, insensitive, selfish, cowardly, unjust, and so forth. A truthful narrative may reveal not only our virtues but also our vices, and it may compel us to recognize that our vices have overwhelmed our virtues. It may make us recognize that our life has been deplorable, that its unity and direction have been provided by irrational, immoral, destructive, or vindictive aims, that we are accountable for our depredations, and that our knowledge of good and bad leads us to conclude that we have been opting for the bad. A truthful narrative may lead to self-loathing, despair, debilitating shame, guilt, or regret. Less dramatically, it may lead us to realize that our life has been banal, pedestrian, and unimaginative, or that it has been made thoroughly dishonest by self-deception, wishful thinking, rationalization, and other stratagems for falsifying the facts. A narrative may lead us to understand that we are set in bad ways, that it is too late for us to change, or that we lack the will to embark on the hard task of self-transformation. The adverse evaluation that may follow from a narrative could lead us to become resigned to our bad life and make do as well as we can with it, or it may lead us to become embittered, cynical, or misanthropic. It cannot be reasonably supposed in the light of these possibilities that a narrative would make our life better. It may do that, or it may make it worse.

Consider the Civil Servant as a case in point. Suppose he realizes that he has not constructed a narrative of his life. Ideal theorists will tell him that he should set about doing so. But he could reasonably ask why he should do that if the narrative might transform his mild dissatisfaction with his life into a strong condemnation of it. He knows that his life could be better than it is, but he also knows that he is not sufficiently dissatisfied with it to take the risk of making it worse. Why would reason require him to take that risk? Why would reason not allow him to go on living as he has been doing? I have found no acknowledgment, let alone an answer, to these questions in the writings of ideal theorists who defend the construction of a narrative as an overriding ideal that reason requires everyone to pursue.

Are Narratives Reliable?

I promised earlier to return to the question of the reliability of narratives. MacIntyre's view, as we have seen, is that "the only criteria for success or failure in a human life as a whole are the criteria of success or failure in a narrated or to-be-narrated quest." He asks: "a quest for what?" (209) and answers that it is for the realization of some conception of the good derived from "the settings which make intentions intelligible" (206). And Taylor repeats and endorses MacIntyre's view that for human beings this quest for the good is "the spiritual source they connect their lives with"; they "see themselves as, in a sense, seeking. They are on a 'quest' in Alasdair MacIntyre's apt phrase."[15] The claim, then, is that this quest takes a narrative form and it is the source of the benefits that, according to its defenders, the narrative ideal is supposed to provide. The success or failure of human life depends on how this quest is going.

There is a sense in which this view is obviously true. Whenever we aim at anything that matters, we do so believing that it would be in some way good, or at least better than something else we might aim at. But this does not get us very far. For we may be lazy, fearful, or passive and have only unambitious aims. Or we may aim at what we believe would be bad for us because we want to punish ourselves, expiate for wrongdoing, or sacrifice ourselves for a cause or for someone we love. Of course, it may be said that even if we have these other aims, we still pursue them because we think it would be better than the alternative. In that case, however, the claim that we are on a quest for the good remains true whatever we do, and thus becomes vacuous.

The way to avoid this vacuity is to specify the content of what we regard as good. A nonvacuous conception of the good must have substance; it may be happiness, duty, salvation, justice, truth, goodness, beauty, or something more mundane. But then the claim that we always aim at the good fails. We may be stupid, weak, perverse, vindictive, or whatever, and have an aim contrary to our substantive conception of good. Should we, then, dismiss as either vacuous or false the claim that we are all on a quest and that the intelligibility of our actions depends on what our quest is? No, we should not, because MacIntyre recognizes the possibility that a quest can fail, so his claim is not vacuous. And he might say that one reason why it might fail is the sort of character defect I have just mentioned. He would insist, however, that when a quest fails, it does so on its own terms, in terms of the criteria of success and failure implicit in the quest itself.

I want to consider now the possibility that a quest might fail even if it is successful in its own terms. Surely, it must be possible that a quest aims at a mistaken conception of the good, or that the cultural pattern, say the religion or the politics, from which the vocabulary, criteria, and the aim of the quest are derived is indefensible, or that the intentions that drive our quest are unrealistic, irrational, destructive, or misunderstood by us. MacIntyre explicitly rules out these possibilities by stressing that "the only criteria of success or failure in a human life as a whole are the criteria of success or failure in a narrated or to-be-narrated quest" (209). If, however, these possibilities are recognized, then the question of the reliability of narratives must be faced. Defenders of the narrative ideal owe an answer to the question of why it is more reasonable to live according to a narrative that is the joint product of possibly mistaken cultural patterns, intentions, and a conception of the good than to try cope with our conflicts in some other way.

There are two reasons for supposing that a narrative that is successful in its own terms may still be an unreliable guide to how we should live and cope with our conflicts. One is that we change and come to see our hitherto successful narrative as contrary or irrelevant to how we now want to live. The other is that a narrative that is successful at a certain time may be based on mistaken descriptions, interpretations, and evaluations of the significance of facts.

Consider first that the contents of our narrative change as time passes, and our circumstances, responses to them, and intentions change. If a narrative we form is reliable, it must reflect these changes. But then it could not be a reliable guide to our life "as a whole," but only to a passing phase of it. A reliable narrative would have to be as changeable as our circumstances and intentions are. Even if we continue to aim at the good, our understanding of what the good is and of how it is best to pursue it would have to change as our understanding, character, intentions, and circumstances change.

What might these changes be? They might be changes in the significance we attribute, say, to sex, money, death, work, comfort, risk, and similar ubiquitous facts of life. Travel may broaden us. Grief or personal encounter with horrendous evil may strengthen or weaken our religious faith, if we have any. The glitter of a desired way of life may fade when we learn more about it. Our need may grow for the consolation of music, nature, art, or literature as we are buffeted by life. We may grow in our appreciation, loyalty, and need for old friends with whom we share experiences and memories. We may become more understanding and tolerant of human weaknesses. The more we know about some area of life, such as politics, the law, or history, the more we recognize its complexity and the difficulty of making firm judgments within it. Our tolerance, discipline, concentration, tact, generosity, energy, dedication, and flexibility ebb and flow as the years pass and as our experiences change. These are common examples of significant changes in our life, and if some lives are not changing in these particular ways, they will be changing in others. A reliable narrative must reflect these changes, not only in retrospect but as going on now and as, in all likelihood, will be going on in the future. A reliable narrative, therefore, will continually have to change to accommodate the shifting significance of such facts.

This has the consequence that it is a mistake to suppose that we can construct a narrative that will be *the* narrative of our life and of *the* significance of the facts. Biographers may be able to construct a retrospective narrative of a life as a whole, but they can do it only because they view the life from a distance, as observers who can tell about the life but cannot change it. We cannot do it ourselves, because we are living the life and are the active and passive subjects who at once make and undergo the significant changes in it. We can construct a narrative of a particular phase of our life and perhaps even use it to guide how that phase unfolds. But we cannot construct a narrative of our life as a whole while we are living it, because we and our life are changing as we are living it. If the unity and direction of our life, our accountability, and our knowledge of what is good and bad depend on a narrative we construct of our life as a whole, as defenders of the narrative ideal claim, then a narrative could not possibly deliver what its defenders promise.

Consider next that the descriptions, interpretations, and evaluations of the significance of facts that form the content of our narrative may be mistaken. It is not merely a logical possibility but an ever-present temptation to skew the facts of our life by stressing the significance of what allows us to think well of our efforts and minimize the significance of our faults by excusing our failures or blaming others or circumstances for them. It is hard to form a realistic view of ourselves and our life, especially when it is unlikely to be entirely favorable. We tend to give ourselves the benefit of the doubt and often falsify the significance we attribute to the autobiographical facts that form our narrative. If we rely on the guidance of such a skewed narrative, our life will not be successful even if it conforms to "the criteria of success and failure in a narrated or to-be-narrated quest." The criteria of success and failure derived from a cultural pattern and our conception of the good may be just as mistaken, and mistaken in the same skewed way, as are the supposed facts that we judge by the criteria. Virtually all of us are biased in our own favor. We want to think well of ourselves and tend to convince ourselves of descriptions, interpretations, and evaluations of our life and actions that will make how we live and act understandable, justifiable, or excusable.

Many volumes have been filled with psychological, literary, and biographical accounts of the ways in which we tend to falsify our judgments of ourselves. I am not going to add to them, but hope that some reminders will suffice. We often deceive ourselves about our strengths and weaknesses, motives, how we are seen by others, and how we see ourselves. We regard our cowardice as prudence, greed as taking our fair share, vindictiveness as just punishment, tactlessness as the oversensitivity of those we have offended, vulgarity as being down to earth, and so on. We invent reasons for doing what we want to do contrary to reason; assuage disappointed hopes by convincing ourselves that we did not really want what we hoped for; explain our self-indulgence as enjoying deserved rewards; confuse what we need with what we love; regard our prejudices as well-founded beliefs; and take wishes to be probabilities. Self-deception, wishful thinking, rationalization, and sentimentality are some of the many ways in which we falsify the facts so that we can avoid forming an unfavorable narrative of some part of our life.

The result of these two ways in which the narratives we construct may be unreliable is that we should be guided by a narrative only if we have good reasons to suppose that it is reliable. And that depends on having good reasons to suppose that a narrative ascribes the right significance to the facts and that its descriptions, interpretations, and evaluations of the facts are not falsified by our desires, fears, and cognitive or emotive shortcomings. Since it is normally doubtful whether these conditions are met, narratives are normally unreliable guides to life.

The Ideal and the Real

By way of concluding this chapter, I will consider the narrative ideal in the light of lives we actually live, bearing in mind great variations in our psychology and contexts. Defenders of the narrative ideal may acknowledge that both we and our narratives are fallible and often unreliable. They will claim, however, that just for that reason it is important to have an ideal that guides how we should live and to construct a narrative to chart and guide our progress toward the ideal. This would give unity and direction to our life, enable us to justify or criticize how we actually live, and provide a standard for resolving conflicts between our commitments. None of this needs to involve unreasonable claims about the infallibility of the ideal and the reliability of the narrative. It would suffice for their purposes to insist that we should make them as free of mistakes as we can and correct them as the need arises.

I accept that this a possible and attractive ideal, even if we have reason to contest the details of any particular formulations of it. But I do not accept the exaggerated claims made by its defenders that "in the end we *become* the autobiographical narratives by which we 'tell about' our lives";[16] "that the unity of a human life is the unity of a narrative quest" (219); and that it is "the basic condition of making sense of ourselves that we grasp our lives in a *narrative*."[17] It is not true that "we all live out narratives in our lives" (211), nor that narratives are an "inescapable feature of human life."[18] I think most of us live without a consciously or otherwise constructed narrative. If we do so, we need not be helpless in the face of conflicts, our life need not lack unity and direction, and we can have ways of justifying and criticizing how we live and identifying what is and is not good and significant. Here is a sketch of many such lives.

We have commitments to our parents, children, and partners; to whatever work we do; to protecting our health, house, and belongings; to politics, morality, religion, art, and personal projects; to physical and financial security; to beauty, truth, goodness, integrity, self-respect, and loyalty; to enjoyments we value; and so forth. Since our time, energy, and resources are limited and circumstances are often unfavorable in various ways, we cannot always meet our commitments as fully as we would like. We then have to opt for one over another or, more often, meet one commitment to a greater and another to a lesser extent. Having to make these choices is a familiar part of most lives. On rare occasions, we have to make tragic choices and violate some commitment we regard as essential to living as we want in order to honor another commitment we regard as even more essential. In civilized societies and normal circumstances, however, many of us go through life without encountering such wrenching conflicts. Nontragic conflicts among commitments are frequent, routine, and expected, and as we mature, we learn more or less well how to balance various commitments' claims on us by making some judgment about their relative importance in a particular context.

We make such judgments by trying to arrive at a modus vivendi that allows us to honor both commitments to the extent to which circumstances allow. We seek a compromise rather than meet one commitment fully and the other not all, since they are both important to how we want to live. We balance them by considering how far we can go in favoring one without betraying the other. Such judgments are context-dependent. Contexts change, and if the conflict recurs, we may make a different judgment. This is just the way in which most of us, most of the time, cope with our conflicts between marriage and work, morality and prudence, the old and the new, ambition and comfort, enjoyments and responsibilities, and so forth.

Decisions about how we should cope with ordinary conflicts between our commitments are not precedent-setting policies that bind us to follow them in the future. What we do here and now need not guide what we will do then and there. The decisions do not require us to appeal to an overriding ideal that we value above all else. Many of us are committed to many ideals and do not think that any of them is overriding. We can cope with our conflicts quite reasonably without relying on a narrative whose guidance is mistakenly claimed by ideal theorists to be essential to living a human life. Most of us live without such a narrative. Our decisions about everyday conflicts are mundane. They need have no momentous significance, no serious implications for the future, and need not compel us to reexamine our past.

Assume that we live without an overriding ideal and a narrative. Do we then have a conception of the good, does our life have unity and direction, are our actions intelligible, are we accountable for them, can we tell what is and is not good or significant if we cope with our conflicts in this way? I think the answer is obviously yes. Our conception of the good is to meet our various commitments as fully as circumstances allow. That is one of our ideals and one direction our life may take. Our actions are intelligible because they are motivated by our commitments, and we are accountable for them because they express our intentions. None of this requires us to make a commitment to an overriding ideal, to have constructed a narrative, and to be guided by it. But does our life have unity if our commitments are various and conflicting? If having unity means that we have an overriding ideal to which we have subordinated all other ideals and commitments, then our life lacks unity. I see no reason, however, why unity should depend on an overriding ideal, rather than on the balanced pursuit of various ideals.

In conclusion, the practical approach that I have been recommending as an alternative to ideal theories can acknowledge that reason allows us to live by aiming at an overriding ideal, constructing a narrative, and being guided by it. Living this way has its dangers, as we know from the lives of fanatics, and it has its rewards, as we know from the fine lives in which a single-minded pursuit has led to great achievements in art, literature, and science. I have been arguing against defenders of the narrative ideal that reason only allows but does not require us to live this way. And it is in order to make this argument concrete that I have sketched how many real lives are actually lived, with varying degrees of success, without aiming at an overriding ideal and the guidance of a narrative.

8 Practical Reason

> The delicate and difficult art of life is to find, in each turn of experi-
> ence, the *via media* between two extremes: to be catholic *without* being
> characterless; to have and apply standards, and yet to be on guard against
> their desensitizing and stupefying influence, their tendency to blind us
> to the diversities of concrete situations and to previously unrecognized
> values; to know when to tolerate, when to embrace, and when to fight.
> And in that art, since no fixed and comprehensive rule can be laid down,
> we shall doubtless never acquire perfection.
>
> ARTHUR O. LOVEJOY, *The Great Chain of Being*[1]

The delicate and difficult art of how we should live is to find a via media
between absolutist ideal theories, according to which reason is an ideal
that should always override whatever consideration conflicts with it,
and relativist theories, which claim that reasons ultimately come to an
end and we have to decide how we should live on some other basis. The
practical approach I am defending is an alternative to absolutism and
relativism about reason. It is in partial agreement and partial disagreement with both absolutism and relativism thus understood.

Defenders of the practical approach agree with absolutists that
conformity to practical reason is a necessary condition of living as we
should, but they also agree with relativists that practical reason cannot
yield an overriding ideal of how we should live. The via media proposed
by the practical approach is that how we should live depends on meeting the requirements of practical reason, but many ideals meet those
requirements, none of them is overriding, and all of them are allowed
by practical reason.

In this chapter I will consider only Donald Davidson's epistemological theory of practical reason. There is a vast body of scholarly and epistemological work on the nature of practical reason, but this chapter is not intended as a contribution to it. I will discuss only how practical reason bears on we should live, and only by considering Davidson's widely accepted theory. According to it, practical reason requires that our decisions about how we should live be based on taking into account all relevant considerations.[2] A decision reached in this way is reasonable, and decisions contrary to it are unreasonable. As Davidson puts it: "Why would anyone ever perform an action when he thought that, everything considered, another action would be better?" And his answer is that "if the question is read, what is the agent's reason for doing *a* when he believes it would be better, all things considered, to do another thing, then the answer must be: for this, the agent has no reason" ("Weakness," 40). According to Davidson, practical reason requires that if we arrive at a decision about how we should live on the basis of having considered all relevant things, then it should override any other consideration that may conflict with it. That is why his is an ideal theory of practical reason.

I will argue that practical reason cannot yield such an overriding decision. I do not deny that we should take into account all relevant considerations in making a decision about how we should live. I deny that if we do that, then practical reason will yield an overriding decision. I think that by considering all things, practical reason will eliminate some unreasonable decisions, but it will allow a diversity of reasonable decisions, each of which may lead to a reasonable way of living. I acknowledge that practical reasons may be overriding in eliminating some unreasonable ways of living.

In arguing this way, I take a further step toward showing that the practical approach is preferable to both absolutist ideal theories and relativist claims that reasons come to an end. Defenders of the practical approach do, while absolutists and relativists do not, practice the delicate and difficult art of finding a via media between regarding reason as an overriding ideal and as ultimately arbitrary. I begin with a story about a woman whose conflicting commitments make her ambivalent, and then I argue that following Davidson's ideal theory could not help her to resolve her conflicts and overcome her ambivalence.

The Divided Woman

The Divided Woman is in her mid-thirties, married, and has two children, aged ten and twelve. She has a university degree and a talent for writing, and she would like to become a writer, but she has never held a job or concentrated on writing. She got married soon after graduation, had the children, and has been raising them, while postponing serious attempts at writing. She feels responsible for her aging and widowed father, who lives nearby and relies on her in various ways. Her husband has a demanding job. He earns enough for the usual household expenses, annual vacations, a new car or roof when the time comes, and to go out to dinner and a movie occasionally, but not enough to make them affluent. They have to be careful about expenses. The marriage is good but not perfect. Her husband's job requires him to travel from time to time, and she does not inquire too closely about what he does alone in another city. She loves the children, but they are difficult in their different ways. The boy is hyperactive, hard to control, and has little sense of danger. The girl has reached the stage when she is sure that whatever life she will have, it will not be like her mother's, and she is not reluctant to show how she feels. Nevertheless, in the midst of these not unusual tensions, the Divided Woman, as wife, mother, and daughter, knows that her family loves, needs, and depends on her. And she has the same feelings toward them.

Her family, however, is not her sole concern. She is committed to protecting the environment, and she regularly does volunteer work for a national organization. She also wants to devote herself to writing. And she needs to get out of the house, have a job, use her mind and writing talent, see new faces, have new experiences, earn some money, and be more independent than she has been during the past years. She envies her friends with careers who are confident, successful, and have plenty of money. She is restless, wants to see Java, ski in the Alps, wonders what casual sex would be like, and whether she has enough talent to make it as a writer. She is fearful about her untried writing talent and about her ability to do well in a job if she had one. She knows that her family could use the money she might earn, but she also knows that a job would not allow her to continue to meet her many and demanding commitments to her husband, children, father, writing, and the environment. She has daily evidence of her family's dependence on the love, peace, and comforts she has been providing, and she does not want to let them down.

She is determined to do as well as she can to meet the various commitments she has willingly made. She knows that she could do more for all of them, but her time and energy are limited, and she sees her life passing. She is busy, her life is full, yet there is much she lacks. She feels guilty for not doing enough for those she loves, shame for not doing more for herself, and frustration because of the relentless demands on her. Her frustrations sometimes break through, she loses her temper about some minor thing, and that makes her more guilty and ashamed. She nevertheless continues to do as well as she can by all concerned. Yet the joint forces of her needs, love, fear, and sense of responsibility prevent her from making some basic change to her life.

Here then is the Divided Woman: competent and fearful; loving and yearning for some independence; desiring to prove herself and anxious about not being able to do so; curious about the world and timid about exploring it; counting on her husband but not wanting to be just his appendage; uncertain whether, after years of baby talk, enough has been left of her mind and talents; worried about her father; envious of her friends with careers; outraged by the failure to protect the environment; desperate for stimulus from the outside world and weary of the routine of quiet nights at home; hoping for a better future and protective of her family's present life. The beliefs, emotions, and desires that guide her life are many and various, shift in importance from day to day, often conflict, and make her ambivalent.

She is not sure what she does or ought to want, and whether she could and would be able to get whatever that may turn out to be. She has no clear idea of how she really wants to live and no realistic view of how her life is going; no single ideal motivates her more than others, and she does not know how to arrive at one. She minds having conflicts and being ambivalent about how to cope with them but does not know how to do better. She lives in this state of confusion, even though she has a firm sense of whom she loves and needs and what her commitments are to them. She is dissatisfied with herself and her life, but not enough to make some basic change to it, and, in any case, she is confused also about what that would be. Her life goes on and is filled with many satisfactions and dissatisfactions.

Practical Reason

The Divided Woman has not arrived at her conflicting commitments and ambivalence on the basis of a consciously formulated, articulate policy to consider all that is relevant to how she should live. She knows that her life would be better if she could resolve her conflicts and overcome her ambivalence, but she does not how to do it. Davidson would say that she should be more reasonable: consider all relevant things, make a decision about how she should live, and then live that way. I do not think this is good advice. I acknowledge, of course, that it is better to be more rather than less reasonable, and that the Divided Woman might make her life better by becoming more reasonable. But I deny that the consideration of all things would enable her—or those of us who are like her in facing our own conflicts and ambivalence—to overcome her conflicts and ambivalence. Practical reason may enable her and us to understand why she and we have such conflicts and are ambivalent about resolving them, but it will not resolve them.

Davidson writes that "the underlying paradox of irrationality, from which no theory can entirely escape, is this: if we explain it too well, we turn it into a concealed form of rationality; while if we assign incoherence too glibly, we merely compromise our ability to diagnose irrationality by withdrawing the background of rationality needed to justify any diagnosis at all" ("Paradoxes," 303). Davidson thus assumes that reason forms the background and the failure to be reasonable is the exception that requires explanation. Being reasonable needs no more explanation than using language, whereas being unreasonable, like dyslexia, is exceptional and needs to be explained.

Now consider some facts. Self-deception, wishful thinking, rationalization, and sentimentalism are frequent. Self-destructive actions, drug addiction, foolish risk-taking, obesity, prejudice, smoking, superstition, alcoholism, and belief in magic, astrology, and witchcraft are widespread. Many people are prejudiced, rely on unexamined stereotypes, follow the guidance of charlatans, and allow themselves to be manipulated by advertising, catchy slogans, and rabble-rousing politicians. Such facts make it very hard to believe that reason is the norm and unreason is deviation from it.

Nor is it plausible to believe that being reasonable frees us from ambivalence and conflicts and being unreasonable leads to them. Many of us are ambivalent precisely because we understand and feel the force of the reasons for and against our conflicting commitments. And unreasonable fanatics, dogmatists, or ideologues may be quite free of conflicts and ambivalence about how they should live. Yet, contrary to the evidence for widespread unreasonable beliefs, emotions, and desires dictated by unreasonable commitments, the illusion persists that being reasonable is the rule and being unreasonable is the exception. Why? Because, as Kant says, the illusion is "*natural* and inevitable . . . inseparable from human reason, and which, even after its deceptiveness has been exposed, will not cease to play tricks with reason and continually entrap it into momentary aberrations ever and again calling for correction."[3] The illusion is that reason is a more widespread and powerful guide to how we should live than in fact it is.

One implication of Davidson's theory that shares this illusion is that understanding human actions depends on finding the reasons for doing them. As he says, "What is the agent's reason for doing *a* when he believes it would be better, all things considered, to do another thing, then the answer must be: for this the agent has no reason" ("Weakness," 40). Given the illusion that reason is the norm, understanding unreasonable actions becomes a serious problem. Why would we act unreasonably, when we believe that it would be better to act reasonably? Davidson's attempt to deal with this problem must be understood against the historical background of the problem.

A widely accepted solution is to deny that unreasonable action can occur. As Plato's argument in the *Protagoras* may be paraphrased, we always do what we believe is best.[4] If what we do is in fact worse than the best we might have done, then the belief on which we acted must be mistaken, but we nevertheless did what we believed was best. As against this, it has been pointed out again and again—beginning with Aristotle[5]—that we may fail to do what we correctly believe is the best, because our emotions or desires prompt us to do what we know is not the best.

The proposed Platonic explanation, then, of why we may act contrary to what we believe is best is that either we have reason for the action, but the reason is bad because it is derived from a false belief; or we have reason for the action, derived from a true belief, but we act contrary to it because emotions or desires overpower the belief. In the first case, the action is not unreasonable, because it does not go against what we believe is best, yet it is nevertheless mistaken, because it is based on a false belief that we take to be true. But what about the second case? When an action is based on emotions or desires that are contrary to our belief about what is best, do we then have a reason for it?

The Platonic view is that emotions and desires are merely causes, and would count as reasons only if accompanied by beliefs. Otherwise, acting on them is unreasonable. Plato has Socrates ask Protagoras: "What is your attitude to knowledge? . . . Most people think in general terms, that it is nothing strong, no leading or ruling element. . . . They hold that it is not the knowledge that a man possesses which governs him, but something else — now passion, now pleasure, now pain, sometimes love, and frequently fear. . . . Would you rather say that knowledge is a fine thing quite capable of ruling a man, and that if he can distinguish good from evil, nothing will force him to act otherwise than as knowledge dictates?" And of course Plato holds that knowledge should rule us.[6]

The Humean view, by contrast, is that emotions and desires, independently of beliefs, may be reasons for actions. Hume rejects the Platonic view:

> Nothing is more usual in philosophy, and even in common life, than to talk of the combat of passion and reason, to give precedence to reason, and to assert that men are only so far virtuous as they conform themselves to its dictates. Every rational creature, 'tis said, is oblig'd to regulate his actions by reason; and if any other motive or principle challenge the direction of his conduct, he ought to oppose it, 'till it be entirely subdued, or at least brought to conformity with that superior principle. On this method of thinking the greatest part of moral philosophy, ancient and modern, seems to be founded.

He thinks that this is a mistake: "reason is, and ought only to be the slave of the passions, and can never pretend to any other office than to serve and obey them."[7]

Davidson's contribution to this old and persistent dispute between the Platonic and the Humean views forms the basis of his theory, according to which reasonable decisions are based on taking into account all relevant considerations. He recognizes that such a decision may or may not be the best one possible. For we can consider only what is available to us, and all relevant considerations may not be available. Reasonable decisions, therefore, are conditional on what considerations are available to us when we deliberate. The best decision would be unconditional because it would be based on all the relevant considerations. Since all of them may not be available, we may be able to make only the second-best decision, based on taking into account all the considerations available to us then. Such a decision would be reasonable, even though it may be mistaken, because it may not be based on all relevant considerations. But if a decision is reasonable, then, according to Davidson, acting contrary to it is unreasonable.

Davidson asks: "Why would anyone ever perform an action when he thought that, everything considered, another action would be better?" And his answer, as we have seen, is that "if the question is read, what is the agent's reason for doing *a* when he believes it would be better, all things considered, to do another thing, then the answer must be: for this, the agent has no reason" ("Weakness," 40). Davidson thinks, co-opting the Humean view, that the consideration of all that is available should include not just our beliefs, but also our emotions and desires. "We perceive a creature as rational," says Davidson, "in so far as we are able to view his movements as part of a rational pattern comprising also thoughts, desires, emotions, and volitions" (40).

This defuses the old dispute between the Platonic and the Humean views by making room for emotions and desires in reasonable decisions and by accepting that they may give us reasons for actions. Acting on emotions and desires is unreasonable only if they do not fit into "a rational pattern comprising . . . thoughts, desires, emotions, and volitions." And this is what happens when we act contrary to what we believe is best. Davidson's theory, therefore, is consistent with the Humean view that emotions and desires motivate, while reason guides, our actions in the appropriate direction, and with the Platonic view that emotions and desires should be controlled by reason.

Given Davidson's theory, the Divided Woman's conflicts are not between her beliefs that prompt her to act reasonably and her emotions and desires that prompt her to act unreasonably. Her conflicts are between the joint motivating force of the beliefs, emotions, and desires she has for remaining the mainstay of her family, becoming more independent by pursuing a career in writing, and protecting the environment. Making a reasonable decision and resolving her conflicts requires her to take into account all the considerations relevant to how she should to live, and then weigh the relative strengths of all her beliefs, emotions, and desires for and against particular decisions. If she did that, she would no longer be ambivalent. She might follow her emotions and desires and go against her beliefs, and neither that decision nor its opposite would have to be unreasonable. What would be unreasonable would be for her to decide how the relative weights of the reasons she derives from her beliefs, emotions, and desires motivate her to live and then act in a way that is contrary to it.

It would be premature, however, to accept Davidson's ideal theory that regards reason as the overriding ideal of how we should live and how we should resolve our conflicts and ambivalence about it. The theory is much too simple. If the complexities it glosses over are recognized, it must be substantially revised. And, as we will see, the revision has far-reaching implications for the dispute between ideal theories and the practical approach. Davidson's theory rests on two questionable assumptions. The first is that beliefs, emotions, and desires are discrete parts of our psychological condition, that we can identify which of them motivates a particular action, and that if we have considered all that is relevant, then we can resolve their conflicts and our ambivalence about which we should follow. The second is that being reasonable involves making decisions based on the consideration of all that is available and bears on how we should live and that it is unreasonable to live contrary to the decision we have reached in this way. I now turn to these assumptions, argue that they are mistaken, and consider the implications.

Complexities

According to Davidson, the explanation of why anyone would ever perform an action when he thought that, everything considered, another action would be better is that "the mind contains a number of semi-independent structures, these structures being characterized by mental attributes like thoughts, desires, and memories" ("Paradoxes," 290). If these structures are coherent and guide our actions, then we act reasonably. If they are incoherent and motivate us to act in conflicting ways, we are ambivalent and act unreasonably. Reason requires that we "perform the action judged best on the basis of all available relevant reasons" ("Weakness," 41). Davidson's theory, then, assumes that beliefs, emotions, and desires are semi-independent structures and that we can weigh the reasons for and against them independently of one another and thereby reach a reasonable decision about how we should live. I do not think that beliefs, emotions, and desires are semi-independent structures, and, consequently, I do not think that the theory can lead to a reasonable decision of this kind.

The beliefs, emotions, and desires that concern us here are only those that guide how we should live. In our typical decisions about such matters, our beliefs, emotions, and desires are intermingled and cannot be sharply distinguished. Beliefs like that all is well, that we are threatened, have acted stupidly, prudently, morally, or insensitively, that we deserve praise or blame, have been lucky or unlucky, or that we are healthy or unhealthy, are normally inseparable from emotions and desires. Pride, jealousy, indignation, fear, hope, joy, confidence, shame, and guilt are based on our beliefs about their objects. Desire for pleasure, revenge, self-improvement, rest, or the triumph of a cause is unavoidably connected with beliefs and emotions. It is, in fact, a symptom of estrangement from our life if our beliefs about some aspect of our life that we regard as important leave us emotionally flat or without desires.

I stress that the relevant contexts in which beliefs, emotions, and desires routinely occur together are those in which something important is at stake, because it concerns how we should live. This is the context in which unreasonable actions typically occur. There is not much point in deceiving ourselves, rationalizing, bemusing ourselves with wishful thinking, sentimentalizing some aspect of the world, or refusing to follow our own decisions if trivial matters are at stake. It is a costly expenditure of psychic energy to contrive to ignore our own beliefs, emotions, or desires. We normally do so because, often without being aware of it, we want to disguise from ourselves something that might seriously threaten how we live. When we are surprised, threatened, pleased, or chagrined by the way our actions conform to or violate our view of how we should live, our reactions form a complex whole of which beliefs, emotions, and desires are interdependent, overlapping, and reciprocally reinforcing aspects. Our ordinary experience of what is involved in making an important decision about how we should live provides obvious reasons to think that beliefs, emotions, and desires are connected aspects of the same psychological process, not semi-independent structures.

The facts to which I have just appealed are common and well-known. Why, then, does Davidson assume, contrary to these facts, that the beliefs, emotions, and desires involved in unreasonable actions are semi-independent structures? Because he thinks that if we do not make that assumption we cannot answer the question of "What is the agent's reason for doing *a* when he believes it would be better, all things considered, to do another thing?" He assumes that unreasonable actions are signs of conflicts that could not occur if the conflicting items were not semi-independent. But this assumption is mistaken.

It is true that beliefs, emotions, and desires often conflict, that their conflicts may lead us to act contrary to our judgment of what is best, and that the resulting action may be unreasonable. But these truths do not require that the conflicting beliefs, emotions, and desires should be semi-independent structures. They are typically interlocking aspects of complex psychological processes, and they may conflict and prompt us to act in incompatible ways. The explanation of their conflicts is not that they are semi-independent structures that clash, but that we are confused about how to evaluate the relative importance of the overlapping aspects of our deliberations about how we should live. If we must act, we have to make a decision either in favor of beliefs, as the Platonic view says we should, or in favor of desires, as the Humean view has it, or in favor of emotions, as Rousseau and his followers claim. Each of these decisions may or may not be reasonable, depending on how strong the reasons are in favor of the interlocking and conflicting beliefs, emotions, and desires.

A belief that we are being unjustly treated may overwhelm conflicting patriotic emotions and desires and lead us to leave the country. Love may dominate conflicting beliefs and desires about getting divorced. Desire for a quiet life may prove much stronger than conflicting beliefs about civic responsibilities and emotions of shame and guilt for lack of political engagement. Such conflicts are frequent, familiar, and most of us encounter them in some form. When we decide in favor of or against a belief, emotion, or desire in a particular context, we may or may not be reasonable. But there is no reasonable way of assigning priority to one of the conflicting aspects of our complex psychological states before we know their relative strengths and the context in which we must make a decision.

It is certainly true, just as Davidson claims, that the resolution of such conflicts may be unreasonable if it does not take into account all the relevant considerations. But the result of that may be that we find that emotions or desires are more important than beliefs for resolving their conflicts in particular cases. If that happens, we acknowledge the relevant facts, but we may well be ambivalent about the relative importance we attribute to conflicting beliefs, emotions, and desires. We may or may not continue to love someone even if we realize that it is undeserved, or fear snakes if we believe that it is phobic, or desire that justice be done if we believe that it is unlikely. Such ambivalence is common, not merely a theoretical possibility, as the case of the Divided Woman shows.

She is ambivalent because she does not know how she should resolve the conflict between her beliefs, emotions, and desires about her family, writing career, and the environment. She ignores none of them, but she is ambivalent about what relative importance she should ascribe to her beliefs, emotions, and desires about them. If she were overpowered by strong emotions or desires that lead her to ignore her contrary beliefs, she would be unreasonable. But if she did not ignore them and had reasons for regarding her emotions and desires as more important than her conflicting beliefs, then she would not be unreasonable. She may reasonably decide that her love for her children should override her belief that she should be independent; or that her desire to do the best she can for her father should override her belief that she has a responsibility to try to protect the environment.

Generally, it need not be unreasonable to be led by love to override what we rightly believe would serve our self-interest. Nor need it be unreasonable to act as prompted by something we desire very much, like a good marriage, even if we believe that it would be detrimental to a successful career. And whether we have such reasons depends on the evaluations embedded in how we believe, feel, and desire to live. These evaluations may reasonably lead us, in particular circumstances, to regard any one of our beliefs, or emotions, or desires as more important than the others. And we may have good reasons in some cases to regard our emotions and desires as more important than conflicting beliefs. Of course, opting for emotions and desires over beliefs could be unreasonable, but whether it is in fact unreasonable in a particular context depends on weighing the reasons for and against them. Much has been written about the moral weakness of allowing our emotions or desires to override our beliefs. It is true that this often happens, and it may be a sign of weakness. But it is also true that it may show moral strength to be moved by love, fellow feeling, or generosity to override our conflicting beliefs and prompt us to give more than what we believe we owe or not to express what we believe is deserved condemnation because it would be harsh or vindictive.

The conclusion that emerges from these criticisms is that the consideration of all that is relevant need not lead to a decision that reason requires us to follow. It may lead only to a better understanding of the conflicts we face and of the ambivalence we have about how to resolve the conflicts. The consideration of all things may leave us with a number of contrary possibilities each of which is allowed but none of which is required by reason. The implication is that Davidson's ideal theory according to which the consideration of all things will yield a decision that reason requires us to follow is mistaken. The consideration of all things may leave us as ambivalent as we were before we considered all things.

These considerations are strong enough, I think, to justify rejecting the first assumption on which the standard view rests. Beliefs, emotions, desires are not semi-independent structures. It need not be unreasonable to resolve their conflicts in favor of emotions or desires. Whether or not it is reasonable depends on what the beliefs, emotions, and desires are, what relative importance we think they have, and the context in which we have to make the decision. I agree with Davidson that acting against what we believe would be the best may be unreasonable and needs to be explained, but the same is true of acting against what we feel or desire would be the best. Either may show moral weakness or moral strength.

Davidson may concede all this and continue to hold that reason requires doing what we judge to be the best. The problem of the Divided Woman and of us who are like her in having conflicts and being ambivalent about how we should live is that our consideration of all things has not gone as far as it should. This leads to the second mistaken assumption on which Davidson's theory rests, and I will now turn to it.

All Things Considered

Defenders of Davidson's theory may say that conflicts and ambivalence will persist only for those who fail to take into account all relevant considerations. In particular, they fail to consider that the emotions and desires that supposedly override beliefs actually presuppose them. As David Pears puts it, emotions and desires are "quasi-cognitive" in that they are essentially connected with beliefs about their objects.[8] If these beliefs are false, the emotions and desires that presuppose them are misdirected and lead to unreasonable actions. Reason requires, therefore, considering all that is relevant in order to make as sure as possible that our emotions and desires do not presuppose false beliefs. It may be reasonable to let emotions and desires override conflicting beliefs, but only if we have good reasons to believe that the presupposed beliefs are true.

There are two reasons why this defense fails. One is that while it is true that emotions and desires are quasi-cognitive and presuppose beliefs, it is also true that beliefs about how we should live are typically quasi-emotive and quasi-conative because they presuppose emotions and desires. The other is that although decisions arrived at by considering all that is relevant are more reasonable than decisions that do not, the ones based on considering all that is relevant remain inconclusive and actions based on them may still be unreasonable.

Beliefs about how we should live are typically quasi-emotive and quasi-conative because it is natural for us to have emotions of approval or disapproval, satisfaction or dissatisfaction about how we believe we have been living, and it is no less natural to want to change how we live in appropriate ways. Our beliefs about how we live are not merely factual, but also evaluative. They concern the quality of our life, and it is exceptional to be indifferent to that. It is unusual and needs to be explained if we do not care whether we are true to our commitments, satisfied with our life, and whether we want to change it in some way. Such beliefs, emotions, and desires are not semi-independent psychological structures but essentially connected evaluative aspects of our attitude toward our life. Reason requires taking into account the relevant facts, but it also requires evaluating the facts, because the evaluations guide how we live. And that is also a fact that reason requires us to take into account.

The beliefs, emotions, and desires involved in such evaluations often conflict, and we need to find some way of coping with their conflicts. If we fail, we cannot make reasonable decisions about how we should live. But, as I have argued against the first assumption, it is a mistake to assume that reason always requires us to resolve the conflicts in favor of any one of beliefs, emotions, or desires. And it remains a mistake even if it is true that emotions and desires are quasi-cognitive, because, as we have just seen, these beliefs are quasi-emotive and quasi-conative. If the conflicts are resolved by ignoring any one of the relevant beliefs, emotions, or desires, then we act unreasonably. But the cause of that could just as easily be that beliefs stifle contrary emotions or desires that guide how we should live as that emotions or desires overwhelm contrary beliefs that should guide us.

Might this mistake be avoided by relying on the consideration of all that is relevant? No, because all that is relevant may be considered from many different points of view. It may be our individual well-being, or the well-being of those we love, or the standards of our profession, or the interest of our party, country, or religion. Or we may consider them from an aesthetic, economic, legal, moral, personal, political, prudential, religious, or scientific point of view, or from the point of view of what we take to be justice, or God's will, or beauty, or duty, or honor, or the common good, and so forth.

If we deliberate from one of these points of view, we may agree about the relevant facts but evaluate them and rank their relative importance in accordance with the different beliefs, emotions, and desires prompted by the particular point of view from which we proceed. We and others may acknowledge all the relevant considerations, and yet evaluate them in conflicting ways on the basis of different points of view. And these conflicting evaluations may be our own, since only fanatics evaluate the relevant facts from a single point of view. We typically have moral, political, religious, personal, economic, prudential, professional, and other concerns, and they typically lead us to evaluate the same facts differently. For these reasons the consideration of all that is relevant need not resolve our conflicts, but simply move them to a different level. The conflicts will be transformed then into conflicts among the various points of view from which we evaluate the relative importance of our conflicting beliefs, emotions, and desires.

The transformed conflicts cannot be finessed by saying that reason requires that the decision about the point of view from which everything should be considered is included in considering all that is relevant. For the decision about what that point of view should be must also be made from the variety of conflicting points of view to which we, or we and others, are committed. Making such a decision reasonably, therefore, cannot merely consist in the consideration of all that is relevant. How we evaluate the relative importance of our beliefs, emotions, and desires depends on the point of view from which we evaluate them, and these points of view may be as conflicting as are the beliefs, emotions, and desires whose relative importance we try to evaluate.

This does not mean that it is useless to try to make reasonable decisions. It means that not even the most reasonable decision we can make in a particular case will allow us to conclude once and for all which of our beliefs, emotions, or desires, if any, should be always overriding. Nor will the most reasonable decision allow us to conclude that one among the variety of points of view to which we are committed should always override any other that conflicts with it. These are the reasons that count against Davidson's theory that the consideration of all things will yield a decision that should override any conflicting consideration and resolve our conflicts and ambivalence about which of our beliefs, emotions, or desires should guide how we live.

To make these reasons concrete and particular, consider again the Divided Woman. Davidson would say that she should take into account all that is relevant, evaluate how she should cope with her conflicts and ambivalence, and thereby make herself less confused. But this will not help her. For if she evaluated all from the point of view of the writing career she wanted to have, she would decide one way; if she evaluated it from the points of view of her beloved husband, children, and father, she would decide another way; and if she evaluated it from the point of view of her commitment to the environmental cause, she would decide in a third way. And if she left behind these personal points of view and asked more abstractly whether self-interest, family, or civic responsibility is more important than the others, then she would still have to decide from which of the more abstract points of view she should evaluate all the relevant facts.

Whichever of these personal or impersonal points of view she might reasonably adopt, she would have to take into account all the relevant facts. But that alone would not enable her to arrive at a reasonable evaluation, because she would also have to decide about the relative importance of the relevant facts. And the source of her conflicts and ambivalence is precisely that she does not know how to decide about their relative importance. She has beliefs, emotions, and desires about how she should live, but they are conflicting and prompt her to act in incompatible ways. Telling her that reason requires her to rely on the evaluation of all the relevant facts is to tell her that she should do what she does not know how to do.

Suppose, however, that she is more reflective than I have described her as being, has a clear understanding of her conflicts and options, and considers whether it might not be best to make a decision even if it would be arbitrary. If her conflicts and ambivalence weighed on her heavily enough to want to put an end to them, then an arbitrary decision might be better than continued dithering. This would give her a reason to proceed one way. But she would also have a reason against it. For whatever her arbitrary decision would be, it would require her to act contrary to two of the three things she deeply cares about in her life. She would have to be untrue either to her lifelong desire to be a writer, or to the love she feels for her husband, children, and father, or to the environmental cause to which she is passionately committed. And if she were indeed reflective, she would realize that the guilt, shame, and loss of self-respect that might result from her decision could be worse than putting up with the conflicts and ambivalence of her present life. Her problem, then, would be transformed from having to decide what arbitrary decision she should make into the problem of having to decide whether it would be worse if she did than if she did not make an arbitrary decision. And she would have these problems precisely because she has been trying to evaluate how she should live by taking into account all the relevant facts.

Davidson assumes that the outcome of such deliberations will be a decision. I have been trying to show that their outcome may well be indecision. There is no reason to assume that the consideration of all relevant things would lead to closure by yielding a decision that would override all conflicting considerations. It is likely to lead to a much better understanding of our commitments to valued but incompatible ways of living, yet it need not bring us closer to making a decision than we were before. And that the outcome will be indecision becomes more likely as the difficulty of the decision increases. It is an illusion to suppose that if we reason scrupulously and well, it will enable us to understand what would be the best thing to do. It may lead us to understand that there is no best thing to do, that there is only a problem, that whatever we do, we will have to cope with conflicts and ambivalence, and that life is like that.

It may be thought that these criticisms of Davidson's ideal theory of reason as the consideration of all things lead to the relativist view that reasons come to an end. If we must make a decision after we find that reasons come to an end and leave us with conflicts and ambivalence, then we must decide in some other way than by reason. I will now argue that this relativist confusion does not follow from the reasons I have given against Davidson's theory.

What Reason Requires and Allows

Pears rightly observes that "the writ of reason does not extend so far as is commonly assumed." I think he is right, but I do not think he is right when he adds that the commonly held assumption fails because "the more primitive systems of appetite and emotion often run their own affairs."[9] It is, of course, unquestionable that emotions and desires are often not controlled by reason and lead to unreasonable actions. But the writ of reason is limited not only by unruly emotions and desires, but also by the inconclusiveness of reasons even if we reason well and our emotions and desires are under control. Reason may allow us to make contrary decisions about how we should live, without requiring any one of them. This may happen not only because we fail to reason as well as we should, but also because, even if we meet the basic requirements of reason, we may not arrive at conclusive decisions about how we should live.

It is one of the great advantages of living in a civilized society that there are several reasonable, possible, and yet incompatible ways of living open to us. I cannot improve on Peter Strawson's way of putting this point: "Men make for themselves pictures of ideal forms of life. Such pictures are various and may be in sharp opposition to each other; and one and the same individual may be captivated by different and sharply conflicting pictures." This is because "the region of the ethical is the region where there are truths but no truth." "The region of the ethical, then, is a region of diverse, certainly incompatible and possibly practically conflicting ideal images or pictures of a human life."[10] These incompatible ideals are among the riches of the possibilities of civilized life, not a shortcoming of reason. To accept this is not to deny that reason has requirements, but to recognize that once its requirements are met, there often remain several different and contrary possibilities, each allowed by reason.

As far as I know, the distinction between what reason requires and allows was first made explicit by Bernard Gert.[11] I leave aside the question of whether the distinction can be drawn in a general way that applies in all contexts, as, for instance, modus ponens does, and concentrate on drawing it in the context of what reason requires and allows in the context of deciding how we should live.

The minimum requirements of reason in this context are straightforward. The propositional content, if any, of the decisions we make should be logically consistent; take into account the relevant facts; weigh the relative importance of the beliefs, emotions, and desires that guide how we should live; and lead to possible actions that have a realistic chance of achieving their aim. If any of these requirements is not met, the resulting action will be unreasonable. In normal circumstances, barring emergencies, there are many actions that meet these minimum requirements, and all of them are allowed by reason. Reason, however, also requires us to decide which, if any, of the actions that reason allows we should actually perform. One way of making such decisions is to be guided by aesthetic, moral, personal, political, religious, or other points of view, which, of course, may result in decisions that vary from person to person. Reason may also allow us to make no decision, or to make different decisions that follow from different points of view to which we attribute different importance about which of the possibilities reason allows us to adopt. And even when reason requires us to make a decision, it need not require any particular decision.

One implication of the distinction between what reason requires and allows is that questions about what is reasonable are systematically ambiguous. They may be questions about what reason requires or what it allows. To fail to live as reason requires is unreasonable, but it need not be unreasonable not to live in one of the ways that reason allows, because another way of living allowed by reason may also be reasonable.

Davidson's theory ignores this ambiguity, and that is the source of the two mistaken assumptions that I questioned earlier. The theory rightly requires that our decisions about how we should live take into account the relevant facts, including our beliefs, emotions, and desires. But it wrongly assumes that after we have done that we will reach a decision that reason requires us to act on. The consideration of all that is relevant may leave us with a number of alternative ways of acting, each of which is allowed by reason. Reason may allow any one of our beliefs, emotions, or desires to override the conflicting ones, depending on the contents of the beliefs, emotions, and desires that guide how we should live and on the point of view from which we evaluate the relevant considerations. The distinction between what reason requires and allows is uncommitted about the relative importance of the beliefs, emotions, and desires and of the points of view that are allowed, but not required, by reason.

Defenders of the practical approach accept that beliefs should override emotions and desires, but only if they presuppose false beliefs. And they also accept that emotions or desires should override beliefs if the beliefs presuppose misguided emotions or desires, such as overwrought hopes or fears or self-stultifying desires. According to the practical approach, beliefs, emotions, and desires are intermingled; none of them should be deemed always overriding, independently of the context and of the relative importance that we, who have to cope with their conflicts in our life, attribute to them. They stand jointly before the tribunal of reason.

The second mistaken assumption made by Davidson's theory is that the reasonable decisions we make on the basis of all relevant considerations about how we should live will be required by reason. They need not be. They may be decisions that recognize that there are various ways of living that are allowed, but not required, by reason. Consequently, the consideration of all that is relevant may be inconclusive, because it may tell us only what ways of living are allowed by reason. The writ of reason does not extend as far as Davidson supposes, not merely because beliefs, emotions, and desires may be unreasonable, but also because, if we are as reasonable as we could possibly be, we may still not be able to decide which of the decisions allowed by reason we should actually follow.

These reasons against Davidson's theory, however, do not lead to the relativist view that reasons ultimately come to an end and the decisions we then make cannot be based on reasons. In the first place, all decisions that we make can and should meet the minimum requirements of reason. Decisions about how we should act have aims, and the actions they prompt are supposed to be instrumental to achieving the aims. Unless the decisions meet the minimum requirements of reason, the resulting actions cannot be instrumental to achieving whatever their aims are. Practical reasons, therefore, do not come to an end so long as we have aims and make decisions about ways of achieving them.

In the second place, the practical approach does not deny that our conflicts between particular beliefs, emotions, and desires can be reasonably resolved in particular contexts. Very often we have and can give strong reasons why a particular conflict between beliefs, emotions, and desires should be resolved in one way rather than another. But such reasonable conflict-resolutions are particular, context-dependent, and may vary with individuals, times, and societies. This is contrary to the relativist view that reasons come to an end. What comes to an end is the possibility of generalizing to other contexts a particular conflict-resolution that is reasonable in a particular context.

The importance of the distinction between what reason requires and allows is considerable for the dispute—one main concern of this book—between ideal theories and the practical approach, quite independently of what the supposedly overriding ideal is taken to be by ideal theorists. Ideal theories are committed to an ideal that reason requires recognizing as always overriding. The practical approach is committed to denying that reason requires recognizing any ideal as always overriding. According to the practical approach, any ideal allowed by reason may be overriding in a particular context, under particular conditions, but no ideal is always overriding in all contexts, under all conditions. I do not think there is a general way of resolving this dispute between ideal theorists and defenders of the practical approach. It must be resolved by discussing the reasons for and against regarding particular ideals as overriding. This is what I have tried to do in all the preceding chapters, as well as in this one.

Where, then, does this leave the Divided Woman? I think it leaves her conflicts and ambivalence pretty much as they were. Of course she, like virtually all of us, could and probably should be more reasonable than she typically is. My point is that there is no guarantee that if we were as reasonable as we could be, then we could free ourselves from our conflicts and ambivalence. We could and should rely on reason to exclude ways of coping with our conflicts and ambivalence that fail to meet the requirements of reason. In most circumstances, however, many ways allowed by reason remain. Reason would enable us to eliminate the conflicts and ambivalence that encumber us only if it provided a way of making a conclusive decision about which of the various decisions allowed by reason is the most reasonable. But the writ of reason does not extend that far. Even if we carry reason as far as we can, it may leave us with conflicts and ambivalence about which decisions allowed by reason we should act on.

Consider some of the various decisions that reason allows the Divided Woman to make. She may reasonably decide that she should continue pretty much as she has been doing, trying as well as she can to meet her many commitments and enjoy the love, comforts, and security she has. But that, of course, would leave her without the independence she desires, with a frustrated writing career, and with much too much to do. Or she may bite the bullet, neglect her husband, children, father, and the environmental cause, and try her best to become a writer. That would leave her with guilt and shame for being untrue to those she loves and who need and depend on her. Or she may opt for full-time environmental activism, forget about writing, and let her loved ones fend for themselves as well as they can. Reason allows her to make any one of these decisions but requires none of them. So what decision should she make? She has reasons for and against each one. If she continues as before, she in fact makes the first decision with its attendant pros and cons, and the same is true if she makes any of the other decisions.

She could and perhaps should force herself to carry her reasoning further. This would require her to make guesses about the likely consequences of the various decisions she might make. She would have to guess how wrenching her guilt and shame might be, how well or badly her family would be able to cope without her, how important her support for the environmental cause is, how much talent she actually has as a would-be writer, how likely it is that she has the strength of will to actually carry through with whatever she decides, and so on. These are imponderables, and they remain so even if she is as reasonable as it is in her to be.

The upshot is that she will have conflicts and remain ambivalent whatever she decides to do. She will have to live with them even if she makes a decision and concludes in retrospect, perhaps after some years have passed, that it was the best one possible and that if she had to she would make the same decision again. This is not because the Divided Woman is particularly unfortunate or not reasonable enough. It is because she is human and her condition, allowing for differences in particularities, is the human condition. We are all encumbered by conflicts and ambivalence, which we can perhaps ameliorate but not eliminate.

9   Inescapable Reflection

Very refin'd reflections have little or no influence upon us. . . . The *intense*
view of these manifold contradictions and imperfections in human reason
has so wrought upon me, and heated my brain, that I am ready to reject all
belief and reasoning. . . . Most fortunately it happens, that . . . nature herself suffices . . . and cures me of this philosophical melancholy and delirium. . . . I dine, I play a game of backgammon, I converse, and am merry
with friends; and when after three or four hour's amusement, I would
return to these speculations, they appear so cold, and strain'd, and ridiculous, that I cannot find in my heart to enter into them any farther.

DAVID HUME, *A Treatise of Human Nature*[1]

This chapter and the next are critical of Bernard Williams's work on
ethics.[2] Williams is a pivotal contemporary thinker about how we
should live in our present circumstances. He defends the antitheoreti-
cal view shared by the practical approach I am defending. Williams,
therefore, is not an ideal theorist. But he is not a defender of the practical approach, either. He occupies an intermediate position between
ideal theories and the practical approach. His earlier *Ethics and the
Limits of Philosophy* is closer to the practical approach, while his later
Truth and Truthfulness is closer to being an ideal theory. I will concentrate on the earlier work in this chapter and on the later work in chapter 10. The aim of these two chapters, however, is not simply criticism
of Williams's work. I have learned a great deal from it and I agree with
much of it. My aim is to make clearer what the practical approach is
by distinguishing it from Williams's approach, which, I think, remains

too close to ideal theories, contrary to his intention to distance his approach from them.

Here are some illustrations of the tension between his remarks indicating views for and against ideal theories. *Against*: "It is my view, as it is Berlin's, that value-conflict is not necessarily pathological at all, but something necessarily involved in human values, and to be taken as central by any adequate understanding of them" (*Luck*, 72). *For*: "My genealogical story aims to give a pedigree to truth and truthfulness. Some of it aims to be, quite simply true. As a whole, it hopes to make sense of our most basic commitment to truth and truthfulness" (*Truth*, 19). Is our commitment to truthfulness basic, or is it merely one among the variety of conflicting ideals to which we are committed?

Against: "We have an ambivalent sense of what human beings have achieved, and have hopes for how they might live (in particular, in the form of a still powerful ideal that they should live without lies). We know that the world was not made for us, or we for the world, that our history tells no purposive story, and that there is no position outside the world or outside history from which we might hope to authenticate our activities" (*Shame*, 166). *For*: characterizing his genealogical approach, Williams writes, "[It] proceeds by way of abstract argument from some very general and, I take it, indisputable assumptions about human powers and limitations" (*Truth*, 39). Are our assumptions about human powers and limitations indisputable, or are we unable to authenticate them?

Against: "A truthful historical account is likely to reveal a radical contingency in our current ethical conceptions. Not only might they have been different from what they are, but also the historical changes that brought them about are not obviously related to them in a way that vindicates them against possible rivals" (*Truth*, 20–21). *For*: "Our outlook" has "fixed points within it"; "we know that most people in the past have not shared it; we know that there are others in the world who do not share it now. But for us, it is simply there. This does not mean that we have the thought: 'for us, it is simply there.' It means that we have the thought: 'it is simply there.' (That is what it is for it to be, for us, simply there.)" ("Philosophy," 194–95). Does our outlook have fixed points which are simply there, or are they, as other points are, radically contingent?

The *against* passages about "value-conflict" being "necessarily involved in human values," our inability to "authenticate our activities," and the "radical contingency" of our ethical views indicate that he favors the practical approach. And, of course, I agree with them. The *for* passages about "our most basic commitment," "indisputable assumptions," and "our outlook" having "fixed points" indicate that Williams is closer to being an ideal theorist than he intends to be. And these are the parts of his work with which I disagree. I do not know whether he is inconsistent or whether he changed his mind between his earlier and later works. But it is clear, I think, that the *against* and the *for* passages are incompatible and indicate an unresolved tension in Williams's work. If the tension is resolved one way, it veers toward ideal theories. If resolved in the other way, it is close to the practical approach. I now turn to the tension as it appears in Williams's earlier work, represented chiefly by *Ethics*. As before, I begin with a story.

The Dean

The Dean was a much-respected historian of political ideas before he became a dean. The faculty rose up in rebellion against the former dean because he lacked understanding of what a university ought to be. The old dean resigned and the search began for a new one. The faculty wanted one of their own, and the consensus emerged after much discussion that the historian should be the new dean. He was respected, trusted, and known to be reasonable, fair, and tolerant of disagreement. He did not want to be a dean. He wanted to continue his research and teaching, which he enjoyed, cared about, and was good at. But his friends and colleagues impressed on him that he was the best candidate, that they trusted and wanted him, that reforms were needed, that their shared view of what a university should be needed to be protected and pursued, and that if responsible people like him did not accept important positions, then far worse people would, and the conditions of the university would go from bad to worse. He thought hard, hesitated, and consulted his wife and friends outside of the university, and they all agreed that he should accept the unwanted responsibility that had been thrust on him. He did accept it, and now he has been dean for some years.

Being a historian of political ideas, he knew well the conflicts of institutional life, but he knew them from the outside as a scholar and an observer. Being the Dean, he is now personally subject to them day in and day out. He has learned firsthand how it feels to have to grapple with controversial and unpopular decisions. He has to distribute scarce resources, set priorities, mediate between the demands of the administrators above him and those of the faculty over whom he is supposed to preside, pacify the disgruntled who do not get what they genuinely need, and make painful decisions that lead to people losing their jobs or not getting the tenure or promotion they think they deserve.

He chafes under all this. He wants to go back to being a historian and resume his quiet thinking, writing, and teaching. He wants to study controversial decisions and how and why they were made, not to make them himself. He hates being the Dean. He knows that he cannot always hide his dissatisfactions. He is often irritable and has little time for himself, and when he has some breathing space, he is too tired to take advantage of it. But he is a conscientious man. He tells himself that he took the job knowing what it was likely to be, and that it would be irresponsible to resign when the going gets hard, as he knew perfectly well it might become. He is experienced and knowledgeable about academic life, and he freely accepted the position, knowing how onerous it might turn out to be. Still and all, he has only one life to live, it is passing quickly, and many of the decisions he has to make are more or less routine and could be made by any reasonably competent person.

There I leave the Dean for the moment, immersed in academic life. He is forced by his conflicting commitments—to history, to his colleagues, to the view of what a university should be, to his sense of responsibility, and to how he wants to live—to reflect on his life and decide whether he should continue as dean. He knows that he needs to make a decision, because if he makes none, he will in fact have decided to continue. He knows that whatever he decides will have serious consequences for his life and self-respect. He knows that he must decide how he wants his life to go in the future and where his responsibilities to others and to himself lie.

Williams would say that the Dean's predicament, mutatis mutandis, is typical in the modern world. We are all forced by our participation in the institutions and activities of life as it now is in the civilized world to cope with our conflicting commitments to a variety of constantly changing ideals, conditions, and contexts. Their conflicts make us ambivalent about how to resolve the resulting conflicts. That, in turn, forces us to become reflective about them, and "there is no route back from reflectiveness." In the modern world, life has become fraught, and there is "no way in which we can consciously take ourselves back from it" (*Ethics*, 163–64). Let us now consider Williams's view of the consequences of what he supposes is the inescapability of reflection in the modern world.

Reflection

I think Williams is right: conflicts, ambivalence, and contingency are deep truths about our condition. But they are not the whole truth, they do not have the consequences Williams thinks they have, and they do not force reflection on us. Most of us in the modern world, including the Dean, live our lives unaffected by these truths, and we are not unreasonable in doing so. Just as Hume says, these "very refin'd reflections have little or no influence" on us, and most of us would find "these speculations . . . cold, and strain'd and ridiculous" and we would not wish to enter into them.

This is not to say that most of us are not bothered by our vulnerability to conflicts, ambivalence, and contingencies. Of course we are, and of course we have many problems, but they are not the result of reflection on deep truths about our condition. They are just our problems. They are caused by our conflicts and ambivalence that handicap our efforts to take advantage of shifting possibilities and cope with the limits that constrain us in our forever changing context. Conflicts and ambivalence are typically personal and social, and only a few of us, and those only rarely, reflect on their philosophical implications. Williams thinks differently, and I will now consider the reasons for and against his views on the inescapability of reflection.

Williams's fullest account of reflection and its inescapability in modern life is in *Ethics*. He writes, "The basic question is how we are to understand the relation between practice and reflection. The very general kind of judgment that is in question here — a judgment using a very general concept — is essentially a product of reflection, and it comes into question when someone stands back from the practices of the society and its use of these concepts and asks whether this is the right way to go on, whether these are good ways in which we assess actions, whether the kinds of character that are admired are rightly admired" (146). This is indeed a basic question, but Williams's answer stresses the importance of reflection, while the practical approach stresses the importance of practice. Williams thinks that "the modern world is marked by a peculiar level of reflectiveness. . . . The urge to reflective understanding of society and our activities goes deeper and is more widespread in modern society than it has ever been before." And once we embark on reflection, "there is no *route* back, no way in which we can consciously take ourselves back from it" (163–64).

I think these claims are mistaken: the modern world is not marked by a peculiar level of reflectiveness, most people do not stand back and reflect on the practices of their society, and there is a route back from reflection. I begin with the supposed peculiarly high level of reflectiveness in the modern world. The modern world includes about 6 billion people, most of whom live in dire poverty in China, India, some other parts of Asia, Africa, and South America. They do not have the leisure, energy, or education on which reflection depends. Their problem is to obtain the necessities of life, not to assess the practices of their society or ponder the relation between practice and reflection. These billions are certainly part of the modern world, but it is absurd to ascribe to them a peculiarly high level of reflectiveness.

Let us charitably assume that Williams means by the modern world the Western one. Is there a peculiarly high level of reflectiveness here and now? The roughly 300 million Americans are certainly part of the modern Western world. A quick search on Google at the time of writing this (December 2012), informs me about Americans that 35 million adults are below the basic level of literacy; 18 million suffer from some form of mental disorder that significantly disrupts their ability to function from day to day; 20 million are addicted to, as opposed to being occasional users of, drugs and alcohol; a little less than half of the total population believe that God created man pretty much in his present form at one time within the past ten thousand years; about 45 million believe that an evil eye exists and people can cast spells; more than half of all adult women and a little less than half of all adult men believe in ghosts; a substantial majority of the 160 million religious believers accept that the Bible or the prescriptions of their religious authorities are literally true. No one can reasonably ascribe to the many millions of illiterate, insane, addicted, ignorant, superstitious, or simpleminded people the high level of reflectiveness that Williams says is characteristic of the modern world and involves standing "back from the practices of the society" and asking "whether this is the right way to go on, whether these are good ways in which we assess actions, whether the kinds of character that are admired are rightly admired" (*Ethics*, 146).

If we leave statistics behind and consider individuals, we encounter a very large group of poorly or moderately educated people who are immersed in everyday life whose conventional practices guide them to live decently with greater or lesser satisfactions or dissatisfactions. They rarely if ever ask the sort of reflective questions that Williams thinks are inescapable in modern life. They want to get on with their lives. They struggle with their conflicts, make better or worse decisions when they have to, hope that contingencies in the form of good luck will favor them and that they will not have the bad luck of getting some terrible disease, being maimed by drunk drivers or crazed terrorists, or being betrayed by those they trust. They certainly think about their choices, decisions, and difficulties, but they think within the conventional possibilities and limits of their society. They may question particular ones piecemeal, but they do not question all the prevailing possibilities and limits wholesale. They are nonreflectively immersed in whatever form their everyday life takes and are never or rarely engaged in the sort of reflection that Williams thinks is prevalent in modern society and basic to its institutions. Very few people need to be cured of the sort of "philosophical melancholy and delirium" from which Hume intermittently suffered, a malady that is familiar to many philosophers and unfamiliar to most others.

Consider the Dean as a case in point. He is among the best educated and most thoughtful people in modern society, and he certainly thinks about his dissatisfactions with being a dean and the responsibilities of his position. But this kind of thinking is not what Williams means by reflection. The Dean thinks within the framework in which he lives, a framework comprising the university as an institution, history as a profession, and the conditions of public and private life as they exist in his society. His thinking and questioning are internal to that framework. He does not question its possibilities and limits. He questions what is the best thing for him to do, given the possibilities and limits of the framework that he accepts and, on the whole, values. He is committed to what he thinks a university should be, to the precepts that should govern the historical profession, and to the way he wants his private life to go. Educated and thoughtful as the Dean is, he is immersed in the form everyday life takes for him. He is not reflective in the sense

Williams claims is prevalent in the modern world, reflection that involves questioning the whole framework of our life. If the Dean does not qualify as being reflective, then, except for a handful of philosophers or philosophically minded people, there are very few to whom Williams's description applies.

How is it possible that such a fine philosopher as Williams can go so very wrong about what he takes to be the prevalent condition of so many of us in the modern world? The fault lies, I believe, in his failure to bear in mind the large gap between his philosophical views of our condition and the extent to which most people's lives are affected by that view. Williams is right, I think, that our condition includes our commitment to conflicting and contingent ideals and that we are ambivalent about resolving the conflicts we individually happen to face. That this is our condition is not good news. It is not easy to face — really face — its implications.

Most of us in the modern world, however, do not face it, for various reasons. Many may be just ignorant of the facts; or concentrate on earning a living, pursuing a career, and attending to their private affairs. They may lack sufficient education; prudently shy away from radical questioning; find meaning and purpose in religion, family life, or some personal project; seek relief in self-deception or wishful thinking; cultivate cynicism, resignation, irony, or some other form of bad faith. Or they may be content to enjoy the benefits that modern life in affluent circumstances affords those who live here and now in fortunate circumstances. Williams is no doubt reflective in just the way he describes, but it is a mistake to suppose that what he does so well is the same as what others in the modern world also do. And those who do not reflect as Williams does need not be simpleminded, naive, or poorly educated. They may have made a considered decision not to pursue the sort of reflection that Williams thinks is inescapable in the modern world and instead to do as well as they can, given the possibilities and limits of their form of everyday life, just as Sextus, Montaigne, Descartes, Hume, Berkeley, and Murdoch have recommended.[3]

We may acknowledge that conflicts make us ambivalent, that the circumstances that have formed our commitments are contingent, and yet refrain from radically questioning the framework in which we live. The resulting attitude may be to accept that the world was not made for us, nor we for the world, and to realize that even if, impossible as it is, we were to radically alter our present condition, any future condition, given the nature of the world and our psychological constitution, would leave us as subject to conflicts, ambivalence, and contingency as we are now. Radical alteration could change only the particular conflicts we face. We would be ambivalent also about how to cope with the new conflicts. And we would be as vulnerable to contingency as we were before the radical alteration. We can and should do what we can to improve our present condition, but that does not depend on radically changing it. We can use the available possibilities to ameliorate our dissatisfactions without embarking on a Promethean revolt that would destroy the possibilities in the vain hope of overcoming the limits. Nothing we can do will free us from the limits set by conflicts, ambivalence, and contingency. And that nothing includes the reflection Williams advocates. Reflection may make us understand that our present condition is just one form the human condition takes and that part of that condition is that neither it nor our lives will be affected by that understanding of it. As Hume saw, "very refin'd reflections have little or no influence upon us."

Knowledge

I leave the question of how widespread reflection is in the modern world to consider now what Williams thinks are the consequences of reflection for those, many or few, who do reflect. One consequence, he says, is that "reflection characteristically disturbs, unseats, or replaces traditional concepts; and if we agree that, at least as things are, the reflective level is not in a position to give us knowledge we did not have before—then we reach the notably un-Socratic conclusion that, in ethics, *reflection can destroy knowledge*" (*Ethics*, 148). Williams thinks that in the modern world reflection not only can destroy knowledge but has done so. In contrast with the premodern world that existed before "the growth of reflection and the naturalist view of society," now "a certain kind of knowledge with regard to particular situations which used to guide them [people in the premodern world] round their social world and helped them form it, is longer available. Knowledge is destroyed because a potentiality for a certain kind of knowledge has been destroyed." This happens because "thick ethical concepts that were used in a less reflective state might be driven from use by reflection, while the more abstract and general ethical thoughts that would probably take their place would not satisfy the conditions of propositional knowledge" (166–67).

These remarks are more than a little obscure, but, for better or worse, here is how I understand them. Examples of the more abstract and general concepts—Williams calls them thin in contrast with thick ones—are good and bad, right and wrong. What we say about them does not satisfy the conditions of propositional knowledge because reflection has supposedly led us to understand that they are the contingent products of changing contexts. We also have thick concepts, which are concrete and specific, such as treachery, promise, brutality, and courage (*Ethics*, 129), and coward, lie, and gratitude (*Ethics*, 140). Thin concepts also fail to satisfy the conditions of propositional knowledge, because they express our evaluations, which reflect how we see the world, not how the world is. Reflection supposedly reveals this about both the thick and the thin concepts that we use, and that is how reflection destroys knowledge.

Williams thinks that thick concepts have a better chance of standing up to reflection than thin ones. Even thick ones are "open to being unseated by reflection, but [to] the extent that they survive it, a practice that uses them is more stable in face of the general, structural reflections about the truth of ethical judgments than a practice that uses them. The judgments made with these concepts can straightforwardly be true" (*Ethics*, 200). As I understand it, Williams claims that although reflection on the conventional framework of our lives has destroyed knowledge of what is good and bad and right and wrong, we can still know whether someone has made a promise, told a lie, acted brutally or cowardly, or shown or failed to show gratitude.

This contrast between the consequences of reflection for our knowledge and use of thick and thin concepts seems to me unconvincing. If reflection destroys knowledge of thin concepts, then, for the very same reason, it would destroy knowledge of thick concepts. To be sure, we may know that in our context certain acts are, for example, lies, but we also know that in our context those acts are bad or wrong. What we do not know, if what Williams says about the destructiveness of reflection is true, is whether we are justified in characterizing the acts as lies and regarding them as bad or wrong. Perhaps the acts are not lies but familiar exaggerations of advertisements, prudent misinformation about dangerous matters, polite flattery, or tactful evasion of what would hurt someone's feelings. And perhaps even if they are lies, they are not bad or wrong, because the conventional view in that context may be that it is permissible to lie to outsiders, inquisitive busybodies, children, competitors, the authorities, or sick patients, or that all is fair in love and war. If Williams were right, we would not know how we should evaluate such matters, because reflection would make it transparent that our conventional ideals were contingent and conflicting and could not be justified.

According to Williams, the problem is not that reflection leads us to doubt that we in our context know how to describe and evaluate actions, practices, and institutions, but to doubt that our evaluations are justified and, even worse, justifiable. And if we reflect, as we all inescapably do, according to Williams, then we will see the arbitrariness not just of the supposed justification of other people's evaluations, but of our own as well. We will know no better whether our own evaluations are justified than we know it about other people's evaluations. Reflection supposedly makes it transparent to all of us in the modern world that the ideals that guide how we live are ultimately arbitrary. But contrary to Williams's claim, this would be true regardless of whether the evaluations involve the use of thick or thin concepts.

If true, the consequences would be extremely serious, because they would cast doubt on all of our ideals, be they moral, political, legal, religious, aesthetic, economic, or medical. It would make matters worse that the ideals that reflection reveals as arbitrary often make conflicting claims on us and make us ambivalent twice over: once because we understand that they are all arbitrary, and twice because they conflict. And since the ideals are ours and we rely on them to guide how we live, whatever we do to cope with their arbitrariness and conflicts would involve losing something essential to how we want to live. If Williams were right, we should all live in an unrelieved state of confusion about how we want and should want to live. And we would suffer this calamity because we would be reaping the bitter harvest of the reflection to which we are doomed by the understanding of our condition.

These consequences would follow if Williams were right, but I do not think that he is right. Not that he is totally wrong: he is half right and half wrong. He fails to distinguish between our theoretical and our practical knowledge of ideals. Even if he is right and reflection destroys our theoretical knowledge of ideals — the kind of knowledge ideal theories aim at — it need not destroy our practical knowledge of them. Theoretical knowledge of ideals is to know that certain propositions about ideals are true and others are false. Practical knowledge of ideals is to know how to act or not act if we accept them. If Williams is right about the destructive consequences of reflection, then we cannot have theoretical knowledge of our ideals, because our theories will be just as contingent and context-dependent as our ideals are. But we can still have practical knowledge of how to act in accordance with the ideals we have accepted. And, of course, the practical approach relies on practical, not theoretical, knowledge.

Practical knowledge does not consist in knowing that the claims about our ideals are true. It consist in knowing how to act in our context toward "the right person, to the right extent, at the right time, with the right aim, and in the right way." That knowledge "is not for everyone, nor is it easy; that is why goodness is both rare and laudable and noble."[4] Practical knowledge is not for everyone, because it is derived from upbringing and the experiences that some of us might gain from much trial and error, success and failure, familiarity with the context in which we live, and sensitivity to differences in the characters and circumstances of those who are affected by our actions. It is difficult to acquire this kind of practical knowledge. It requires the cultivation of intelligence, attentiveness, imagination, patience, and moderation that follows from acknowledging our fallibility. But this practical knowledge, difficult though it is, remains as available — and rare — in the modern world as it has ever been, because it remains unaffected by reflection that reveals that our ideals are contingent, conflicting, and cannot be justified by an ideal theory or a standard that is not itself context-dependent and contingent.

If we see the Dean — who is like the large majority of more or less comfortable middle-class people in our society — as making use of practical, rather than theoretical, knowledge, then we can see that he is trying to live and act in a reasonable way. He relies on the practical approach to balance the many demands on him, and he does as well as he can to satisfy as many of them as much as he can. He does not live and act in a way that, according to Williams, is characteristic in the modern world. He is not "someone who stands back from the practices of the society and its use of . . . concepts and asks whether this is the right way to go on, whether these are good ways in which we assess actions, whether the kinds of character that are admired are rightly admired" (Ethics, 146). He participates in the conventional practices of our society and uses its concepts, as they exist in the institutional context of a university. He knows perfectly well what acts are loyal or disloyal, friendly or hostile, honest or dishonest, prudent or imprudent, thoughtful or thoughtless, and he knows most of the time that the first in each of these pairs is right and the second wrong. He does not stand back "from his own dispositions" and does not ask "whether there is anything in the view of things he takes from the outside that conflicts with the views he takes from the inside," and for him no "gap opens between the agent's perspective and the outside view" (51–52). He feels at home in his university context, values its possibilities, rues its limits, and struggles with his conflicts, ambivalence, and the contingencies of his life, as we all do in our contexts.

If Williams is right, as I think he is in this regard, then reflection reveals that theoretical knowledge of ideals is unjustified and that it is an illusion to try to construct an ideal theory. But that leaves practical knowledge of ideals and the question of whether reflection shows that it, also, is unjustified. Its justification, of course, cannot be derived from a theory that is independent of the supposedly known ideals, because that would falsely assimilate practical to theoretical knowledge, just as I have criticized Williams for doing. What, then, could justify our practical knowledge and our reliance on it?

The answer is obvious: the success of actions that are guided by it. And it is also obvious what constitutes success: coping with our conflicts and ambivalence and improving our lives in our context and in particular ways. There is no general answer to what constitutes coping and improvement, because there are many differences in our own and other people's characters, circumstances, and contexts. There are reasonable answers to the question of whether particular actions aid, hinder, or do not affect some particular aspect of our life, but the answers vary with contexts and persons. Those in the modern world who are familiar with the academic context, as the Dean is, do know how to evaluate the priorities that guide the Dean's actions. He would be a fool if he fell for the young and sexy Assistant Professor who is seeking tenure and had a torrid affair with her, or if he decided to take time off and hitchhike to California. Naturally, not all evaluations of what is and is not reasonable for the Dean to do are as simple as these.

It is often unclear how much frustration warrants resignation from a responsible position; how far downhill universities have gone to make it reasonable for senior academics to despair of their future; to what extent the Dean, or others in like positions, should use their limited resources to promote excellence or alleviate existing injustice; how to balance the responsibilities of public and private life; how to distinguish between a reasonable compromise and caving in under pressure; and so forth. But in each of these and other difficult cases, there are reasonable and unreasonable decisions that can be made, even if it happens, as it often does, that more than one decision would be reasonable. We often have to choose between reasonable decisions about how we should act in complex circumstances when our knowledge is imperfect and the available evidence is insufficient. This is a fact of life that we need to face. It is often difficult to make reasonable decisions. And even if we succeed in making them, they may turn out to be mistaken. The improvement we rightly want to make may elude us even if we do the best we can. None of this, however, is news. Living reasonably is and has always been difficult. It is not a curse inflicted on us by inescapable reflectiveness in the modern world. And it is not a reason to stop trying to make reasonable decisions. The alternatives are much worse.

The upshot of these considerations is that Williams's view that reflection is widespread in the modern world and that it destroys knowledge of ideals leads to a basic problem that Williams can neither avoid nor satisfactorily resolve. If he claims that reflection is inescapable in the modern world and destroys knowledge of ideals, then it should destroy all knowledge of all ideals. But, as I have argued, it does not, because even if it destroys theoretical knowledge of ideals, practical knowledge of them remains unaffected. If, contrary to what Williams claims, reflection in the modern world is not inescapable and the amount of reflection there is does not destroy practical knowledge of ideals, then Williams is mistaken about his description of "the state of affairs on which the argument of [his] book . . . turn[s]" (*Ethics*, 53). And this mistake, of course, invalidates the argument of *Ethics and Limits of Philosophy*.

Confidence

Regardless of whether reflection is prevalent in the modern world, as Williams mistakenly thinks, or whether it is merely the predilection of a handful of intellectuals, as I believe, Williams claims that those who do reflect understand that our ideals are many, contingent, and conflicting; that we are ambivalent about how to resolve their conflicts; and that we cannot rely on a context-independent ideal theory about how we should live because there can be no such theory. Of course, I agree with him about all this; this is precisely what I have been claiming. It seems to me, however, that the obvious consequence of understanding and accepting these truths is that they reinforce our ambivalence about how to resolve our ubiquitous conflicts. One consequence of reflection, therefore, seems to be that ambivalence emerges as the most reasonable attitude to understanding that all but the most basic ideals—those that concern the satisfaction of basic and universal human needs—are unavoidably many, conflicting, contingent, and context-dependent.

Remarkably, however, Williams thinks that the most reasonable attitude to what reflection leads us to understand is the virtual opposite of ambivalence, namely confidence. What does he mean by confidence? "It is basically a social phenomenon. This is not to deny that when it exists in a society, it does so because individuals possess it in some form." Philosophy cannot "tell us how to bring about confidence. . . . It is a social and psychological question what kind of institutions, upbringing, and public discourse help to foster it" (Ethics, 170). "One question we have to answer is how people, or enough people, can come to possess a practical confidence that, particularly granted both the need for reflection and its pervasive presence in our world, will come from strength and not from the weakness of self-deception and dogmatism" (171). For this we need "a satisfactory way of life (not one that was uniquely so, perhaps)—but what made it so would be the fact that we could live stably and reflectively in it." And this way of life "would have to grow from inside human life" (172). Apart from some remarks about what confidence does not involve—coercion, knowledge, objectivity, dogmatism—this is all Williams says (in Ethics) about confidence.

I must now say that this is barely the beginning of an adequate justification of Williams's surprising claim that reflection may reasonably lead to confidence, rather than to ambivalence. We are told nothing about the content of confidence or about the beliefs, emotions, or desires that are supposed to lead to it. What exactly is it that we are supposed to be confident about if our ideals are as various, conflicting, and contingent as Williams thinks they are? What would show that our confidence is misplaced, excessive, or deficient? Why does reflection lead to confidence rather than to despair, resignation, cynicism, indifference, denial, or, indeed, ambivalence? If confidence is so important, why does Williams not value the unreflective confidence of people who are immersed in everyday life and unquestioningly follow the conventional ideals of their context? Who are some of the real people who are confident in the right way and what is the basis of their confidence? Williams does not ask or answer these questions. He expresses instead—what is for him very uncharacteristic—vague wishes and promises, which he claims make confidence a reasonable alternative to other attitudes we may hold if we accept his view that all but the most primitive of our ideals are various, conflicting, and contingent.

I am not the first to dissent from Williams on this point. In a fine article, Altham poses some tough questions.[5] Williams replies to them and adds the clarification that he claimed in *Ethics* "that modern societies tend to use less thick concepts and rely more on thin concepts, such as 'good,' 'right,' 'obligatory,' that are, significantly, the materials of typically modern ethical theories." "I also claimed," Williams writes, "that, to the extent that our ethical outlooks rely simply on those concepts, they will not give us knowledge. We shall need, rather, something I called 'confidence.' Altham has asked why we need confidence" and "how we could . . . [have] confidence that does not take the form of knowledge" (*Replies*, 207). Williams's answer is that thin concepts do not survive reflection, but some thick concepts do, and we can be confident about our use of them, not of all of them but only some: chastity does not survive reflection, but cruelty and despicability do. He writes that he did not mean that a thick "concept properly deployed is turned by reflection into reflective knowledge: it will not have been validated." "It survives reflection just in the sense that we would not have encountered any consideration that led us to give it up, lose hold on it, or simply drift away from it, as modern societies in the past two centuries or less have, for instance, done one or more of those things in relation to the concept of *chastity*" (207).

Reflection leads us to be "aware, when we think of it, of something that less reflective people were not aware of, that these concepts are not simply given, and this leaves space where confidence, again, is indeed, confidence in seeing the world in these evaluative terms. The thick concept under which we have some pieces of ethical knowledge are not themselves sustained by knowledge, but by confidence" (*Replies*, 208). However, "we do not have any very robust sense of there being a collective cognitive enterprise in ethics, such that we can represent our rejection of alien concepts and our use of our own as in itself an advance in knowledge. Again, this does not mean that we need to be hesitant or double-minded in using our own; if we are not, this just means that we can sustain them with a certain measure of confidence" (208).

I find this answer quite unconvincing. Williams first claims that reflection destroys ethical knowledge (*Ethics*, 147) and that "knowledge is destroyed because a potentiality for a certain kind of knowledge is destroyed" (166). Then he claims that "we have some pieces of ethical knowledge" and those pieces are sustained by our confidence (*Replies*, 208). How could confidence reasonably sustain thick concepts if they have not been validated by some form of knowledge? His answer is that some of them survive "reflection just in the sense that we would not have encountered any consideration that led us to give [them] up, lose hold on [them], or simply drift away from [them]" (207). I repeat this passage because I find it plainly inconsistent with Williams's defense of his influential, persuasive, and repeated argument in *Ethics* that reflection undermines confidence in our conventional ideals and that there is no route back once we start reflecting.

His reply, however, not only is inconsistent with what he claims elsewhere, but it is a poor argument. Imagine a bishop in medieval Europe saying about the then thick concepts of immaculate conception, witchcraft, and heresy that he has not encountered any consideration that leads him to give them up, lose hold on them, or simply drift away from them. We would want to say to the bishop that he should be more inquiring and that he is not entitled to be as confident as he is, unless he has considered the reasons for and against the continued use of these thick concepts. And why should we not say the same thing about thick concepts we now have, such as prosperity, equality, and the free press?

Surely, as Mill rightly argued, it is in everyone's interest to question our ideals; if no one does, then we should have Devil's advocates who will perform the much-needed service. No one who is reflective, in just the sense Williams claims, should say, as he does, that

> there will be some elements in our outlook which are fixed points within it. We believe, for instance, that in some sense every citizen, indeed every human being . . . deserves equal consideration. Perhaps this is less a propositional belief than the schema of various arguments. But in

either case it can seem, at least in its most central and unspecific form, *unhintergehbar*: there is nothing more basic in terms of which to justify it. We know that most people in the past have not shared it; we know that there are others in the world who do not share it now. But for us, it is simply there. ("Philosophy," 194–95)

This is dogmatism pure and simple, and if this is what entitles us to be confident, then it is far more reasonable to be ambivalent.

If reflection indeed destroys theoretical knowledge, if it leads us to understand that our ideals are various, conflicting, and contingent and that they cannot be justified by an ideal theory, then what else could we reasonably be but ambivalent if reflection leads us to understand that our ideals lack the authority we have long supposed they have? To insist nevertheless, as Williams does, that we should be confident is to refuse to face the consequences of his own arguments.

These doubts about confidence are strengthened by another consideration that Williams rightly stresses in other contexts. He writes about unbearable suffering: "The first thing that must be said and never forgotten throughout the discussion is that some suffering is simply unbearable. It can break people. . . . The idea that meaning, or purpose, or understanding, or even, perhaps, a true philosophy could make all suffering bearable is a lie, whether it is told by recruiting sergeants or by ancient sages" (*Past*, 333–34). Further, "There are some areas of philosophy which might be supposed to have a special commitment to not forgetting or lying about the horrors, among them moral philosophy. No one with sense asks it to think about them all the time, but in addressing what it claims to be our most serious concerns, it would do better if it did not make them disappear. Yet this is what in almost all its modern forms moral philosophy effectively does" (54). And lastly, "We have to acknowledge the hideous costs of many human achievements that we value, including this reflective sense itself" (*Shame*, 166).

I find these eloquent passages deeply right, and I wish that Williams had not forgotten them. But the unbearable suffering, past and present horrors, and hideous costs he recognizes in these passages are not acknowledged and are incompatible with the confidence he finds reasonable in *Ethics*. How could it be reasonable to be confident of our ideals, thick or thin, and about our institutions and practices, in view of the facts to which Williams rightly calls attention. The awful truths about the modern world should strengthen our ambivalence and weaken our confidence in our ideals, institutions, and practices.

The Route Back

When Williams says that "there is no route back from reflectiveness," he means that there is "no way in which we can consciously take ourselves back from it" (*Ethics*, 163–64). I interpret him to say that reflection makes us lose innocence, and once lost, it is lost irretrievably. Once we understand that our ideals are various, conflicting, and contingent, we cannot undo that understanding. We can, of course, forget it, deceive ourselves about it, or ignore it, but we cannot return to a state prior to understanding. I believe that it is not an "obvious truth that reflection characteristically disturbs, unseats, or replaces those traditional concepts" that we have accepted prior to reflection (148). Reflection may or may not lead to the loss of innocence, depending on whether we understand innocence as guiltlessness, naïveté, and what may be called a childlike state of mind. Its rough synonym then is purity. Alternatively, it may be understood as a simple, trusting, spontaneous manner of conduct that is without artifice and calculation. Its approximate synonym then is simplicity. Reflection characteristically leads to the loss of innocence as purity, but it need not lead to the loss of innocence as simplicity.[6]

Montaigne insightfully distinguishes between three kinds of innocence, which I will call prereflective, unreflective, and postreflective. Prereflective innocence is "to be simply provided with a nature easy and affable," with a mind that is uninquiring and wants that are moderate. This "makes a man innocent, but not virtuous, exempt from doing ill, but not apt to do good." Unreflective innocence is to live immersed in everyday life, unquestioningly accept its ideals, control oneself "by main force, and, having let oneself be surprised by the first commotions of passions, to arm and tense oneself to stop their course and conquer them" and be like Cato, whose "nature had endowed him with incredible firmness, and he had strengthened it by perpetual constancy." Such people successfully use part of their nature to subdue another part of their nature. Postreflective innocence is possessed by those who no longer have to subdue any part of their nature. They have acquired "so perfect a habituation to virtue that it has passed into their nature. It is no longer a laborious virtue, or one formed by the ordinances of reason and maintained by a deliberate stiffening of the soul; it is the very essence of their soul; its natural and ordinary gait" (*Essays*, 309–10). Such people's carefully cultivated second nature has become their first nature. Reflection has led them to conclude that living by the conventional ideals of their society is preferable to available alternatives. This is the state of mind that Sextus, Montaigne, Descartes, Hume, Berkeley, and Murdoch find more reasonable than the "philosophical melancholy and delirium" to which "very refin'd reflections" lead.[7]

If we are prereflective, we are likely to lose our innocence if reflection leads us to understand that the ideals by which we have been naively living are various, conflicting, and contingent. If we are unreflective, then reflection may or may not lead us to lose our innocence, because we may respond to what we have understood about our ideals by ignoring it, or deceiving ourselves about it, or relying on an authority to assure us that we have misunderstood what we fear reflection has shown us. Reflection need not lead to the loss of post-reflective innocence, not because we may contrive some stratagem for dismissing what we understand, but because we may find that there are good reasons for maintaining our post-reflective innocence, by remaining committed to our ideals, even though we accept that they are various, conflicting, contingent, that we are ambivalent toward them, and that confidence in them would be unwarranted. There are two such reasons.

The first is that reflection may lead us to understand that although it is possible to survive outside of a society and its system of conventional ideals, it is not possible to live a recognizably human life without the countless possibilities and limits that societies provide for those who live in them. We can, of course, leave our society, but if we want to live a civilized life, we must leave it for another society, and that society will also have its system of conventional ideals, which will also be various, conflicting, and contingent, and we will be ambivalent about them too, just as we are about the ideals of the society with which we are familiar.

Reflection will make us understand, then, that if life in our society is not made intolerable by great poverty, severe repression, drastically curtailed opportunities, insecurity, or terror, if it has a tolerably civilized system of conventional ideals, then it is far more reasonable to take advantage of such possibilities as we can and put up with such limits as we must than to exchange its familiar system of conventional

ideals for the unfamiliar ones of another society. Our reflective understanding that the conventional ideals are various, conflicting, and contingent will not weaken the reason we have for accepting that any society in which we might live will have a system of conventional ideals,
so that we might as well live by those that have been made familiar to
us by our upbringing and experiences. This is not to deny the obvious
fact that life in our society has many dissatisfactions. But reflection may
lead us to understand that the dissatisfactions we find and the improvements we think there should be presuppose those ideals of the prevailing conventional system that are unaffected by the dissatisfactions.

We may arrive at the second reason if reflection leads us to seek a system of ideals that are not conventional, a system formed of ideals that
are not various, conflicting, and contingent but in some sense natural,
necessary, and independent of all particular contexts, ideals whose acceptance is required by reason. We will then look for an ideal theory
that will provide such a system of ideals. I have argued throughout this
book that such a theory cannot be found. Suppose reflection leads us to
understand that as well. Then we might mistakenly think that we have
a choice between two possible responses. One is disenchantment with
the human condition, and it may take the form of despair, cynicism, or
seeking refuge in some form of transcendental consolation. The other
is to make the best we can of the unavoidably imperfect system of conventional ideals of the society in which live. But the fact is that we do
not have such a choice.

The second reason whose force reflection may lead us to understand
is that it is not humanly possible to maintain a consistent attitude of disenchantment. Such an attitude must be a pose, because as long as we
are alive, we must live as if we were not disenchanted. We must earn a
living, respond to others, live in some dwelling, clothe ourselves, find
some way of satisfying at least our basic needs, rely on others to do for
us what we cannot do for ourselves, and so on for the countless unavoidable activities of everyday life. Immersion in everyday life is part
of the human condition, and we do not have a choice about its being
the condition in which we live. We can opt out of it, but that is to opt
out of living a human life. And that means that we have no alternative
to accepting that whatever ideals guide how we live will be various, conflicting, and contingent and that because they are, we will be ambivalent about them. If we understand this, then postreflective innocence
about our participation in everyday life becomes possible for us. And

that is the route back from reflection. I do not mean that then we will no longer reflect.

> We shall not cease from exploration
> And the end of all our exploring
> Will be to arrive where we started
> And know the place for the first time.[8]

10 Necessary Truthfulness

The greatest virtue of all — is what existentialists call authenticity, and what the romantics called sincerity. . . . Anyone who is sufficiently a man of integrity, anyone who is prepared to sacrifice himself upon any altar, no matter what has a moral personality which is worthy of respect, no matter how detestable or how false the ideals to which he bows his knee.

ISAIAH BERLIN, *The Roots of Romanticism*[1]

In chapter 9 I gave reasons why, although Williams's earlier work is close to the practical approach, it is nevertheless not close enough because it remains much too sympathetic to ideal theories. In this chapter I will focus on Williams's last book, *Truth and Truthfulness*.[2] It is even closer to ideal theories, because he is concerned with making a case for the necessity of truthfulness for civilized life.

Williams writes that in "modern thought and culture . . . there is an intense commitment to truthfulness . . . an eagerness to see through appearances to the real structures and motives that lie behind them" (1); "we need to understand that there is indeed an essential role for the notion of truth in our understanding of language and of each other. We need to ask how that role may be related to the larger structures of thought which are essential to our personal, social, and political self-understanding" (6). Williams "hopes to make sense of our most basic commitment to truth and truthfulness" (19); he "proceeds by way of abstract argument from some very general and . . . indisputable assumptions about human powers and limitations" (39). He claims that "every society not only needs there to be dispositions [of truthfulness] . . . but needs them to have a value that is not purely functional" (42); "the concept of truth itself—that is to say, the quite basic role that truth plays in relation to language, meaning, and belief—is not culturally various, but always and everywhere the same" (61); "everywhere, trustworthiness and its more particular applications such as that which concerns us here, Sincerity, have a broadly similar content" (93); "truthfulness has an intrinsic value. . . . It can be seen as such with good conscience. Living with truth is just a better way to be" (263).

I think these passages show that in *Truth and Truthfulness* Williams comes very close to being an ideal theorist. But why only close? Because most of the time, but not by any means always, when he discusses our "intense commitment to truthfulness," its "essential role," our "basic commitment" to it, and its "intrinsic value," and says that "living with truth is just a better way to be" he restricts his claims to the context of "modern thought and culture" and "our current ethical conceptions" (20), he concentrates mainly on truthfulness in the context of "a liberal society" (263–on), and he recognizes "a radical contingency in our current ethical conceptions." "Not only might they have been different from what they are," he adds, "but also the historical changes that brought them about are not obviously related to them in a way that vindicates them against possible rivals" (20).

Ideal theorists, being absolutists, insist on the context-independence of the overriding ideal they favor. They regard that ideal as necessary and overriding always and in all contexts. Williams hedges on this. Sometimes he writes as if truthfulness were necessary and overriding in all contexts, and sometimes as if it were necessary and overriding only in our context. I will not dwell on this inconsistency but argue instead that truthfulness is not necessary in our context. I recognize, of course, the importance of truthfulness in our context. But there are also other important ideals that often conflict with truthfulness, and it is not a requirement of reason that such conflicts be always resolved in favor of truthfulness.

The case Williams makes for the importance of truthfulness takes the form of a "genealogical story" (19) that "aims to give a pedigree to truth and truthfulness. Some of it aims to be, quite simply true. As a whole, it hopes to make sense of our most basic commitment to truth and truthfulness" (19). The genealogical approach "proceeds by way of abstract argument from some very general and . . . indisputable assumptions about human powers and limitations" (39). As before, I start with a story about a real person and then consider Williams's genealogical story with reference to it.

The Betrayed Woman

The Betrayed Woman is in her forties, the mother of three children, aged fourteen, twelve, and ten. She is a university graduate who worked for a few years immediately after graduation in a lowly capacity for a corporation, but her heart was not in the job. She wanted a conventional marriage and motherhood. She met her future husband, they discussed and agreed about their plans for the future, and then acted accordingly. The children were born, the years passed, he was earning enough for a not-too-lavish middle-class existence, and she was fully engaged in housewifery and motherhood. The marriage had its ups and downs and the children had the usual growing problems, but on the whole their lives were going as planned. But then her husband had an affair with an attractive, sexy, much younger woman and decided to get a divorce and live with his newfound lover. The divorce settlement awarded the wife custody of the children, the house, their very limited savings, and half the husband's future income. That meant, however, that she and the children had to make do with drastically reduced income. She cannot afford a housekeeper, must struggle to make ends meet, and has to look after and console the children, who are as devastated as she is about her husband's and their father's betrayal. Her age, lack of skills and work experience, and the children's needs make it very difficult for her to get a decent, well-enough-paying job. So she is left trapped in her unfortunate circumstances, approaching middle age, with children who are as miserable and needy as she is herself.

The truth about her condition is that underneath her depression, self-pity, panic, and doubts about her attractiveness and ability to get a decent job, her deepest emotion is rage. She nurtures murderous thoughts about her ex-husband, fantasizes about revenge, and loves the children but resents their incessant and yet understandable demands of her, while feeling desperately sorry for them and for herself. Time passes in their miserable condition and she is becoming a prickly termagant, filled with suspicion, bad temper, and a readiness to blow up at the often-imagined insults she thinks are heaped upon her. She is often overpowered by her rage, makes her children fear what has become her unpredictable awful temper, alienates her few remaining friends and acquaintances, and worsens the already bad conditions of her own and the children's lives.

She neglects the children, fails to manage their inadequate finances, allows the house to fall into disrepair, barely cooks and cleans any more, and has stopped caring about her physical appearance and manners. She is intelligent and honest enough to know all this, and she is as truthful to herself about her and the children's condition as she can be. She thinks and thinks, of course, about what she might do to make matters better. She dismisses out of hand the temptation to cultivate some stratagem for denying the truth about her condition. And that leaves her, she concludes, with two possible courses of action.

One is to continue to be as truthful as she can be about her condition and accept that there is no realistic prospect of improvement, that her rage is justified, and that she can only live on miserably one day at a time, without self-deception, false hopes, and the unwarranted expectation of a miracle. She vaguely remembers a philosophy course from her student days in which she was told to her surprise that according to Sartre, sincerity was a form of bad faith.[3] This leads her to understand that truthfulness about her wretched condition is no remedy of it and that dwelling on it is in fact an obstacle to trying to improve it. She understands that truthfulness is not even the first step toward improving it, because, being truthful, she recognizes that she lacks what it takes to make their condition less wretched. The more truthful she is, the more hopeless she will see her condition.

The second possibility is to stop dwelling on the truth of her condition. Having been truthful, she of course cannot make herself fail to know the truth, but she can stop herself from having it in the center of her attention. She can, instead, take to heart another vaguely remembered philosophical advice, this one given by Hume to men, but it no doubt applies to women as well: "Let a man propose to himself the model of a character, which he approves. Let him be acquainted with those particulars in which his own character deviates from this model. Let him keep constant watch over himself, and bend his mind, by continual effort, from the vices, towards the virtues; and I doubt not but, in time, he will find, in his temper, an alteration for the better."[4] She realizes that improving her condition depends on acting as if she were what she is not, namely, confident, in control of her life, courageously facing the odds against her, cheerful in face of her misfortune, controlling her feelings, and doing what an admirable person that she is not would do if that person were in her ghastly condition. If she were to follow that course of action, she would not be less truthful, but she would ignore the truth about what she is in order to focus on becoming what she knows she is not. That would make it more likely that she might approximate the model of the person she would like to be.

The first course of action is to focus on the truth about her condition as centrally important. The second is to stop dwelling on the truth and focus instead on what she might do to improve her condition. I ask: is it not obvious that in her case there is good reason not to dwell on the truth? If truthfulness were as necessary as Williams thinks, then the answer is that it is not obvious. I think that is not a reasonable answer. Let us now consider the reasons for it that follow from Williams's account of the genealogy of truthfulness.

Genealogy

Williams writes, "I use a method which I call 'genealogy.' It is a descendant of one of Nietzsche's own methods" (18). He uses this method "to give a decent pedigree to truth and truthfulness. Some of it aims to be, quite simply, true. As a whole, it hopes to make sense of our most basic commitment to truth and truthfulness" (19). What, then, is genealogy? "A genealogy is a narrative that tries to explain a cultural phenomenon by describing a way in which it came about, or could have come about, or might be imagined to have come about" (20). But "genealogy is not simply a matter of what I have called real history. There is also a role for a fictional narrative, an imagined developmental story, which helps to explain a concept or a value or institution by showing ways in which it could have come about in a simplified environment containing certain kinds of human interests or capacities, which, relative to the story, are taken as given" (21). Such a fictional account is "an imaginary genealogy." It "proceeds by way of abstract argument from some very general and . . . indisputable assumptions about human powers and limitations" (39).

Here are some examples of genealogies: Hobbes in the *Leviathan* on the state, Hume on justice in the *Treatise*, Hegel on history as the self-realization of *Geist*, and Marx on history as the dialectic of class conflict; more recently, Nozick on the minimum state,[5] Craig on knowledge,[6] and also Williams on truth and truthfulness. Williams calls such genealogies vindicatory. They may or may not be true. But if a vindicatory genealogy is true, it shows that the ideal whose historical development it describes serves a function that is necessary for civilized life. This is the sense in which we cannot live in peace with others unless we have a political organization we can call, very broadly, a state; we cannot do without rules protecting us, so we need justice; and, according to Craig and Williams, we cannot do without knowledge, truth, and truthfulness.

Genealogies may be subversive, not vindicatory. Some examples are Thrasymacus in *The Republic* on justice as the rule of the strong over the weak; Hume in *The Natural History of Religion* on religion as the product of fear; Rousseau in the second *Discourse on the Origin of Inequality* on civilization as the corruption of innocence; and Nietzsche in *The Genealogy of Morals* on Christianity as the product of *ressentiment* and on morality as the revenge of the weak on the strong. Subversive genealogies unmask an ideal by showing that its real function is very different from what its defenders strategically claim for it. The ideal is not a condition of civilized life, but a way of protecting the interests of its defenders. Like vindicatory genealogies, subversive ones may be true or false. If true, they show that the unmasked ideal is not valuable.

Williams, of course, intends his genealogy of truthfulness to be vindicatory and true. It "was designed to bring out, in an abstract form, functional elements in the explanation of truthfulness; that every society not only needs there to be dispositions of this kind but needs them to have a value that is not purely functional" (42). The reason why it cannot be purely functional is that if it were, then something else could possibly perform the same function better, but truthfulness is so basic that nothing else could perform its function. It is impossible, given human nature and our condition, that we might have civilized life without it. "No society can get by . . . with a purely instrumental conception of the values of truth" (59). "The concept of truth itself—that is to say, the quite basic role that truth plays in relation to language, meaning, and belief—is not culturally various, but always everywhere the same" (61). Williams's vindicatory genealogy is meant to explain that this is so because no form of civilized life is possible without truth and truthfulness. And close to the end of the book, he writes that "if the genealogy of truthfulness is vindicatory, it can show why truthfulness has an intrinsic value; why it can be seen as such with a good conscience; why a good conscience is a good thing with which to see it" (263).

Criticisms

I now turn from Williams's account of the genealogy of truthfulness to criticisms of it. To begin with, let us agree that Williams is right about the importance of truthfulness. We really cannot do without it, and we must value it. I ask: why then do we need a genealogy of it? Why bother constructing an imaginary narrative of how truthfulness gets us from the state of nature to civilized life? If we recognize that we cannot live with others without being truthful in most of our dealings with each other, if we see that truthfulness is necessary for civilized life, then why not just say that instead of constructing a fictional narrative whose credentials are admittedly imaginary? We can recognize the necessity of truthfulness by thinking about our lives here and now. There is no need to start with a mythical prehistory and tell a fictional story that traces imaginary steps that we are to assume have taken us from there to here. The necessity of truthfulness does not depend on a true vindicatory genealogy. It depends on facts about basic human needs and about the conditions we need for satisfying them. And those facts make vindicatory genealogies entirely dispensable for our recognition of the importance of truthfulness.

Next, it is a mistake to suppose that the importance of truthfulness is so great as to override any other consideration that may conflict with it. I think there may be good reasons for overriding the claims of truthfulness if more important considerations conflict with it. One such reason emerges if we consider the Betrayed Woman. She has a choice between being truthful, thereby dooming herself to focus on her justified rage, and ceasing to be truthful, thereby allowing herself to focus instead on what she might become and try to improve her life. Surely, she has a good reason to stop herself from dwelling on the wretchedness of her condition. This would not make her untruthful, but it would enable her to focus on more practical matters.

Generalize this. We all know that we will die, may get some terrible disease, or have a serious accident. If we are truthful, we will admit it. But that does not mean we should keep thinking about it. And when we stop thinking about it, we do so because we also have other concerns and thinking about adversities that might befall us would interfere with them. Of course, in some situations being truthful is more important than any other concern we may have then and there. But many situations are not like that.

Do not think only about not dwelling on unpleasant truths that we cannot do anything about. Think also about large areas of civilized life in which few of us are truthful: money matters; sexual fantasies; infidelities; responding to intrusive questions; or admitting, even to ourselves and certainly not to others, that we are envious, crude, vulgar, or hypocritical. If truthfulness about our income and expenses were widespread, there would be no need for vast bureaucracies to enforce the tax code; crimes would not have to be detected; students would not have to examined; witnesses would not have to be sworn in; physicians and lawyers would not have to be admonished to be truthful; and so on and on. Remember, further, the many areas of life that truthfulness would make impossible, such as making jokes, paying compliments, writing satires, playacting, storytelling, bargaining, negotiating, advertising, exaggerating, consoling, writing letters of reference, and the like. Sometimes truthfulness is more important than other concerns, sometimes not. And when it is not, that is because some other concern is more important than it. This does not detract from the importance of truthfulness, but it does show that it is not always more important than anything else that may conflict with it.

All this may be conceded by defenders of the importance of truthfulness, but they can go on to claim that there is always a prima facie reason for being truthful. They may acknowledge that the reasons for it may sometimes be defeated by a stronger countervailing reason but unless defeated, the prima facie reason holds. It may be claimed to be the default position. But this claim will not yield what it is meant to provide.

There are many areas of life, some of them mentioned above, in which there is a prima facie reason not to be truthful. That reason is not a reason for being untruthful, but for not dwelling on the truth. Furthermore, the prima facie reason for truthfulness leaves open the question of what reasons may be stronger than the reason for being truthful. If there are many reasons that may be stronger, as the examples above show that there are, then the general claim that there is always or most of the time a prima facie reason for truthfulness is destroyed. It might be said with equal plausibility that there is a prima facie reason for not dwelling on the truth, but it may be defeated by stronger reasons for dwelling on it. Saying that there is a prima facie reason for something is justified only if the reason holds most of the time and if what needs to be justified are the occasional exceptions to it. But the many examples above and the others that may given show that the prima facie reason for being truthful often does not hold and that the exceptions to it are not rare but a constant feature of civilized life.

There is a prima facie case for truthfulness when we make an assertion that we intend to be believed. But, as Williams rightly, and I think inconsistently, says, we should not fetishize assertion (100). It is true that civilized life would not be possible if we could not most of the time believe one another's assertions. But there are many areas of civilized life other than making assertions. Furthermore, even if the prima facie reason for truthfulness were to hold most of the time, it would not show the necessity of truthfulness. For there are also no less strong prima facie reasons for many other ideals we rightly value, such as security, cooperation, privacy, pursuing happiness in our own way, the rule of law, intimate relationships, and moral, political, religious, and aesthetic concerns. These rightly pursued ideals, or many of them, are also necessary for civilized life. And as we all know, rightly pursued ideals often conflict. We must resolve their conflicts in some way or lose what we rightly value. It is not a foregone conclusion that when truthfulness conflicts with one or another of these ideals, truthfulness should always in all circumstances override whatever conflicts with it. Truthfulness is not always the most important consideration. Williams's genealogy, as an attempt to show that it is, fails.

This conclusion is strengthened by considering what Williams writes about Accuracy and Sincerity. He capitalizes them and calls them virtues of truth (57). Accuracy "consists in the desire for truth 'for its own sake'—the passion for *getting it right*." And "getting it right can be a matter of conscience, honour, or self-respect" (126). That is "the basic reason why Accuracy can be properly treated as a *virtue*, and not simply as a disposition to pick up reliable information" (124). "Sincerity consists in a disposition to make sure that one's assertion expresses what one actually believes" (96), and thus it is virtually a synonym of truthfulness. "We want people to have a disposition of Sincerity which is centred on sustaining and developing relations with others that involve different kinds and degrees of trust." "The disposition itself enables the agent to think clearly and without self-deceit." "Much of one's thought, if one is such an agent, looks outward, to the other people involved and to the relations they have to one" (121). Williams thinks that Sincerity, that is, truthfulness, is compatible with deceit. Part of truthfulness is to know when we ought to be truthful and when it is permissible, or perhaps even required, not to be truthful.

Williams thinks that truthfulness involves Accuracy that aims at the truth. I think there is a serious problem here about truthfulness. Accuracy and truthfulness often pull us in different directions. If we are Accurate in our beliefs about the truth and truthful about their expression, then all should be fine, but we will see in a moment that all may still not be fine. Furthermore, it may be reasonable to be untruthful in the expression of our Accurate beliefs, as well as to be truthful and inaccurate about them. The passion for getting it right may reasonably go together with the unwillingness to be truthful about expressing it. The urge to be truthful may do more harm than good if what we truthfully express is not the truth but what we culpably or inadvertently mistake for it. And these considerations, of course, show that truthfulness does not have "intrinsic value" (263), that "our most basic commitment" cannot be just to "truth and truthfulness" (19) because there are many and various considerations that may reasonably override truthfulness.

I start with doubts about truthfulness in the expression of Accurate beliefs. What could be unreasonable about that is that it must be qualified and curbed by considerations of importance. It is certainly reasonable to be truthful in the expression of Accurate beliefs if the beliefs are important, and if they are truthfully expressed at the right time, in the right context. But of course they may not be. The truthful expression of Accurate beliefs may be a self-indulgent, boring, and pedantic exercise to say what everybody knows or no one apart from oneself cares about. This happens when philosophers write like G. E. Moore; when chroniclers assemble lists about who begat whom; when psychologists compile responses to questionnaires and use a sophisticated statistical technique to show that people can be influenced by the opinions of others, or be manipulated, or be disturbed by traumas; when economists claim to have discovered that people are guided by what they think of as their interests; or when game theorists construct complex mathematical models to demonstrate that civilized life goes better if people trust each other than if they do not.

It is important to be truthful only when something important is at stake. However, it may also be important not to be truthful, especially when something important is at stake. It would not be reasonable to be truthful about secrets entrusted to one in confidence, safeguards against terrorist attacks, the location of nuclear and biological weapons, defensive strategies in case of hostilities, the identity of informants who risk their lives in providing crucial information, or the combinations of safes in which large sums of money are kept. These considerations make it obvious that the truthful expression of Accurate beliefs is not and ought not to be our "basic commitment," because it may conflict with and be overridden by other no less basic commitments. And even if we acknowledge that truthfulness is, in some sense of that far-from-clear term, an intrinsic value, there are also other ideals that have the same claim to having intrinsic value, and these other ideals may, in many cases and contexts, prove to be more important than truthfulness.

Remember further that it may be kind and a testimony to our integrity not to be truthful about Accurate beliefs that we have about the indiscretions of colleagues, competitors, or others. Being truthful about information that will damage others is often malicious, not virtuous. Before Sincerity and authenticity became cults, it used to be thought that reticence was often admirable, spouting Accurate information about ourselves was self-indulgent, and doing so about others was a culpable failure to respect their privacy. Of course there are times when we ought to be truthful even about damaging information, but there are many times when we ought not to be. Nor is it a foregone conclusion that we should always be truthful even to ourselves about our failures, missed opportunities, and embarrassing past moments. It is not that we should deceive ourselves about them. Rather, we should not dwell on them, because doing so may undermine our confidence and present efforts. There are episodes in all of our lives that we wish had not happened, but if we cannot undo them and if they are not symptoms of character defects, then we might reasonably let sleeping dogs lie. This, of course, is what makes it reasonable for the Betrayed Woman not to dwell on her justified rage but, instead of focusing on that incubus, do what she can in order to become a person who can be more confident and better motivated.

A further reminder is needed of our fallibility. It often happens that our truthfully expressed beliefs are inaccurate, not only because many people are inarticulate, but because the beliefs may be false. They may be based on self-deception, wishful thinking, fantasies we take to be real, misremembered episodes, or imagined insults, and then their expression may cause serious harm. They may lead to giving false testimony, to accusing innocent people of imagined offenses, or to being untrustworthy parents, lovers, or friends. But these harms are small-scale. Far more serious harm is caused by dogmatic ideologues, religious fanatics, and perfervid nationalists who indoctrinate followers and persecute supposed enemies on the basis of their truthfully expressed false beliefs. I take these consideration to show that although truthfulness is important, its importance is not always overriding because more important considerations may conflict with and override it.

Vindicatory Genealogies

Assume for the sake of argument that Williams's genealogy of truthfulness somehow has a satisfactory response to the criticisms I have so far expressed. I will now argue that there are strong reasons against accepting any vindicatory genealogical justification or subversive genealogical criticism of any ideal. Before turning to these reasons, I want to get a pseudo-problem out of the way. The genealogical approach is not a new version of the genetic fallacy. It remains a fallacy to confuse the reconstruction of the history of anything with a justification of it. The genealogical approach *is* concerned with the historical development, for instance, of security, justice, knowledge, or truthfulness, but its concern is a special one, namely, to identify the function of its subject and ask whether it is necessary for civilized life. Only if it is necessary could its genealogical account be vindicatory; otherwise, it is not.

The first general reason against relying on the genealogical justification of any ideal has to do with conflicts between ideals that have been genealogically vindicated. Let us grant that Hobbes's genealogy of the state, Hume's of justice, Craig's of knowledge, and Williams's of truthfulness are vindicatory. Their defenders correctly identify each as serving a function that is necessary for civilized life. The state provides security, justice defines and protects rights, and knowledge and truthfulness enable us to cope with the facts of life. Having granted all this, have we granted that the prevailing evaluations of security, justice, knowledge, and truth are justified? Genealogists can give a clear answer to this question only if they specify what the justification of security, justice, knowledge, and truthfulness involves.

If their justification amounts to no more than showing that they are necessary for civilized life, then no one can reasonably disagree with the claim that they are justified. The problem is that vindicatory genealogies can be constructed of many other ideals necessary for civilized life, such as enjoyment, freedom, health, hope, love, meaning, order, responsibility, and so forth. It is a fact of life that these and other necessary ideals of civilized life often conflict. The claim that they are all justified because vindicatory genealogies can be constructed of them amounts to very little unless we are told how to resolve conflicts between genealogically vindicated ideals. Without providing an account of how their conflicts can be reasonably resolved, all vindicatory genealogists have done is to express the no doubt correct wish that it would be good to protect security, justice, knowledge, and truthfulness. We can accept that platitude, however, without relying on a historical reconstruction of how the present conditions of security, justice, knowledge, truthfulness, and all the other ideals we value have been arrived at. If we already value them, we do not need their genealogical vindication. And if we doubt their value, then our doubt will be carried over to the genealogies that are intended to vindicate them. No one in the civilized world would nowadays take seriously a vindicatory genealogy of monarchy, primogeniture, or compulsory church attendance, although each was thought in the past to be necessary for civilized life.

Genealogists may say that we need genealogies not to understand the necessity of an ideal we value, but to understand what its function is. This, however, is not a persuasive claim. We reasonably value protection against murder, assault, theft, and fraud, and we rightly prefer knowledge to ignorance and truth to falsehood without having any information about the past social conditions and the many changes in them that have led to the present conditions of security, justice, knowledge, and truthfulness.

Suppose, then, that genealogists go beyond platitudes, acknowledge that vindicatory genealogies of various ideals we value often conflict, and attempt to provide some reasonable approach to how we should resolve their conflicts. Whatever that approach may be, it would have to provide some reason for valuing one of the conflicting ideals more than another. But if both of them have been justified by vindicatory genealogies, then the justification of preferring one of the conflicting ideals to the other cannot be merely genealogical, because both ideals have already been genealogically vindicated. The consequence is that as a result of conflicting ideals, vindicatory genealogies unavoidably fall short of the justification of whatever they have vindicated. I ask: What then is the point of vindicatory genealogies beyond the intrinsic interest of the historical account implicit in them? If the genetic fallacy is indeed avoided by the genealogical approach, as it certainly should be, then vindicatory genealogies must always fall short of the justification of whatever ideal they aim to vindicate.

To make this concrete, consider again the Betrayed Woman. Assume that Williams's genealogy vindicates truthfulness. It would not be hard to construct a vindicatory genealogy of the need to control rage, to try to rise above adversities, and to take control of one's life. But the Betrayed Woman's predicament is that these genealogically vindicated ideals conflict and she finds it difficult to choose between them. Since these vindicatory genealogies conflict in her case, she cannot resolve her predicament merely by relying on genealogies. She needs something more than ideals vindicated by genealogies: she need to choose between them. Furthermore, it is absurd to suppose that vindicatory genealogical accounts of the historical conditions that shaped the development of truthfulness and self-control in the Western world are necessary for her to find the more that she needs.

Subversive Genealogies

The reason against accepting the genealogical criticism of any ideal has to do with the identification of subversive genealogies. Consider the not-entirely-imaginary examples of Catholic orthodoxy, utilitarian morality, and socialist ideology. Suppose that a genealogy traces the historical development of each and shows that its real function is not what its defenders claim it is. Catholic orthodoxy is intended to coerce others to accept certain dogmas as the sole means of salvation. Utilitarian morality awards to itself exclusive moral authority to decide what the common good is and how it ought to be pursued. And socialist ideology is a means of seizing power and dictating policies that lead to the ideal of egalitarian justice that takes precedence over all considerations that may conflict with it. These subversive genealogies unmask the unfounded dogmatic certainties of their defenders and show that again and again they have led to persecuting dissenters and imposing on others The Way they should live their lives.

If this were the end of the matter, these versions of Catholicism, utilitarianism, and socialism should be consigned to the dustbin of history to join countless other dangerous human follies. But, of course, the last word is far from having been spoken. Catholics, utilitarians, and socialists can acknowledge with various degrees of chagrin the regrettable excesses of the past and explain that they were caused by misguided dogmatists who should have known better. Catholics can leave the complexities of theology to theologians and endeavor to live a Christian life modeled on Christ. Utilitarians can accept a pluralistic view of the common good and acknowledge that there are deontological constraints on how the common good ought to be pursued. And socialists can resist dictatorial tendencies and opt for socialism with a human face. By means of these corrective strategies, which may be sincere and not merely stratagems, they can defuse what the supposedly subversive genealogies are doing and transform them into vindicatory genealogies that have been strengthened by correcting past mistakes.

Moreover, Catholics, utilitarians, and socialists can rightly claim that they are not guilty of special pleading. All ideals and evaluations always have and always will be in need of post hoc corrections and improvements, since we are all fallible and likely to make mistakes. It is unreasonable to abandon important components of the prevailing evaluative framework if they can be corrected in appropriate ways. But it is usually a hard question when that can and cannot, should and should not, be done. Answering it requires making the difficult judgment of whether the status quo can be reformed by small, incremental changes, or whether it is beyond reform and should be abandoned. Cherished ideals rarely disappear suddenly. They usually sink, if they do, slowly under the weight of hundreds of small corrections.

It seems to me that this is one of the reasonable conclusions we can form if we reflect on genealogies that reconstruct historical processes. They can help us understand how and perhaps why what we now have has become what it is. But genealogies will not subvert the ideals because they can be interpreted as spurs to correction, rather than as reasons for condemnation. Nor will they often enable us to say whether a particular genealogy being offered is vindicatory or subversive when we live with slowly changing ideals. Revolutionary changes of the prevailing evaluative dimension of life are rare. What happened during the emergence of philosophy in fifth-century BC Athens, Christianity, the Renaissance, the scientific revolution, and the Enlightenment were momentous but exceptional. They have all been preceded and followed by centuries of gradual changes of sensibility. In the light of the then contemporary uncertainties of those who lived through these times, about where such historical changes might lead, I do not see how most genealogies could be reasonably identified as subversive rather than corrective. Apparently subversive genealogies may become vindicatory by prompting small changes that correct whatever the defects are that all status quos always have.

The claims made on behalf of subversive genealogies, however, are far more ambitious. They aim at revolutionary changes of the prevailing ideals, not at their correction. In the *Republic* Thrasymachus aims to subvert *dikaiosyne*; Hume in *Natural History* wants to unmask religion as the product of fear; Nietzsche in *Genealogy* is bent on destroying conventional morality; and the various genealogies constructed by Pyrrhonian skeptics, Rousseau, Marx, psychoanalysts, Foucault, and other would-be subverters aim to bring about evaluative revolutions. All these apparently subversive genealogies are inconclusive, however, because defenders of each of their targets can reasonably interpret the genealogy as warranting only the correction, not the abandonment, of whatever they aim to subvert. Of course, there have been and are obviously vile and incorrigible ideals that should be unmasked and abandoned. As we learn from history, however, that is not what happens most of the time.

Let us return once more to the Betrayed Woman. Suppose that she becomes convinced by subversive genealogies that truthfulness is a strategy by men to oppress women and that self-control is a non-chemical tranquilizer aimed at the suppression of righteous rage. That will do nothing to enable her to cope with her predicament. For she will still have to decide how she should live, given the wretched circumstances in which she finds herself. And she may come to see that even if truthfulness and self-control have been misused to oppress women, they can be corrected and used well. But this will not help her get out of her predicament. She will still have to decide whether she should opt for rightly used truthfulness or rightly used self-control. So she will still need more than subversive genealogies that have been corrected.

I conclude that no vindicatory genealogies can be relied on as an adequate justification, because genealogically vindicated ideals conflict and justified conflict-resolutions must go beyond genealogies. And I conclude also that no subversive genealogy can be an adequate criticism of any ideal because genealogically subverted ideals can be corrected and thus no longer liable to previous criticisms.

The Very Idea of Genealogies

Williams writes, "History is central to my argument not just because history is central among humanistic disciplines, but because, I am going to argue, philosophy has some very special relations to it."[7] And one very special relation philosophy has to history is illustrated by genealogy, which may be "an imagined developmental story, which helps to explain a concept or value or institution by showing the ways in which it could have come about" (21). I strongly agree that the relation between philosophy and history is special. I cannot think of any other subject, except history itself, whose connection to its history is as intimate and formative. But I do not think that genealogy is an acceptable instance of the intimate connection. I think the use Williams makes of genealogy combines bad history with questionable philosophy.

If genealogies aimed to be real historical accounts, they would be obviously bad histories, because they are fictional or imagined. Good histories get the facts right. If the supposed facts of genealogies are fictional or imagined, then they are rightly scorned by historians. Williams of course makes clear that the genealogies he favors are not meant to be factual historical accounts. But then the connection between history and genealogies is severed. Genealogies are historical only in the sense that they are about the past—but it is an imagined, fictional past, not the real one. Genealogies, then, are philosophical reconstructions of how some of the ideals we now value "could have come about, or might be imagined to have come about" (20). I think that such philosophical reconstructions are questionable.

Kipling's delightful and whimsical children's stories, collected in a volume called *Just So Stories*, tell tales about how the whale got its throat, the camel its hump, and the leopard its spots. Just so, genealogies tell fictional, imaginary stories about how various ideals got to be what they now are. What reason is there for taking these stories seriously? Williams says, "It is a good question how a fictional narrative can explain anything" (21). His answer is that "the power of imaginary genealogies lies in introducing the idea of function where you would not necessarily accept it, and explaining in more primitive terms what the function is" (32). Imaginary genealogies, then, are functional explanations of ideals that proceed "by way of abstract argument from some very general, and . . . indisputable assumptions about human powers and limitations" (39). They are indisputable because they have "such a basic role in human thought that our . . . understanding of human beings in general can take it for granted" (53).

Given indisputable assumptions about human nature, we know that some functions follow from human nature. Imaginary genealogies reconstruct these functions. Human beings must live together, and the indispensable function of the state is to secure order; of justice to protect rights; of knowledge to cope with the environment; and of truthfulness to make communication and cooperation possible. So imaginary genealogies are not "just so" stories, but reconstructions of functions that are required by human nature and civilized life.

Philosophical arguments that proceed from the requirements of human nature and civilized life have been well known since Aristotle first gave them systematic formulation. They are not "just so" stories, but reasonable conclusions based on our understanding of human nature and civilized life. Why, then, do I say that the philosophical reconstructions of genealogies are questionable? Because even if we accept that the ideals serve functions that follow from human nature, it does not follow that these functions are valuable. Williams assumes that their genealogical reconstructions are sufficient to show that the ideals are valuable, but there are strong reasons why they are not sufficient. Some of these reasons are as follows.

First, the fact that an ideal rests on "certain human interests and capacities" and "indisputable assumptions about human powers and limitations" (21) is compatible with deploring those interests, capacities, powers, and limitations. Human nature has been formed by a long evolutionary process. Even if these traits have been valuable in our struggle to adapt to past conditions, our conditions have changed, and some of the traits are no longer valuable. Consider some examples. All societies known to us have to contend with wars and crimes. Wars have been waged throughout history, and violent crimes have been ubiquitous features of civilized life. It is not unreasonable to attribute wars and crimes to human aggression and acquisitiveness. These traits are likely to have been formed in the course of evolution, and they may have served valuable functions, but they are clearly not valuable now, and there are strong reasons for thinking that we would much better off if these functions were no longer served.

Not all human capacities, interests, powers, and limitations are benign and instrumental to our well-being, and consequently not all of them are valuable. A philosophical reconstruction of their genealogy, therefore, is not sufficient to show that the valuable functions they used to serve in the past are valuable now in quite different conditions. Showing that what served a valuable function in past conditions still serves a valuable function in present conditions requires more than a genealogical reconstruction. It requires showing that the ideal is now valuable. Suppose that is done in the cases of the state, justice, knowledge, and truthfulness. But showing that cannot be done by genealogical reconstructions of why they were valuable in the past. If we have reasons for regarding them as valuable now, then genealogical reconstructions are irrelevant and can neither strengthen nor weaken the reasons we now have. And if we have no reasons for regarding them as valuable now, then "describing the way in which [they] came about, or could have come about, or might be imagined to have come about" (20) could not give us reasons in our different conditions now.

Second, assume that the function an ideal serves now is rightly recognized as valuable. From this it does not follow that we have reason to value it more than some other ideal that serves the same function but does it better. Consider an example. All large industrialized societies must have some system of taxation to provide funds for the protection of security, health, and the infrastructure. So we have reason to regard taxation as valuable. But from that it does not follow that a particular system of taxation is more valuable than some other system. The U.S. tax code, for instance, is seventy-five hundred pages long, and only a handful of experts have adequate understanding of it. Surely, a much simplified system of taxation would be more valuable than the present complicated one.

A genealogical reconstruction of the present U.S. tax code would show that it is the outcome of several centuries of political bargaining and compromises, hundreds of small additions and deletions, the success of various interest groups in influencing legislators by means fair or foul, the often intentionally vague formulations of lawyers, and the judgments of those momentarily in power about how great a burden taxpayers could be expected to bear before they would rebel. A genealogical reconstruction of this sordid history will not show that the particular way taxation now serves a necessary function is more valuable than some other way.

To strengthen these reasons, let us go back to the plight of the Betrayed Woman. Suppose that she constructs or, more likely, is told of a genealogy that gives her a deeper understanding of what led to her predicament. She believes that it explains to her satisfaction how in the institution of marriage the expected roles of husbands and wives, the responsibilities for earning a living, raising children, the upkeep of housing, and so forth, came to be divided. The Betrayed Woman, then, will see her predicament as the consequence of the developments that the genealogy reconstructs. I ask: will that improve her condition? will it lessen her rage? will it somehow defuse the conflict between the love and resentment she feels toward her children? will it make her more confident? The reasonable answer to all these questions is obviously no. Why, then, should she take the slightest interest in the construction of a genealogy?

Why would the vast majority of people living in contemporary societies have the slightest interest in the genealogy of the state, when they feel oppressed by impersonal bureaucratic rules? Why should they care about the genealogy of justice, when they are enraged by not getting what they deserve? Why should they be concerned with the genealogy of knowledge when they are trying to understand how a computer program works? And how could they be helped by the genealogy of truthfulness if they wonder whether they should cheat on their income tax? I ask these rhetorical questions not to call into question the value of understanding the conditions under which we live. I ask them to point out that such understanding has a very low priority in the lives of the vast majority of reasonable people living reasonable lives. This is not because they are negligent or culpably ignorant, but because they can cope with their everyday problems quite well without genealogies. Genealogies serve a theoretical purpose that has few and insignificant practical consequences. Williams writes as if the theoretical understanding a genealogical account of truthfulness yields may make us more truthful. It will not.

It will be said by defenders of genealogies that, apart from their intrinsic interest as studies in the history of ideals, the point of genealogies is to raise the question whether some of the prevailing ideals in the context of a society are or are not justified. A subversive genealogy may show that the apparent function of an ideal called into question is not its real function. If a genealogy is subversive, it will show that the ideal is unjustified, and that will be a spur to reforming it. It may show, as many think, that the real function of the U.S. tax code is to protect the wealth of the rich, not the security of all the citizens. If a subversive genealogy shows this, then it is important and needed. But of course it has to show it, not just speculate about it. And it cannot show it by giving an imaginary, fictional account of how the ideal actually came about. The only way of showing that is by a factual account of the function the tax code actually serves now in the present context and by showing that one of the available alternatives to it would better serve the function the tax code ought to have. Such a subversive account will be political and economic, not genealogical or philosophical.

Suppose, however, that the genealogy is not subversive but vindicatory. It would show then that the real function of the U.S. tax code is what its defenders claim: the protection of security, health, and the infrastructure. Showing that, of course, also depends on a factual account of contemporary political and economic realities, and not a genealogical one. But the reasons against the claim that vindicatory genealogies may provide a justification of necessary functions are even stronger than those against subversive genealogies really subverting prevailing practices. For, even if a vindicatory genealogy actually rested on factual research, it would not show that the way the necessary function is really performed by the U.S. tax code is the best available way. Vindicatory genealogies can justify what they vindicate only if they also show that of the available ways the prevailing ones are the best. Vindicatory genealogies, however, cannot show that. They can, at best, only contribute to the identification and evaluation of present possibilities. I conclude that genealogies, regardless of whether they are subversive or vindicatory, cannot be reasonably accepted either as criticisms or as justifications of prevailing ideals. They are speculative "just so" stories that at best may raise questions about ideals that should be asked and answered, but they will not be answered—if they are—genealogically.

Truthfulness and the Practical Approach

Nothing I have argued for in this chapter is intended to disparage the importance of truthfulness. Williams is right: truthfulness is an ideal, and valuing it is necessary for civilized life. The critical part of my argument has been that he goes wrong in two ways. One is by ignoring the fact that other ideals are also necessary for civilized life, that the ideals conflict, and that their conflicts cannot be reasonably resolved always in all circumstances in favor of truthfulness. The other way Williams goes wrong is by supposing that a vindicatory genealogy of truthfulness will show that if other ideals conflict with truthfulness, then reason requires that the conflicts should always be resolved in favor of truthfulness. I have given numerous concrete examples, among them the conflict of the Betrayed Woman, in which reason allows us to recognize that other considerations may be more important than truthfulness. I repeat: none of this detracts from the importance of truthfulness. It detracts only from the inflated importance Williams attributes to it.

There has also been a constructive part of my argument. It is to show how defenders of the practical approach go about resolving conflicts between truthfulness and other ideals. They do not look for a theoretical conflict-resolution that could be generalized to other conflicts between other ideals in other contexts. They focus on the particular context in which truthfulness about a particular matter conflicts with another rightly valued particular ideal, and they weigh the reasons for and against resolving that conflict in that context between those ideals in favor of one or the other. And, of course, my intention was to use this approach to conflict-resolution to strengthen the arguments I have been giving in preceding chapters in favor of the practical approach.

However, I must qualify the arguments I have been giving against Williams's defense of the ideals of reflection and truthfulness in this chapter and the previous one. In chapters 2–8 my arguments have been directed against various versions of ideal theories, but Williams's defense of these two ideals, although close to an ideal theory, is not a full-blown ideal theory. Why, then, have I considered it in a book whose critical targets are ideal theories? For two reasons. One is that Williams shares a basic assumption with ideal theorists, and I think it is mistaken. The assumption is that reason requires that a rightly valued ideal should override any other ideal that conflicts with it. The ideal theories I have discussed claim this for absolutist morality, individual autonomy, reflective self-evaluation, unconditional love, strong evaluation, and practical reason. Williams, like ideal theorists, but without being a full-blown one, claims this for reflection and truthfulness. And that is one reason why I have discussed both of his ideals.

The other reason is to enlarge the scope of the practical approach by showing that it is an alternative not only to ideal theories, but to all attempts to find an ideal so necessary for how we should live that reason requires that it should override any other consideration that may conflict with it. The constructive aim of my argument throughout the book has been to show that the practical approach is a better guide to how we should live and cope with conflicts between ideals. I emphasize, as I have done throughout the book, that the practical approach is practical, not theoretical, and an approach, not yet another competing theory. The form it takes varies with contexts. There can be no authoritative statement of it because that would have to be context-independent, and the possibility of such a statement is just what defenders of the practical approach deny. My argument has been that reason allows, but does not require, following the practical approach. I have claimed that following the practical approach is more reasonable than continuing the fruitless search that has gone on for millennia to find an ideal of how we should live that always overrides all other ideals. There are many reasonable ideals of how we should live, they often conflict, and we have to struggle with resolving their conflicts. That is often difficult, but the difficulty is a consequence of the richness of life in civilized societies that we should value.

11 Conclusion

My hope is to have written a book that will be useful to those who read it intelligently, and so I thought it sensible to go straight to a discussion of how things are in real life. . . . Many authors have constructed imaginary republics and principalities that have never existed and never could; for the gap between how people actually behave and how they ought to behave is so great that anyone who ignores everyday reality in order to live up to an ideal will soon discover he has been taught to destroy himself.

NICCOLO MACHIAVELLI, *The Prince*[1]

The Practical Approach

The aim of the practical approach is to help us live as we should. It focuses on our conflicts in everyday life and on our ambivalence about how we should cope with them. The stories I tell in the preceding chapters illustrate conflicts between incompatible beliefs, emotions, and desires about how we should live; between the moral, personal, political, religious, and other ideals we hold; and between our present self with which we are in some ways dissatisfied and a future self, which we hope will be better. These conflicts are formidable obstacles to living as we think we should. Any way we try to cope with them unavoidably involves acting contrary to some valued part of ourselves. This makes us ambivalent. Furthermore, our efforts to cope with such conflict will also be subject to the conflicts we are trying to cope with. Our conflicted self is the only resource we have for coping with the conflicts of our conflicted self. We have no option but to rely on the only self we have, which is riddled with conflicts and ambivalence and hence it is unreliable. Throughout the book, I have been concentrating on these conflicts, the ambivalence that results from them, and on how the practical approach may nevertheless be a reasonable way of trying to cope with them. It is a particular, context-dependent, pluralist, and reasonable way that is neither absolutist nor relativist.

It focuses on particular conflicts that occur in particular contexts. Coping with them consists in finding a way that enables us to live as close to how we think we should as our often adverse circumstances allow. This is always difficult, and we are ambivalent about how to do it in all but the simplest cases. Nevertheless, we have a strong reason to overcome our ambivalence and act in one way or another, because the failure to do so is far worse than opting for either of the conflicting alternatives. Inaction makes it impossible to live as we think we should, whereas acting on one of the alternatives at least allows us to be faithful to it to the extent to which it is possible, given our conflicted self and the exigencies of our context. Whatever we do, however, will not, except in the most fortunate and therefore rare cases, resolve the conflict once and for all. It will only enable us to find a temporary expedient in a particular context.

This way of understanding the conflicts and what we can do about them shows the impossibility of the absolutist aim to find a conflict-resolution that is a final solution that can be generalized to all cases in which the conflict occurs. The various absolutist conflict-resolutions I have discussed are guided by one of the supposedly overriding ideals of morality, autonomy, reflective self-evaluation, unconditional love, strong evaluation, narrative unity, practical reason, reflection, and truthfulness. All these ideals are valuable, but all of them conflict with other no less valuable ideals, as I have endeavored to show in the preceding chapters. Relying on them will perpetuate, rather than resolve, our conflicts.

The practical approach is incompatible also with the relativist view, according to which coping with our conflicts ultimately involves making a choice for which no further reasons can be given. Such a choice is arbitrary. The relativist mistake is the mirror image of the absolutist one. Absolutists think there is an ultimate conflict-resolution and our task is to find it. Relativists think that since we cannot find it, ultimately no reasonable conflict-resolution is possible. The practical approach aims to show that there is a reasonable nonarbitrary conflict-resolution, although it is not final and cannot be generalized to other contexts. I have proposed in each chapter a possible way in which the protagonist in the story might find such a resolution of the conflict he or she faces.

These considerations are intended to make evident why defenders of the practical approach insist on the context-dependence of reasonable ways of coping with conflicts. The contexts in which conflicts occur are always and unavoidably particular. The conflicts we each face are between different aspects of our psychological condition, which has been formed by our upbringing and experiences, preferences and aversions, satisfactions and dissatisfactions with our life and circumstances, and the complex mixture of moral, personal, political, religious, and other ideals that guide our evaluations of what we recognize as our possibilities and limits. It is unreasonable to suppose that a reasonable way of coping with such conflicts can be generalized to other persons and contexts whose particularities will be very different. And it is not just that the particular facts will vary. Even if the facts were the same in the lives of different people and in different contexts, the relative importance they attribute to them would likely be different.

Absolutists think there are context-independent conflict-resolutions. But they can think that only by ignoring the complexities of individuals and contexts. Defenders of the practical approach recognize these complexities and reject the absolutist view that there is an overriding ideal that reason requires everyone in all contexts to accept as the key to resolving whatever the conflict is. And they reject also the relativist view that because the conflicts are context-dependent, ultimately no way of coping with conflicts can be more reasonable than any other. According to the practical approach, it is possible to find a particular way of coping with a particular conflict in a particular context that is more reasonable than the other possibilities. But finding it always depends on the particularities of persons and contexts. I have attempted to show in each chapter how such a way of coping may be found in the particular case I have discussed.

The practical approach is pluralist, not absolutist or relativist, about ideals. Defenders of each of these three views acknowledge the obvious fact that there are numerous ideals, some of which are moral, personal, political, and religious. And they acknowledge also that these ideals often conflict. Where they differ is about how to cope with the conflicts between ideals. According to the practical approach, reasonable ways of coping with them depend on finding reasons why one ideal should override the conflicting one in a particular context. In some contexts moral ideals are more important than personal, political, or religious ones. In other contexts, their relative importance shifts in favor of another ideal. There are reasons why an ideal should be overriding in a particular context, but the reasons will not carry over to other contexts and other ideals.

The practical approach rejects the absolutist claim that there is an ideal that should always and in all contexts override any other ideal that conflicts with it. All attempts by ideal theorists to show that reason requires everyone to accept that a particular ideal is always overriding have again and again failed throughout the millennia. This has not been because the critics of ideal theories have been unreasonable, but because their criticisms were based on better reasons than the defenders of the ideals could adduce in favor of them. The history of ideal theories is a graveyard in which candidates for overriding ideals are laid to rest.

The relativist claim is that ideals are merely conventional constructs in particular societies. Ultimately no better reasons can be given for them than that they are valued in that society. This cannot be right for two reasons. One is that not all conventionally valued ideals are valuable. History amply shows that some conventionally valued moral, personal, political, religious, and other ideals have been horrendously mistaken and have led to the immense, avoidable, and undeserved suffering of innocent people. No reasonable person could accept that there are no reasons against the conventionally valued ideals of a society that led to mass murders, concentrations camps, and the torture of dissenters for no other reason than that they were suspected of not being wholehearted supporters of some ideal.

The other reason why the relativist claim is mistaken is that some ideals are not merely conventional constructs but concern the satisfaction of needs necessary for human life. No society can endure unless it satisfies the basic needs of at least very many of those who live in it. Even if there are exceptional cases in which basic needs may be overridden by some other consideration, this cannot become a lasting convention, because it would destroy the possibility of human lives and thus of there being any conventions.

The particular, context-dependent, and pluralist aspects of the practical approach are interdependent and reciprocally reinforcing. Taken together, they are reasonable. The distinction between what practical reason requires and allows is central to understanding how defenders of the practical approach think of reasons. The minimum requirements of reasonable ideals of how we should live are logical consistency, coherence, the recognition of relevant facts, and the practical possibility of actually living according to an ideal. In a civilized society there usually are several ideals that meet these minimum requirements. All of them are allowed by reason, but they may conflict. If the conflicting ideals are followed voluntarily, without manipulation, indoctrination, or deception; if it is realistically possible to reject one ideal in favor of another; and if dissatisfactions with life are not the result of the ideal being faulty but of the failure to live according to it; then reason allows living according to any one of the conflicting ideals that meets these conditions. The choice between them, then, is a matter of personal preference.

The practical approach rejects the absolutist view that if all relevant matters are considered, then we can resolve conflicts between ideals in a way that reason requires everyone to follow. I have argued that this requirement cannot be met. All relevant matters can always be considered from several different and conflicting points of view, which may be moral, personal, political, religious, and so forth. The conflicts between these points of view will persist even if we manage the unlikely feat of considering all relevant matters.

The practical approach also rejects the relativist view that conflict-resolutions are ultimately arbitrary, because any ideal to which we can appeal is no more than a conventional construct of a particular society. I have argued against this that some reasonable ideals must be more than conventional because some conventional ideals are contrary to interests that all human beings have and some other ideals are necessary for the satisfaction of basic needs without which human life cannot go on.

The argument of the book has concentrated mainly on the dispute between the practical approach and ideal theories. I have not said nearly enough about why the practical approach is incompatible with relativism. That is why I now stress that the rejection of ideal theories need not lead to the acceptance of relativism. The practical approach, I claim, is an alternative that we have reason to prefer to both absolutist ideal theories and relativism. In addition to the reasons I have given in the preceding chapters, I will now propose three further reasons for rejecting ideal theories: their error of omission, their impracticality, and their implausibility.

The Error of Omission

Hegel's uncharacteristically eloquent words point at the omission I have in mind.

> When we contemplate [the] display of passions and the consequences of their violence, the unreason which is associated not only with them, but even — rather we might say *especially* — with good designs and righteous aims; when we see arising therefrom the evil, the vice, the ruin that has befallen the most flourishing kingdoms which the mind of man ever created, we can hardly avoid being filled with sorrow at this universal taint of corruption. . . . A simple truthful account of the miseries that have overwhelmed the noblest nations and polities and the finest exemplars of private virtue forms a most fearful picture and excites emotions of the profoundest and most hopeless sadness, counter-balanced by no consoling results.[2]

Ideal theorists write as if evil were not a permanent presence in human life. They make theories about the good and say next to nothing about evil. If they think at all about evil, they treat it as deviation from the good. They assume that the good forms the natural background, evil is a falling away from it, and that requires explanation. They explain it by pointing at deplorable social conventions that corrupt our essentially good and reasonable nature and lead us to be or to do evil. Ideal theorists do not ask the obvious question of how some of the social conventions we create, maintain, and follow could be deplorable if we are indeed essentially good and reasonable. If they are deplorable, it is because we make them what they are. The fearful picture of which Hegel rightly reminds us is a human creation and it is what it is because in our nature good and evil dispositions coexist, and sometime one, sometimes the other dominates. The bright side of life is not more natural and no more dominant than the dark side. We are neither essentially good, nor essentially evil, but essentially ambivalent. That is the profound truth that we, theists, agnostics, and atheists alike, can learn from the religious notion of original sin.

I do not believe ideal theorists have learned that truth, and that is the omission for which I am faulting them. I am not alone in this. Hampshire writes that "the known successes of the Nazi movement in Germany and elsewhere ought to have destroyed forever a previous innocence in moral philosophy: an innocence which is evident in Mill and Sidgwick and G. E. Moore, but which extends backward in time to the first utilitarians, and even to Hume and Adam Smith and to other British moralists of their century. They wrote as if it was sufficient to establish some truths about the great goods for mankind, and then deduce from these truths the necessary human virtues and vices and the necessary social policies. It is not sufficient." It is not sufficient because the "unrestrained natural drive to domination is the greatest source of evil . . . interpreted as involving destruction of life, oppression, and misery."[3] We ought to be aware of the danger of such innocence not merely as a result of the evils of Nazism, but also as a result of Communism and various other murderous, oppressive, and inhumane political, nationalistic, racial, and religious ideologies.

To the best of my knowledge, none of the works I have discussed is without this kind of innocence. The only exception, once again, is Williams:

> Some suffering simply is unbearable. It can break people. This is true of physical pain, as is well known to torturers and to those who send agents into the risk of being tortured. Suffering may be such that, even when you are utterly identified with the purpose for which you are suffering, you would give *anything* for it to end. The same can be true of such things as losing a child in a struggle in which, once again, one thoroughly believes. The idea that meaning, or purpose, or understanding, or even, perhaps, a true philosophy could make all suffering bearable is a lie, whether it is told by recruiting sergeants or by ancient sages.[4]

I cite Williams once more for another passage that is deeply right:

> There are areas of philosophy which might be supposed to have a special commitment to not forgetting or lying about the [world's] horrors, among them moral philosophy. No one with sense asks it to think about them all the time, but, in addressing what it claims to be our most serious concerns, it would do better if it did not make them disappear. Yet this is what in almost all its modern forms moral philosophy effectively does. This is above all because it tries to withdraw our ethical interest from both chance and necessity. . . . Everything that an agent most cares

about typically comes from, and can be ruined by, uncontrollable necessity and chance. . . . Necessity and chance and the bad news they bring
with them are deliberately excluded [from moral philosophy].[5]

If ideal theorists faced the facts to which Hegel, Hampshire, and Williams so rightly and forcibly remind us, they would not largely ignore
the horrors of human life and the serious obstacles they constitute to
the pursuit, let alone the achievement, of the supposedly overriding
ideals that the theorists think should guide how we live. Even if one of
their ideals were indeed all they claim for it, it would not be a sufficient
guide to how we should live. We could follow it only if we countered the
evil dispositions that cause the horrors that stand in the way of even the
most excellent ideal.

Impracticality

The impracticality of ideal theories is another reason against continuing the search for them. What I have to say is easily misunderstood as a
disreputable ad hominem argument accusing ideal theorists of hypoc-
risy. I emphasize that my criticism is very different. What I have in
mind is indicated by what two very different thinkers said in a different context. One is Nietzsche: "The only critique of philosophy that is
possible and that proves something . . . [is] trying to see whether one
can live in accordance with it."[6] The other is Wittgenstein: "What is
the use of studying philosophy if all it does for you is to enable you talk
with some plausibility about some abstruse questions of logic, etc. &
if it does not improve your thinking about the important questions of
everyday life."[7] I cite these passages because I think the practicality of
ideal theories depends on whether they make it more likely that those
who hold them will live as, according to the ideal theory, they should.
I doubt that ideal theories pass the test Nietzsche and Wittgenstein
rightly propose.

I begin with pointing out that no reason has been given to suppose
that Kantians are more autonomous than, say, utilitarians; that Aris-
totelians are more virtuous than socialists; that reflective people are
less ambivalent than nonreflective ones; that absolutists are guided by
ideals more than relativists; that those who construct a narrative of
their lives make better decisions than those who are otherwise occu-

pied; or that ideal theorists of practical reason live more reasonably than those who make decisions without having considered all relevant matters. More generally, I know of no reason to think that ideal theorists are better at living as they should than their critics.

If it is unclear that the lives of ideal theorists are improved by their theories, then why should the rest of us do as ideal theorists claim we should and strive to transform our lives in accordance with the ideal they favor? Could it be that ideal theories serve some other purpose than motivating us to follow them? Or could it perhaps be that ideal theories are intended but fail to motivate even those who obviously accept them? What evidence supports the assumption that the acceptance of an ideal theory improves lives? I repeat: the point of these questions is not that ideal theorists are hypocritical, but that reasons are required but lacking in support of the claim that holding an ideal theory will improve the lives of those who hold it. I know of no attempt by ideal theorists to provide such reasons.

It strengthens the need for such reasons that the acceptance of the right ideal theory is neither necessary nor sufficient for living according to it. It is not necessary because it is absurd to suppose that without familiarity with, say, Kantian theory, no one could live an autonomous life; or that those who are ignorant of Frankfurt's theory of reflective self-evaluation and love could not be self-evaluators or wholehearted lovers; or that people could not have been reflective or truthful before Williams's defense of those ideals; and so on for all the ideal theories that have ever been proposed. Ideal theorists have not created the possibility of living according the ideal they favor but have articulated the ideal they found exemplified in the lives of people who could not have followed their theory because it had not yet existed. Lives exemplifying an ideal come first, and a theory about it can only follow. So the acceptance of an ideal theory cannot be necessary for following its ideal.

Nor is the acceptance of an ideal theory sufficient for following its ideal, as shown by the lives of ideal theorists who fail to follow their own theory. Perhaps they regret, feel guilty, or are ashamed for not following it, but it is obvious that it is possible to hold an ideal theory and not live according to it. The egalitarian Cohen wickedly asked in the title of his book: if you are an egalitarian, how come you are so rich? The same question, suitably rephrased, may be asked of more than a few ideal theorists.

Ideal theorists may concede that the acceptance of an ideal theory is neither necessary nor sufficient for following its ideal, but they may still insist that it predisposes those who accept it to follow it. This may be true. What they need to show, however, is that those who follow the ideal do so because they have accepted the ideal theory. Perhaps they would follow the ideal even if they had never heard of the theory. It does not seem obvious that those who have accepted the strongest available ideal theory of a moral, personal, political, religious, or other ideal are more morally good, personally satisfied, politically savvy, or likely to follow the teachings of their religion than people who never heard of the theories. One test of ideal theories is whether living according to them will make lives better than they would be without the theory. If ideal theories are neither necessary nor sufficient for living as they claim we should, and if there is no reason to suppose that they are needed to improve lives, then there is no reason to accept any of them. We may reasonably suspect that the point of ideal theories is to enable those who hold one of them to talk to others about some abstruse questions that arise out of the theories on offer.

Implausibility

Consider how paradoxical is the claim that there is an overriding ideal that reason requires all of us to follow in how we live, even though we live in vastly different times and contexts and have very different psychological dispositions. The claim requires accepting that the same moral, personal, political, religious, or other ideal should be followed by all lives, in all contexts, throughout the immense changes and differences that have existed in the past and continue to exist in the present of humanity. Why would anyone suppose that historians and acrobats, chivalric knights and Chinese peasants, ayatollahs and mountain climbers, nuns and soldiers, Japanese grandmothers and African shamans are required by reason to follow the same ideal? Why suppose that those who have lived their lives in urban and rural, affluent and impoverished, tyrannical and democratic, Christian and Buddhist, ancient and modern, agricultural and mass-producing industrial societies are all unreasonable and fail to live as they should unless they aim at the ideal favored by defenders of some form of absolutism? What could lead highly intelligent and analytic thinkers to make such an implausible claim?

I think the answer is that they suppose that practical reason guiding how we should live is like theoretical reason guiding what we should believe. What we should believe is the truth. And what is true is true for everyone, always, everywhere. It is universal, context-independent, and absolute. Beliefs contrary to it are mistaken. Absolutists suppose that practical reason should be like theoretical reason and aim at being universal, context-independent, and absolute. That is why they suppose that there is an ideal of how we should live, which is like truth in holding for everyone, always, everywhere. And that is why they suppose that living contrary to it is mistaken. They then search and search for such an ideal, and when they do not find it or when they think they have found it but it is not accepted by others, they blame themselves or the recalcitrant others. But their search is futile, because practical reason is not like theoretical reason.

The essential difference between theoretical and practical reason is that the truth is one, whereas reasonable ways of living are many. The truth is what it is regardless of how it affects us. But how we live is essentially connected with how it affects us. The truth is not up to us, and we have no choice about what it is. But how we live is up to us, at least in civilized societies, and we have choices about it. We can choose reasonably or unreasonably. Practical reason guides us to choose reasonably. And that depends on the possibilities available to us and on the limits that constrain us. In civilized societies our possibilities are many more and the limits are many fewer than in barbaric societies. The great advantage of life in a civilized society is that we can choose among the available possibilities, within the prevailing limits, in accordance with our preferences. Since contexts and preferences differ, so will be how we should live.

Absolutists deny this because they mistakenly assume that practical reason should be like theoretical reason. Their implausible claim that reason requires everyone, always, everywhere to live according to one and only one overriding ideal is a consequence of their mistaken assumption. The practical approach is free of this mistaken assumption, and we can rely on it to guide us to live reasonably in the context of civilized societies in a plurality of ways, each of which is allowed, and none required, by practical reason.

Notes

Chapter One

1 David Hume, "The Sceptic," in *Essays, Moral, Political, and Literary* (1741; Indianapolis: Liberty Press, 1985), 180.

2 Plato, *Apology*, trans. Hugh Tredennick, in *The Collected Dialogues*, ed. Edith Hamilton and Huntington Cairns (c. 370 BC; Princeton, NJ: Princeton University Press, 1989), 38.

3 Aristotle, *Nicomachean Ethics* book I, 13; book VI; book X.

4 Immanuel Kant, *Groundwork of the Metaphysics of Morals*, in *The Cambridge Edition of the Collected Works of Immanuel Kant: Practical Philosophy*, trans. and ed. Mary J. Gregor (1785; Cambridge: Cambridge University Press, 1996).

5 John Stuart Mill, "Utilitarianism," in *The Collected Works of John Stuart Mill*, ed. J. M. Robson (1861; Indianapolis: Liberty Fund, 2006), 10:231.

6 Steven Pinker, *The Better Angels of Our Nature: Why Violence Has Declined* (New York: Penguin, 2011).

7 Niall Ferguson, *The War of the World: Twentieth-Century Conflict and the Descent of the West* (New York: Penguin, 2006), preface.

8 Ibid., 649; and R. J. Rummell, *Death by Government* (New Brunswick, NJ: Transaction, 1994).

9 Michael Howard, *The Invention of Peace: Reflections on War and International Order* (New Haven, CT: Yale University Press, 2000), 1.

10 For example, between 1914 and 1918, the Turks massacred about a million and a half Armenians. In the Soviet Union about 2 million prosperous peasants, called kulaks, were murdered in 1931 or deported to concentration camps where they died slowly as a result of forced labor in extreme cold and on a starvation diet, and during the great terror of 1937–1938, 2 million more were murdered. In 1937–1938, the Japanese murdered about a half million Chinese in Nanking. During World War II, about 6 million Jews, 2 million prisoners of war, and a half million Gypsies, mental defectives, and homosexuals were murdered in Nazi Germany.

After India's independence in 1947, over a million Muslims and Hindus were murdered in religious massacres. In the 1950–1951 campaign against so-called counterrevolutionaries in China, about 1 million people were murdered, and the so-called Great Leap Forward of 1959–1963 caused the death of an estimated 16 to 30 million people from starvation. Pol Pot in Cambodia presided over the murder of about 2 million people. In 1992–1995, about two hundred thousand Muslims were murdered in Bosnia by Serb nationalists. In 1994, almost 1 million people were murdered in Rwanda. To this list of mass murders many more could be added from Afghanistan, Argentina, Chile, the Congo, Iran, Iraq, Sudan, Uganda, and numerous other places.

11   "It requires but very little knowledge of human affairs to perceive, that a sense of morals is a principle inherent in the soul, and one of the most powerful that enters into the composition. But this sense must certainly acquire new force, when reflecting on itself, it approves of those principles, from whence it is deriv'd, and finds nothing but what is great and good in its rise and origin." David Hume, *A Treatise of Human Nature*, ed. P. H. Nidditch (1739; Oxford: Clarendon Press, 1978), 619. "Man is naturally good; I believe I have demonstrated it." Jean-Jacques Rousseau, *Discourses on the Origin and Foundation of Inequality among Man*, trans. Donald A. Cress (1754; Indianapolis: Hackett, 1988), 89. "The fundamental principle of all morality, about which I have reasoned in all my works . . . is that man is a naturally good creature, who loves justice and order; that there is no original perversity in the human heart." Jean-Jacques Rousseau, *Letter to Beaumont*, in *Oeuvres completes*, 5 vols. (Paris: Gallimard, 1959–1995), 5:935; cited in and translated by Timothy O'Hagan in *Rousseau* (London: Routledge, 1999), 15. Man is "*not basically* corrupt (even as regards his original predisposition to good), but rather . . . still capable of improvement," and "man (even the most wicked) does not, under any maxim whatsoever, repudiate the moral law. . . . The law, rather, forces itself upon him irresistibly by virtue of his moral predisposition." Immanuel Kant, *Religion within the Bounds of Reason Alone*, trans. Theodore M. Greene and Hoyt H. Hudson (1794; New York: Harper and Row, 1960), 39, 31. It is "no argument against individual freedom that it is frequently abused. Freedom necessarily means that many things will be done which we do not like. Our faith in freedom does not rest on the foreseeable results in particular circumstances but on the belief that it will, on balance, release more forces for the good than for the bad." Friedrich Hayek, *The Constitution of Liberty* (1960; Chicago: Regnery, 1972), 31. "Men's propensity to injustice is not a permanent aspect of community life; it is greater or less depending in large part on social institutions, and in particular on whether they are just or unjust." And "a moral person is a subject with ends he has chosen, and his fundamental preference is for conditions that enable him to frame a mode of life that expresses his nature as a free and equal rational being."

John Rawls, *A Theory of Justice* (Cambridge, MA: Harvard University Press, 1971), 245, 561. "The essence of evil is that it should *repel* us. If something is evil, our actions should be guided, if they are guided by it at all, toward its elimination rather than toward its maintenance. That is what evil *means*. So when we aim at evil we are swimming head-on against the normative current. . . . From the point of view of the agent, this produces an acute sense of moral dislocation." Thomas Nagel, *The View from Nowhere* (New York: Oxford University Press, 1986), 182. "Moral evil is 'a kind of natural defect,'" "acting morally is part of practical rationality," and "no one can act with full practical rationality in pursuit of a bad end." Philippa Foot, *Natural Goodness* (Oxford: Clarendon Press, 2001), 5, 9, 14. "It is human nature to be governed by morality, and from every point of view, including his own, morality earns its right to govern us. We have therefore no reason to reject our nature, and can allow it to be a law to us. Human nature, moral government included, is therefore normative, and has authority for us." Christine M. Korsgaard, *The Sources of Normativity* (Cambridge: Cambridge University Press, 1996), 66.

12 Friedrich Nietzsche, *Human, All Too Human*, trans. R. J. Hollingdale (1879–1880; Cambridge: Cambridge University Press, 1996), 1:517.

Chapter Two

1 Isaiah Berlin, "The Hedgehog and the Fox," in *Russian Thinkers*, ed. Henry Hardy and Aileen Kelly (New York: Viking Press, 1978), 22.

2 Immanuel Kant, *Groundwork of the Metaphysics of Morals*, in *The Cambridge Edition of the Collected Works of Immanuel Kant: Practical Philosophy*, trans. and ed. Mary J. Gregor (1785; Cambridge: Cambridge University Press, 1996), 76.

3 Immanuel Kant, *The Metaphysics of Morals*, in Kant, *Cambridge Edition*, 378–79.

4 John Stuart Mill, *Utilitarianism*, in *The Collected Works of John Stuart Mill*, ed. J. M. Robson (1861; Indianapolis: Liberty Fund, 2006), 10:255, 257, 259.

5 Kurt Baier, *The Moral Point of View* (Ithaca, NY: Cornell University Press, 1966); Kurt Baier, *The Rational and Real* (Chicago: Open Court, 1995); Lawrence C. Becker, *Reciprocity* (London: Routledge, 1986); Richard B. Brandt, *A Theory of the Good and the Right* (Oxford: Clarendon Press, 1979); Alan Donagan, *The Theory of Morality* (Chicago: University of Chicago Press, 1977); Philippa Foot, *Natural Goodness* (Oxford: Clarendon Press, 2001); Alan Gewirth, *Reason and Morality* (Chicago: University of Chicago Press, 1978); R. M. Hare, *The Language of Morals* (Oxford: Clarendon Press, 1952); R. M. Hare, *Freedom and Reason* (Oxford: Clarendon Press, 1963); R. M. Hare, *Moral Thinking* (Oxford: Clarendon Press, 1981); Christine M.

Korsgaard, *Creating the Kingdom of Ends* (Cambridge: Cambridge University Press, 1996); Christine M. Korsgaard, *The Sources of Normativity* (Cambridge: Cambridge University Press, 1996); Christine M. Korsgaard, *Self-Constitution* (Oxford: Clarendon Press, 2009); Thomas Nagel, *Mortal Questions* (Cambridge: Cambridge University Press, 1979); Thomas Nagel, *The View from Nowhere* (New York: Oxford University Press, 1986); Thomas Nagel, *Equality and Partiality* (New York: Oxford University Press, 1991); Thomas Nagel, *The Last Word* (New York: Oxford University Press, 1997); Thomas Nagel, *Mind and Cosmos* (New York: Oxford University Press, 2012); W. D. Ross, *The Right and the Good* (Oxford: Clarendon Press, 1930); W. D. Ross, *Foundations of Ethics* (Oxford: Clarendon Press, 1939); T. M. Scanlon, *What We Owe to Each Other* (Cambridge, MA: Harvard University Press, 1998); Samuel Scheffler, *Human Morality* (New York: Oxford University Press, 1992).

6   Susan Wolf, "Moral Saints," *Journal of Philosophy* 79 (1982): 419–39. The cited passages are on 422 and 424.

7   Nagel, *Equality*, 14.

8   Michel de Montaigne, *Essays*, in *The Complete Works of Montaigne*, trans. Donald M. Frame (1588; Stanford, CA: Stanford University Press, 1943), 758–59.

9   Bernard Williams, "Persons, Character, and Morality," in *Moral Luck* (Cambridge: Cambridge University Press, 1981), 14.

10   Harry G. Frankfurt, *Taking Ourselves Seriously and Getting It Right* (Stanford, CA: Stanford University Press, 2006), 29.

11   Aristotle, *Nicomachean Ethics* 1109a23–29.

12   Aristotle, *Eudemian Ethics* 1214b6–14.

Chapter Three

1   Robert Burton, *The Anatomy of Melancholy*, ed. Thomas C. Faulkner, Nicolas K. Kiessling, and Rhonda L. Blair, vols. 1–3 (1621; Oxford: Clarendon Press, 1989), 1.1.1.5, 1:137–38.

2   Christine M. Korsgaard, *Self-Constitution* (Oxford: Oxford University Press, 2009). References in parentheses are to the pages of this book.

3   A wonderful work tracing the emergence of autonomy as a moral ideal is J. M. Schneewind's *The Invention of Autonomy* (New York: Cambridge University Press, 1998). He writes: "A new outlook that emerged by the end of the eighteenth century centered on the belief that all normal individuals are equally able to live together in a morality of self-governance. All of us, on this view, have an equal ability to see for ourselves what morality calls for and are in principle equally able to move ourselves to act accordingly. . . . These two points have come to be widely accepted—so widely that moral philosophy now starts by assuming them. In daily life they give us

the working assumption that the people we live with are capable of understanding and acknowledging in practice the reasons for the moral constraints we all mutually expect ourselves and others to respect" (4).

4   Ibid., 5.

5   Perhaps the fullest development of moral particularism at the time of
writing this (2012) is Jonathan Dancy's *Ethics without Principles* (Oxford:
Clarendon Press, 2004). See also the anthology and bibliography in *Moral
Particularism*, ed. Brad Hooker and Margaret Little (Oxford: Clarendon
Press, 2000).

6   Dancy, *Ethics without Principles*, 1.

7   This approach is implicit in Annette Baier's *Postures of the Mind* (Minneapolis: University of Minnesota Press, 1985); *Moral Prejudices* (Cambridge,
MA: Harvard University Press, 1994); and *Reflections on How We Live*
(Oxford: Oxford University Press, 2010); Lawrence A. Blum, *Moral Perception and Particularity* (New York: Cambridge University Press, 1994); most
of the essays in Timothy Chappell, ed. *Values and Virtues* (Oxford: Blackwell, 2006), which explores the Aristotelian roots of moral particularism;
John Cottingham's *Philosophy and the Good Life* (Cambridge: Cambridge
University Press, 1998); *On the Meaning of Life* (London: Routledge, 2003);
and *The Spiritual Dimension* (Cambridge: Cambridge University Press,
2005); John McDowell's *Mind, Value, and Reality* (Cambridge, MA: Harvard
University Press, 1998); Iris Murdoch's *The Sovereignty of Good* (London:
Routledge, 1970); and *Metaphysics as a Guide to Morals* (London: Chatto
and Windus, 1992); several of the essays collected in Iris Murdoch's *Existentialists and Mystics* (New York: Allen Lane, 1998); and Roger Teichman's
Nature, Reason, and the Good Life (Oxford: Oxford University Press, 2011).

8   Dancy, *Ethics without Principles*, 2.

9   An excellent account of this line of thought and of its philosophical implications is Jennifer Radden's *Divided Minds and Successive Selves* (Cambridge, MA: MIT Press, 1996). Its bibliography is a helpful guide to the
enormous literature on this much-debated subject.

10   See Lionel Trilling's fine study *Sincerity and Authenticity* (Cambridge, MA:
Harvard University Press, 1971).

11   Peter F. Strawson, "Social Morality and Individual Ideal," in *Freedom and
Resentment* (1961; London: Methuen, 1974), 26.

12   Burton, *Anatomy of Melancholy*, 1:138.

Chapter Four

1   Isaiah Berlin, "Two Concepts of Liberty," in *Four Essays on Liberty* (1958;
Oxford: Oxford University Press, 1969), 154.

2   Harry G. Frankfurt, *The Importance of What We Care About* (Cambridge:
Cambridge University Press, 1988); Harry G. Frankfurt, *Necessity, Voli-*

tion, and Love (Cambridge: Cambridge University Press, 1999); Harry G. Frankfurt, "Replies," in *Contours of Agency*, ed. Sarah Buss and Lee Overton (Cambridge, MA: MIT Press, 2002); Harry G. Frankfurt, *The Reasons of Love* (Princeton, NJ: Princeton University Press, 2004); Harry G. Frankfurt, *Taking Ourselves Seriously and Getting It Right* (Stanford, CA: Stanford University Press, 2006). I will refer to these works in the text as *Importance*, *Necessity*, "Replies," *Love*, and *Taking & Getting*, along with the page number on which the cited passage appears.

3   See, e.g., Buss and Overton, *Contours of Agency*; David Widerker and Michael McKenna, eds., *Moral Responsibility and Alternative Possibilities* (Aldershot: Ashgate, 2003), and the extensive bibliography in each volume.

4   David Hume, "The Sceptic," in *Essays, Moral, Political, and Literary* (1741; Indianapolis: Liberty Press, 1985), 159–60.

5   Berlin, "Two Concepts," 172.

6   John McDowell, "Virtue and Reason," in *Mind, Value, and Reality* (Cambridge, MA: Harvard University Press, 1998), 55–56.

7   Stanley Cavell, *Must We Mean What We Say?* (1958; Cambridge, MA: Harvard University Press, 1976), 52.

8   Ibid., 60.

9   McDowell, "Virtue and Reason," 61.

10 Ibid., 63.

Chapter Five

1   William Shakespeare, *Othello*, act 5, scene 2, 340–43.

2   Harry G. Frankfurt, *Taking Ourselves Seriously and Getting It Right* (Stanford, CA: Stanford University Press, 2006), 3, 44–45; Harry G. Frankfurt, *The Importance of What We Care About* (Cambridge: Cambridge University Press, 1988); Harry G. Frankfurt, *Necessity, Volition, and Love* (Cambridge: Cambridge University Press, 1999); Harry G. Frankfurt, "Replies," in *Contours of Agency*, ed. Sarah Buss and Lee Overton (Cambridge, MA: MIT Press, 2002); Harry G. Frankfurt, *The Reasons of Love* (Princeton, NJ: Princeton University Press, 2004). I will refer to these works, as I did in chapter 4, as *Taking & Getting*, *Importance*, *Necessity*, "Replies," and *Love*, along with the page number on which the cited passage appears. In the current chapter, parenthetical references are to *Taking & Getting* unless otherwise noted.

3   In discussing sentimentalism, I draw on I. A. Richard's *Practical Criticism* (London: Routledge, 1929); Anthony Savile's *The Test of Time* (Oxford: Clarendon Press, 1982); and Michael Tanner, "Sentimentality," *Proceedings of the Aristotelian Society* 77 (1976–1977): 127–47.

4   Savile, *Test of Time*, 238–39.

Chapter Six

1   Walter Jackson Bate, "Negative Capability," in *John Keats* (Cambridge, MA: Harvard University Press, 1963), 249.
2   R. W. B. Lewis, *The American Adam: Innocence, Tragedy, and Tradition in the Nineteenth Century* (Chicago: University of Chicago Press, 1955), 1–2.
3   Bate, "Negative Capability," 249.
4   Charles Taylor, introduction to *Human Agency and Language* (New York: Cambridge University Press, 1985), 1.
5   References in the text are to the following works by Taylor: "What Is Human Agency?" and "Self-Interpreting Animals," both in *Human Agency and Language* and both referred to as *Agency*; and *Sources of the Self* (Cambridge, MA: Harvard University Press, 1989), referred to as *Self*.
6   Bernard Williams, "The Women of Trachis" (1996), in *The Sense of the Past*, ed. Myles Burnyeat (Princeton, NJ: Princeton University Press, 2006), 54.
7   Adam Smith, *The Theory of Moral Sentiments* (1759; Indianapolis: Liberty-Classics, 1976), 386.

Chapter Seven

1   Stuart Hampshire, *Justice Is Conflict* (Princeton, NJ: Princeton University Press, 2000), 33–34.
2   Some defenders of the narrative ideal are as follows. Jerome Bruner, "Life as Narrative," *Social Research* 54 (1987): 11–32; Jerome Bruner, *Acts of Meaning* (Cambridge, MA: Harvard University Press, 1990); David Carr, *Time, Narrative, and History* (Bloomington: Indiana University Press, 1986), which traces the narrative ideal in the history of European thought from Dilthey to Husserl to Heidegger to Sartre; Gregory Currie, *Narratives and Narrators* (Oxford: Oxford University Press, 2010); Daniel Dennett, "The Self as a Center of Narrative Gravity," in *Self and Consciousness* (Hillsdale, NJ: Lawrence Erlbaum Associates, 1992), 103–15; Owen Flanagan, *Varieties of Moral Personality* (Cambridge, MA: Harvard University Press, 1993); most of the articles in the anthology Daniel D. Hutto, ed. *Narrative and Understanding Persons*, Royal Institute of Philosophy Supplement 60 (Cambridge: Cambridge University Press, 2007); Alasdair MacIntyre, *After Virtue*, 2nd ed. (Notre Dame, IN: University of Notre Dame Press, 1984) (parenthetical references in the chapter are to the pages of this work); Paul Ricoeur, *Time and Narrative*, 3 vols., trans. Kathleen McLaughlin and David Pellauer (Chicago: University of Chicago Press, 1985–1988); Marya Schechtman, *The Constitution of Selves* (Ithaca, NY: Cornell University Press, 1997); Marya Schechtman, "Stories, Lives, and Basic Survival," in Hutto, *Narrative and Understanding Persons*, 155–78; Marya Schechtman,

"The Narrative Self," in *The Oxford Handbook of the Self*, ed. Shaun Gallagher (Oxford: Oxford University Press, 2011), 394–416, which is an excellent survey of the literature; Charles Taylor, *Sources of the Self* (Cambridge, MA: Harvard University Press, 1989); J. David Velleman, "The Self as Narrator," in *Self to Self* (Cambridge: Cambridge University Press, 2006): 203–23.

A more equivocal defense of the narrative ideal by way of genealogy is Bernard Williams, *Truth and Truthfulness* (Princeton, NJ: Princeton University Press, 2002). In "Life as Narrative," *European Journal of Philosophy*, 17 (2007): 305–14, Williams is critical of MacIntyre's version and proposes, but does not develop, an alternative version. Alexander Nehamas, *Nietzsche: Life as Literature* (Cambridge, MA: Harvard University Press, 1985), also connects narratives to Nietzsche's version of genealogy. And William Dray, *Laws and Explanation in History* (Oxford: Clarendon Press, 1957), stresses the centrality of narrative explanation to historiography.

3   Some critics of the narrative ideal are David A. Jopling, *Self-Knowledge and the Self* (New York: Routledge, 2000); John Kekes, *The Human Condition* (Oxford: Clarendon Press, 2010), chapter 4; Peter Lamarque, "On the Distance between Literary Narratives and Real-Life Narratives," in Hutto, *Narrative and Understanding Persons*, 117–32; Donald F. Spence, *Narrative Truth and Historical Truth* (New York: Norton, 1982); Galen Strawson, "Against Narrativity," *Ratio* 17 (2004): 428–52; Galen Strawson, "Episodic Ethics," in Hutto, *Narrative and Understanding Persons*, 85–115.

4   Bruner, "Life as Narrative," 15.

5   MacIntyre, *After Virtue*, 219.

6   Schechtman, "Narrative Self," 395.

7   Taylor, *Self*, 47.

8   MacIntyre, in *After Virtue*, claims that "personal identity is just that identity presupposed by the unity of the character which the unity of a narrative requires"; "all attempts to elucidate the notion of personal identity independently of and in isolation from the notions of narrative, intelligibility, and accountability are bound to fail"; without "accountability narratives would lack that continuity required to make both them and the actions that constitute them intelligible," and "the relationship is one of mutual presupposition." And "to ask 'What is the good for me?' is to ask how best I might live out that unity and bring it to completion," where the "it" is the narrative quest (all on 218). Writing in partial agreement with Sartre, he says, "We agree in identifying the intelligibility of an action with its place in a narrative sequence" (214).

9   Taylor, *Self*, 47; and "making sense of my present action . . . requires a narrative understanding of my life" (48).

10   MacIntyre, *After Virtue*: "A social setting may be an institution, it may be what I have called a practice, or it may be a milieu of some other human kind. But it is central to the notion of a setting as I am going to understand

it that a setting has a history, a history within which the histories of individual agents not only are, but have to be situated" (206).

11 MacIntyre, *After Virtue*: "There is no present which is not informed by some image of some future and an image of the future which always presents itself in the form of a *telos* — or of a variety of ends or goals — towards which we are either moving or failing to move in the present" (215–16).

12 "The heart of my argument is this: eventually the culturally shaped cognitive and linguistic processes that guide the self-telling of life narratives achieve the power to structure experience, to organize memory, to segment and purpose-build the very 'events' of a life. In the end, we *become* the autobiographical narratives by which we 'tell about' our lives." Bruner, "Life as Narrative," 15.

13 "A social setting may be an institution, it may be what I have called a practice, or it may be a milieu of some other human kind." MacIntyre, *After Virtue*, 206.

14 "An individual is constituted by the language and culture which can only be maintained and renewed in the communities he is part of. The community is not simply an aggregation of individuals; nor is there simply a causal interaction between the two. The community is also constitutive of the individual in the sense that the self-interpretations which define him are drawn from the interchange which the community carries on." Taylor, *Self*, 8.

15 Ibid., 17.

16 Bruner, "Life as Narrative," 15.

17 Taylor, *Self*, 47.

18 Ibid., 48.

Chapter Eight

1 Arthur O. Lovejoy, *The Great Chain of Being* (1936; New York: Harper and Row, 1960), 312.

2 Donald Davidson, "How Is Weakness of Will Possible?" in *Essays on Actions and Events* (1970; Oxford: Clarendon Press, 1980), 21–42 (referred to in the text as "Weakness"); Donald Davidson, "Paradoxes of Irrationality," in *Philosophical Essays on Freud*, ed. Richard Wollheim and James Hopkins (Cambridge: Cambridge University Press, 1982), 289–305 (referred to in the text as "Paradoxes"). The bibliography of works discussing Davidson's theory is too large to be listed here. I list only some works that are centrally relevant to it: Alfred R. Mele, *Irrationality* (New York: Oxford University Press, 1987); David Pears, *Motivated Irrationality* (Oxford: Clarendon Press, 1984); Christine Korsgaard, "Skepticism about Practical Reason," in *Creating the Kingdom of Ends* (Cambridge: Cambridge Univer-

sity Press, 1996); and Sebastian Gardner, *Irrationality and the Philosophy of Psychoanalysis* (Cambridge: Cambridge University Press, 1993). For bibliographies and relevant essays, see *The Oxford Handbook of Rationality*, ed. Alfred R. Mele and Piers Rawling (New York: Oxford University Press, 2004); *Weakness of Will and Practical Irrationality*, ed. Sarah Stroud and Christine Tappolet (Oxford: Clarendon Press, 2003); and *Ethics and Practical Reason*, ed. Garrett Cullity and Beryl Gaut (Oxford: Clarendon Press, 1997).

3   Immanuel Kant, *Critique of Pure Reason*, trans. Norman Kemp Smith (1953; London: Macmillan, 1787), A 298.

4   Plato, *Protagoras*, trans. W. K. C. Guthrie, in *The Collected Dialogues*, ed. Edith Hamilton and Huntington Cairns (c. 370 BC; Princeton, NJ: Princeton University Press, 1989), 352–58.

5   Aristotle, *Nicomachean Ethics*, trans. W. D. Ross, rev. J. O. Urmson, in *The Complete Works of Aristotle*, ed. Jonathan Barnes (c. 350 BC; Princeton, NJ: Princeton University Press, 1984), book 7.

6   Plato, *Protagoras*, 352.

7   David Hume, *A Treatise of Human Nature* (1739; Oxford: Clarendon Press, 1978), 413 and 415.

8   Pears, *Motivated Irrationality*, 145.

9   Ibid.

10 Peter F. Strawson, "Social Morality and Individual Ideal," in *Freedom and Resentment* (1961; London: Methuen, 1974), 26, 29.

11 Bernard Gert, *The Moral Rules* (New York: Harper and Row, 1966), revised and expanded as *Morality* (New York: Oxford University Press, 1998).

Chapter Nine

1   David Hume, *A Treatise of Human Nature*, 2nd ed. rev. P. H. Nidditch (1739; Oxford: Clarendon Press, 1978), 268–69.

2   Bernard Williams, *Moral Luck* (Cambridge: Cambridge University Press, 1981); Bernard Williams, *Ethics and the Limits of Philosophy* (London: Fontana/Collins, 1985), 163–64; Bernard Williams, *Shame and Necessity* (Berkeley: University of California Press, 1993); Bernard Williams, "Replies," in *World, Mind, and Ethics*, ed. J. E. J. Altham and Ross Harrison (Cambridge: Cambridge University Press, 1995); Bernard Williams, *Truth and Truthfulness* (Princeton, NJ: Princeton University Press, 2002); Bernard Williams, *The Sense of the Past*, ed. Myles Burnyeat (Princeton, NJ: Princeton University Press, 2006); Bernard Williams, "Philosophy as a Humanistic Discipline," in *Philosophy as a Humanistic Discipline*, ed. A. W. Moore (Princeton, NJ: Princeton University Press, 2006). I will refer to these works in the text as *Luck, Ethics, Shame*, "Replies," *Truth, Past*, and "Philosophy," in each case followed by the page number.

3   Immersion in everyday life, according to Sextus, is "attending to what is
apparent . . . in accordance with everyday observances. . . . These everyday
observances seem to . . . consist in guidance by nature, necessitation by
feelings, handing down laws and customs, and teaching kinds of expertise."
Sextus Empiricus, *Outlines of Scepticism*, trans. Julia Annas and Jonathan
Barnes (c. end of first century BC; Cambridge: Cambridge University
Press, 1994), 9. Montaigne says: "It is an absolute perfection and virtually
divine to know how to enjoy our being rightfully. We seek other conditions
because we do not understand the use of our own, and go outside of ourselves because we do not know what it is like inside. Yet there is no use
mounting on stilts, for on stilts we must still walk on our own legs. And on
the loftiest throne in the world we are still sitting on our own rump. The
most beautiful lives, to my mind, are those that conform to the common
human pattern, with order, but without miracle and without eccentricity."
Michel de Montaigne, *Essays*, in *The Complete Works of Montaigne*, trans.
Donald M. Frame (1588; Stanford, CA: Stanford University Press, 1943),
857. Descartes echoes it: "I formed for myself a provisional moral code . . .
to obey the laws and customs of my country" and of "governing myself in
all other matters according to the most moderate and least extreme opinions—the opinions commonly accepted in practice by the most sensible
of those with whom I should have to live." René Descartes, *Discourse on
the Method of Rightly Conducting One's Reason and Seeking the Truth in the
Sciences*, in *The Philosophical Writings of Descartes*, vols. 1-2, trans. John
Cottingham et al. (1637; Cambridge: Cambridge University Press, 1985),
1:122. Hume expresses it this way: "Custom, then, is the great guide of
human life. It is that principle alone, which renders our experience useful
to us, and makes us expect, for the future, a similar train of events with
those which have appeared in the past." David Hume, *Essay concerning
Human Understanding*, ed. Tom L. Beauchamp (1748; Oxford: Oxford University Press, 1999), 122. Berkeley thinks that "although it may, perhaps,
seem an uneasy reflection to some, that when they have taken a circuit
through so many refined and unvulgar notions, they should at last come to
think like other men: yet, methinks, this return to the simple dictates of
nature, after having wandered through the wild mazes of philosophy, is not
unpleasant. It is like coming home from a long voyage: a man reflects with
pleasure on the many difficulties and perplexities he has passed through,
sets his heart at ease, and enjoys himself with more satisfaction for the
future." George Berkeley, preface to *Three Dialogues between Hylas and
Philonous* (1713; Indianapolis: Hackett, 1979). Murdoch says: "Perhaps the
best that can be said, and that is indeed a great deal, is that [we should] re-
semble the Buddhist master who said that when he was young he thought
that mountains were mountains and rivers were rivers, then after many
years of study and devotion he decided that mountains were not mountains and rivers were not rivers, and then at last when he was very old and

wise he came to understand that mountains are mountains and rivers are rivers." Iris Murdoch, *Existentialists and Mystics* (New York: Allen Lane, 1998), 234.

4   Aristotle, *Nicomachean Ethics*, trans. W. D. Ross, rev. J. O. Urmson, in *The Complete Works of Aristotle*, ed. Jonathan Barnes (Princeton, NJ: Princeton University Press, 1984), 1109a23–29.

5   J. E. J. Altham, "Reflection and Confidence" in Altham and Harrison, *World, Mind, and Ethics*, 156–69.

6   Philosophical discussions of innocence are meager. As we will see, Montaigne is illuminating on the subject, especially in "On Cruelty," in *Essays*. Soren Kierkegaard's *Purity of Heart*, trans. D. V. Steere (1847; New York: Harper and Row, 1948) is a perfervid edifying treatment of it. Nicolai Hartmann's *Ethics*, trans. S. Coit (1926; London: Allen and Unwin, 1932), vol. 2, chapter 18, deals with it. Frances Myrna, "Purity in Morals," *Monist* 66 (1983): 283–97, is a good critical examination of Hartmann's views; Herbert Morris, "Lost Innocence," in *On Guilt and Innocence* (Berkeley: University of California Press, 1976), is a very good modern discussion. And so is Stuart Hampshire's *Innocence and Experience* (Cambridge, MA: Harvard University Press, 1989). Peter Johnson's *Politics, Innocence, and the Limits of Goodness* (London: Routledge, 1988) has a useful bibliography. See also my own "Constancy and Purity," *Mind* 92 (1983): 499–518; and my "Purity and Judgment in Morality," *Philosophy* 63 (1988): 453–69.

7   See note 3.

8   T. S. Eliot, "Little Gidding," *Four Quartets*, in *The Complete Poems and Plays, 1909–1950* (New York: Harcourt, Brace, 1952), 145.

Chapter Ten

1   Isaiah Berlin, *The Roots of Romanticism* (Princeton, NJ: Princeton University Press, 1999), 139.

2   Bernard Williams, *Truth and Truthfulness* (Princeton, NJ: Princeton University Press, 2002). Parenthetical references in the text are to the pages of this work.

3   "What then is sincerity except precisely a phenomenon of bad faith?" and "the essential structure of sincerity does not differ from that of bad faith since the sincere man constitutes himself as what he is *in order not to be it.*" Jean-Paul Sartre, *Being and Nothingness*, trans. Hazel E. Barnes (1943; New York: Philosophical Library, 1956), 63 and 65.

4   David Hume, "The Sceptic," in *Essays, Moral, Political, and Literary* (1741; Indianapolis: Liberty Press, 1985), 170. Hume, of course, relies on Aristotle's *Nicomachean Ethics* in the quoted lines.

5   Robert Nozick, *Anarchy, State, and Utopia* (New York: Basic Books, 1974).

6   Edward Craig, *The Mind of God and the Works of Man* (Oxford: Clarendon Press, 1987).

7   Bernard Williams, "Philosophy as a Humanistic Discipline," in *Philosophy as a Humanistic Discipline*, ed. A. W. Moore (Princeton, NJ: Princeton University Press, 2006), 180.

Chapter Eleven

1   Niccolo Machiavelli, *The Prince*, trans. David Wootton (1513; Indianapolis: Hackett, 1994), chapter 15, 48.

2   G. F. W. Hegel, *Reason in History*, trans. R. S. Hartman (1837; New York: Liberal Arts, 1953), 26–27.

3   Stuart Hampshire, *Innocence and Experience* (Cambridge, MA: Harvard University Press, 1989), 77–78.

4   Bernard Williams, "Unbearable Suffering," in *The Sense of the Past* (Princeton, NJ: Princeton University Press, 2006), 334.

5   Bernard Williams, "The Women of Trachis," in *Sense of the Past*, 54.

6   Friedrich Nietzsche, "Schopenhauer as Educator," in *Untimely Meditations*, trans. R. J. Hollingdale (1874; Cambridge: Cambridge University Press, 1983), 187.

7   Ludwig Wittgenstein, in a letter to Norman Malcolm, cited in Norman Malcolm's *Ludwig Wittgenstein: A Memoir* (Oxford: Oxford University Press, 1958), 39.

Bibliography

Altham, J. E. J., and Ross Harrison, eds. *World, Mind, and Ethics*. Cambridge: Cambridge University Press, 1995.

Aristotle. *Eudemian Ethics*. Translated by J. Solomon. In *The Complete Works of Aristotle*, ed. Jonathan Barnes. Princeton, NJ: Princeton University Press, 1984.

———. *Nicomachean Ethics*. Translated by W. D. Ross. Revised by J. O. Urmson. In *The Complete Works of Aristotle*, ed. Jonathan Barnes. Princeton, NJ: Princeton University Press, 1984.

Baier, Annette. *Moral Prejudices*. Cambridge, MA: Harvard University Press, 1994.

———. *Postures of the Mind*. Minneapolis: University of Minnesota Press, 1985.

———. *Reflections on How We Live*. Oxford: Oxford University Press, 2010.

Baier, Kurt. *The Moral Point of View*. Ithaca, NY: Cornell University Press, 1966.

———. *The Rational and Real*. Chicago: Open Court, 1995.

Bate, Walter Jackson. "Negative Capability." In *John Keats*. Cambridge, MA: Harvard University Press, 1963.

Becker, Lawrence C. *Reciprocity*. London: Routledge, 1986.

Berkeley, George. *Three Dialogues between Hylas and Philonous*. Indianapolis: Hackett, 1979. First published 1713.

Berlin, Isaiah. "The Hedgehog and the Fox." In *Russian Thinkers*, ed. Henry Hardy and Aileen Kelly. New York: Viking Press, 1978.

———. *The Roots of Romanticism*. Princeton, NJ: Princeton University Press, 1999.

———. "Two Concepts of Liberty." In *Four Essays on Liberty*. Oxford: Oxford University Press, 1969. First published 1958.

Blum, Lawrence A. *Moral Perception and Particularity*. New York: Cambridge University Press, 1994.

Brandt, Richard B. *A Theory of the Good and the Right.* Oxford: Clarendon Press, 1979.

Bruner, Jerome. *Acts of Meaning.* Cambridge, MA: Harvard University Press, 1990.

———. "Life as Narrative." *Social Research* 54 (1987): 11–32.

Burton, Robert. *The Anatomy of Melancholy.* Vols. 1–3. Edited by Thomas C. Faulkner, Nicolas K. Kiessling, and Rhonda L. Blair. Oxford: Clarendon Press, 1989. First published 1621.

Buss, Sarah, and Lee Overton, eds. *Contours of Agency.* Cambridge, MA: MIT Press, 2002.

Carr, David. *Time, Narrative, and History.* Bloomington: Indiana University Press, 1986.

Cavell, Stanley. *Must We Mean What We Say?* Cambridge, MA: Harvard University Press, 1958.

Chappell, Timothy, ed. *Values and Virtues.* Oxford: Blackwell, 2006.

Cottingham, John. *On the Meaning of Life.* London: Routledge, 2003.

———. *Philosophy and the Good Life.* Cambridge: Cambridge University Press, 1998.

———. *The Spiritual Dimension.* Cambridge: Cambridge University Press, 2005.

Craig, Edward. *The Mind of God and the Works of Man.* Oxford: Clarendon Press, 1987.

Cullity, Garrett, and Beryl Gaut, eds. *Ethics and Practical Reason.* Oxford: Clarendon Press, 1997.

Currie, Gregory. *Narratives and Narrators.* Oxford: Oxford University Press, 2010.

Dancy, Jonathan. *Ethics without Principles.* Oxford: Clarendon Press, 2004.

Davidson, Donald. "How Is Weakness of Will Possible?" In *Essays on Actions and Events.* Oxford: Clarendon Press, 1980. First published 1970.

———. "Paradoxes of Irrationality." In Wollheim and Hopkins, *Philosophical Essays on Freud.*

Dennett, Daniel. "The Self as a Center of Narrative Gravity." In *Self and Consciousness.* Hillsdale, NJ: Lawrence Erlbaum, 1992.

Descartes, René. *Discourse on the Method of Rightly Conducting One's Reason and Seeking the Truth in the Sciences.* In *The Philosophical Writings of Descartes,* vols. 1–2, translated by John Cottingham et al. Cambridge: Cambridge University Press, 1985. First published 1637.

Donagan, Alan. *The Theory of Morality.* Chicago: University of Chicago Press, 1977.

Dray, William. *Laws and Explanation in History.* Oxford: Clarendon Press, 1957.

Eliot, T. S. "Little Gidding." In *Four Quartets*, in *The Complete Poems and Plays, 1909–1950*. New York: Harcourt, Brace, 1952.

Ferguson, Niall. *The War of the World: Twentieth-Century Conflict and the Descent of the West*. New York: Penguin, 2006.

Flanagan, Owen. *Varieties of Moral Personality*. Cambridge, MA: Harvard University Press, 1993.

Foot, Philippa. *Natural Goodness*. Oxford: Clarendon Press, 2001.

Frankfurt, Harry G. *The Importance of What We Care About*. Cambridge: Cambridge University Press, 1988.

———. *Necessity, Volition, and Love*. Cambridge: Cambridge University Press, 1999.

———. *The Reasons of Love*. Princeton, NJ: Princeton University Press, 2004.

———. *Taking Ourselves Seriously and Getting It Right*. Stanford, CA: Stanford University Press, 2006.

Gallagher, Shaun, ed. *The Oxford Handbook of the Self*. Oxford: Oxford University Press, 2011.

Gardner, Sebastian. *Irrationality and the Philosophy of Psychoanalysis*. Cambridge: Cambridge University Press, 1993.

Gert, Bernard. *The Moral Rules*. New York: Harper and Row, 1966. Revised and expanded as *Morality*. New York: Oxford University Press, 1998.

Gewirth, Alan. *Reason and Morality*. Chicago: University of Chicago Press, 1978.

Hampshire, Stuart. *Innocence and Experience*. Cambridge, MA: Harvard University Press, 1989.

———. *Justice Is Conflict*. Princeton, NJ: Princeton University Press, 2000.

Hare, R. M. *Freedom and Reason*. Oxford: Clarendon Press, 1963.

———. *The Language of Morals*. Oxford: Clarendon Press, 1952.

———. *Moral Thinking*. Oxford: Clarendon Press, 1981.

Hartmann, Nicolai. *Ethics*. Translated by S. Coit. London: Allen and Unwin, 1932. First published 1926.

Hayek, Friedrich. *The Constitution of Liberty*. Chicago: Regnery, 1972. First published 1960.

Hegel, G. F. W. *Reason in History*. Translated by R. S. Hartman. New York: Liberal Arts, 1953. First published 1837.

Hooker, Brad, and Margaret Little, eds. *Moral Particularism*. Oxford: Clarendon Press, 2000.

Howard, Michael. *The Invention of Peace: Reflections on War and International Order*. New Haven, CT: Yale University Press, 2000.

Hume, David. *Essay concerning Human Understanding*. Edited by Tom L. Beauchamp. Oxford: Oxford University Press, 1999. First published 1748.

———. "The Sceptic." In *Essays, Moral, Political, and Literary*. Indianapolis: Liberty Press, 1985. First published 1741.

———. *A Treatise of Human Nature*. 2nd ed., revised by P. H. Nidditch. Oxford: Clarendon Press, 1978. First published 1739.

Hutto, Daniel D., ed. *Narrative and Understanding Persons*. Royal Institute of Philosophy Supplement 60. Cambridge: Cambridge University Press, 2007.

Johnson, Peter. *Politics, Innocence, and the Limits of Goodness*. London: Routledge, 1988.

Jopling, David A. *Self-Knowledge and the Self*. New York: Routledge, 2000.

Kant, Immanuel. *Critique of Pure Reason*. Translated by Norman Kemp Smith. London: Macmillan, 1953. First published 1787.

———. *Groundwork of the Metaphysics of Morals*. In *The Cambridge Edition of the Collected Works of Immanuel Kant: Practical Philosophy*. Translated and edited by Mary J. Gregor. Cambridge: Cambridge University Press, 1996. First published 1785.

———. *Religion within the Bounds of Reason Alone*. Translated by Theodore M. Greene and Hoyt H. Hudson. New York: Harper and Row, 1960. First published 1794.

Kekes, John. "Constancy and Purity." *Mind* 92 (1983): 499–518.

———. *The Human Condition*. Oxford: Clarendon Press, 2010.

———. "Purity and Judgment in Morality." *Philosophy* 63 (1988): 453–69.

Kierkegaard, Soren. *Purity of Heart*. Translated by D. V. Steere. New York: Harper and Row, 1948. First published 1847.

Korsgaard, Christine M. *Creating the Kingdom of Ends*. Cambridge: Cambridge University Press, 1996.

———. *Self-Constitution*. Oxford: Oxford University Press, 2009.

———. *The Sources of Normativity*. Cambridge: Cambridge University Press, 1996.

Lamarque, Peter. "On the Distance between Literary Narratives and Real-Life Narratives." In Hutto, *Narrative and Understanding Persons*.

Lewis, R. W. B. *The American Adam: Innocence, Tragedy, and Tradition in the Nineteenth Century*. Chicago: University of Chicago Press, 1955.

Lovejoy, Arthur O. *The Great Chain of Being*. New York: Harper and Row, 1960. First published 1936.

Machiavelli, Niccolo. *The Prince*. Translated by David Wootton. Indianapolis: Hackett, 1994. First published 1513.

MacIntyre, Alasdair. *After Virtue*. 2nd ed. Notre Dame, IN: University of Notre Dame Press, 1984.

Malcolm, Norman. *Ludwig Wittgenstein: A Memoir*. Oxford: Oxford University Press, 1958.

McDowell, John. *Mind, Value, and Reality*. Cambridge, MA: Harvard University Press, 1998.

Mele, Alfred R. *Irrationality*. New York: Oxford University Press, 1987.

Mele, Alfred R., and Piers Rawling, eds. *The Oxford Handbook of Rationality*. New York: Oxford University Press, 2004.

Mill, John Stuart. *Utilitarianism*. In *The Collected Works of John Stuart Mill*, vol. 10, edited by J. M. Robson. Indianapolis: Liberty Fund, 2006. First published 1861.

Montaigne, Michel de. *Essays*. In *The Complete Works of Montaigne*, translated by Donald M. Frame. Stanford, CA: Stanford University Press, 1943. First published 1588.

Morris, Herbert. "Lost Innocence." In *On Guilt and Innocence*. Berkeley: University of California Press, 1976.

Murdoch, Iris. *Existentialists and Mystics*. New York: Allen Lane, 1998.

———. *Metaphysics as a Guide to Morals*. London: Chatto and Windus, 1992.

———. *The Sovereignty of Good*. London: Routledge, 1970.

Myrna, Frances. "Purity in Morals." *Monist* 66 (1983): 283–97.

Nagel, Thomas. *Equality and Partiality*. New York: Oxford University Press, 1991.

———. *The Last Word*. New York: Oxford University Press, 1997.

———. *Mind and Cosmos*. New York: Oxford University Press, 2012.

———. *Mortal Questions*. Cambridge: Cambridge University Press, 1979.

———. *The View from Nowhere*. New York: Oxford University Press, 1986.

Nehamas, Alexander. *Nietzsche: Life as Literature*. Cambridge, MA: Harvard University Press, 1985.

Nietzsche, Friedrich. *Human, All Too Human*. Translated by R. J. Hollingdale. Cambridge: Cambridge University Press, 1996. First published 1879–1880.

———. "Schopenhauer as Educator." In *Untimely Meditations*, translated by R. J. Hollingdale. Cambridge: Cambridge University Press, 1983. First published 1874.

Nozick, Robert. *Anarchy, State, and Utopia*. New York: Basic Books, 1974.

Pears, David. *Motivated Irrationality*. Oxford: Clarendon Press, 1984.

Pinker, Steven. *The Better Angels of Our Nature: Why Violence Has Declined*. New York: Penguin, 2011.

Plato. *Apology*. Translated by Hugh Tredennick. In *The Collected Dialogues*, edited by Edith Hamilton and Huntington Cairns. Princeton, NJ: Princeton University Press, 1989. Written c. 370 BC.

———. *Protagoras*. Translated by W. K. C. Guthrie. In *The Collected Dialogues*, edited by Edith Hamilton and Huntington Cairns. Princeton, NJ: Princeton University Press, 1989. Written c. 370 BC.

Radden, Jennifer. *Divided Minds and Successive Selves*. Cambridge, MA: MIT Press, 1996.

Rawls, John. *A Theory of Justice*. Cambridge, MA: Harvard University Press, 1971.

Richard, I. A. *Practical Criticism*. London: Routledge, 1929.

Ricoeur, Paul. *Time and Narrative*. 3 vols. Translated by Kathleen McLaughlin and David Pellauer. Chicago: University of Chicago Press, 1985–1988.

Ross, W. D. *Foundations of Ethics*. Oxford: Clarendon Press, 1939.

———. *The Right and the Good*. Oxford: Clarendon Pres, 1930.

Rousseau, Jean-Jacques. *Discourses on the Origin and Foundation of Inequality among Man*. Translated by Donald A. Cress. Indianapolis: Hackett, 1988. First published 1754.

———. *Letter to Beaumont*. In *Oeuvres completes*. 5 vols. Paris: Gallimard, 1959–1995. Translated by Timothy O'Hagan in *Rousseau*. London: Routledge, 1999.

Rummell, R. J. *Death by Government*. New Brunswick, NJ: Transaction, 1994.

Sartre, Jean-Paul. *Being and Nothingness*. Translated by Hazel E. Barnes. New York: Philosophical Library, 1956. First published 1943.

Savile, Anthony. *The Test of Time*. Oxford: Clarendon Press, 1982.

Scanlon, T. M. *What We Owe to Each Other*. Cambridge, MA: Harvard University Press, 1998.

Schechtman, Marya. *The Constitution of Selves*. Ithaca, NY: Cornell University Press, 1997.

Scheffler, Samuel. *Human Morality*. New York: Oxford University Press, 1992.

Schneewind, J. M. *The Invention of Autonomy*. New York: Cambridge University Press, 1998.

Sextus Empiricus. *Outlines of Scepticism*. Translated by Julia Annas and Jonathan Barnes. Cambridge: Cambridge University Press, 1994. Written c. end of first century BC.

Shakespeare, William. *Othello*.

Smith, Adam. *The Theory of Moral Sentiments*. Indianapolis: LibertyClassics, 1976. First published 1759.

Spence, Donald F. *Narrative Truth and Historical Truth*. New York: Norton, 1982.

Strawson, Galen. "Against Narrativity." *Ratio* 17 (2004): 428–52.

———. "Episodic Ethics." In Hutto, *Narrative and Understanding Persons*, 85–115.

Strawson, Peter F. "Social Morality and Individual Ideal." In *Freedom and Resentment*. London: Methuen, 1974. First published 1961.

Stroud, Sarah, and Christine Tappolet, eds. *Weakness of Will and Practical Irrationality*. Oxford: Clarendon Press, 2003.

Tanner, Michael. "Sentimentality." *Proceedings of the Aristotelian Society* 77 (1976–1977): 127–47.

Taylor, Charles. *Human Agency and Language*. New York: Cambridge University Press, 1985.

———. *Sources of the Self*. Cambridge, MA: Harvard University Press, 1989.

Teichman, Roger. *Nature, Reason, and the Good Life*. Oxford: Oxford University Press, 2011.

Trilling, Lionel. *Sincerity and Authenticity*. Cambridge, MA: Harvard University Press, 1971.

Velleman, J. David. *Self to Self*. Cambridge: Cambridge University Press, 2006.

Widerker, David, and Michael McKenna, eds. *Moral Responsibility and Alternative Possibilities*. Aldershot: Ashgate, 2003.

Williams, Bernard. *Ethics and the Limits of Philosophy*. London: Collins, 1985.

———. "Life as Narrative." *European Journal of Philosophy* 17 (2007): 305–14.

———. *Moral Luck*. Cambridge: Cambridge University Press, 1981.

———. "Persons, Character, and Morality." In Williams, *Moral Luck*.

———. "Philosophy as a Humanistic Discipline." In *Philosophy as a Humanistic Discipline*, edited by A. W. Moore. Princeton, NJ: Princeton University Press, 2006.

———. *The Sense of the Past*. Edited by Myles Burnyeat. Princeton, NJ: Princeton University Press, 2006.

———. *Shame and Necessity*. Berkeley: University of California Press, 1993.

———. *Truth and Truthfulness*. Princeton, NJ: Princeton University Press, 2002.

———. "Unbearable Suffering." In Williams, *Sense of the Past*.

———. "The Women of Trachis." In Williams, *Sense of the Past*.

Wolf, Susan. "Moral Saints." *Journal of Philosophy* 79 (1982): 419–39.

Wollheim, Richard, and James Hopkins, eds. *Philosophical Essays on Freud*. Cambridge: Cambridge University Press, 1982.

Index